CREATION, GRACE, AND REDEMPTION

THEOLOGY IN GLOBAL PERSPECTIVE SERIES

Peter C. Phan, General Editor
*Ignacio Ellacuría Professor of Catholic Social Thought,
Georgetown University*

At the beginning of a new millennium, the *Theology in Global Perspective* Series responds to the challenge to re-examine the foundational and doctrinal themes of Christianity in light of the new global reality. While traditional Catholic theology has assumed an essentially European or Western point of view, *Theology in Global Perspective* takes account of insights and experience of churches in Africa, Asia, Latin America, Oceania, as well as from Europe and North America. Noting the pervasiveness of changes brought about by science and technologies, and growing concerns about the sustainability of Earth, it seeks to embody insights from studies in these areas as well.

Though rooted in the Catholic tradition, volumes in the series are written with an eye to the ecumenical implications of Protestant, Orthodox, and Pentecostal theologies for Catholicism, and vice versa. In addition, authors will explore insights from other religious traditions with the potential to enrich Christian theology and self-understanding.

Books in this series will provide reliable introductions to the major theological topics, tracing their roots in Scripture and their development in later tradition, exploring when possible the implications of new thinking on gender and socio-cultural identities. And they will relate these themes to the challenges confronting the peoples of the world in the wake of globalization, particularly the implications of Christian faith for justice, peace, and the integrity of creation.

Other Books Published in the Series

Orders and Ministries: Leadership in a Global Church, Kenan Osborne, O.F.M.
Trinity: Nexus of the Mysteries of Christian Faith, Anne Hunt
Spirituality and Mysticism: A Global View, James A. Wiseman. O.S.B.
Eschatology and Hope, Anthony Kelly, C.Ss.R.
Meeting Mystery: Liturgy, Worship, Sacraments, Nathan D. Mitchell
Globalization, Spirituality, and Justice: Navigating a Path to Peace, Daniel C. Groody, C.S.C.

THEOLOGY IN GLOBAL PERSPECTIVE SERIES
Peter C. Phan, General Editor

CREATION, GRACE, AND REDEMPTION

NEIL ORMEROD

ORBIS BOOKS

Maryknoll, New York 10545

Copyright © 2007 by Neil Ormerod.
Published by Orbis Books, Maryknoll, New York, U.S.A.
All rights reserved.

Scripture quotations are taken from *The Holy Bible* in the New Revised Standard Version, copyright © 1989, Division of Christian Education of the National Council of the Churches of Christ in the United States of America.

Manufactured in the United States of America.

Library of Congress Cataloguing in Publication Data

Ormerod, Neil.
    Creation, grace, and redemption / Neil Ormerod.
        p. cm. — (Theology in global perspective series ; 1)
    Includes bibliographical references and index.
    ISBN-13: 978-1-57075-705-1
    1. Theology, Doctrinal. I. Title.
    BT75.3.O76 2007
    230—dc22

                            2006032584

To my beautiful wife, Thea,
And our shared life of meaning, truth, love, and grace

Contents

Foreword

by Peter C. Phan

What does it mean to be human? Behind every theology, that is to say, "God-talk," lurks the shadow of anthropology, that is, "humanity-talk," and vice versa. The mutual implication of theology and anthropology should surprise no Christian since, according to the Bible, God creates humanity, male and female, in God's image (Gen 1:27). One cannot talk of the original without talking of its image and, conversely, one cannot speak of the image without speaking of its original. The question of course is: Where can one start? From the original or from the image? Or, to use a spatial metaphor, from above or from below?

In recent decades many note what is called an "anthropological turn" or a "turn toward the subject," that is, toward the human person and the experience of self-consciousness, freedom, and responsibility as the launching pad for God-talk. Upon careful reflection, however, the human subject is not an isolated monad but an interpersonal, social being embedded in a network of political and economic structures, intimately related to other human beings in and through the bodies, and dependent on the ecosystems of the Earth. Contemporary theology reflects this turn to the subject in its various concerns, for example, in reflections on transcendental, existential, political, liberationist, and feminist projects.

Moreover, in Christian anthropology, humans are seen to be created not only in the image of God but re-created in the image of Christ, who is himself "the reflection of the Father's glory, the exact representation of the Father's being" (Heb 1:3). From a Christian perspective, in other words, to understand what humans are, one must know who Christ is. As Vatican II puts it concisely, "it is only in the mystery of the Word made flesh that the mystery of the human person truly becomes clear" (*Gaudium et Spes* 22). As anthropology is intertwined with theology, so theology is intertwined inextricably with Christology.

In this book Neil Ormerod develops a Christian anthropology by attending to the classical themes of God's creation of the cosmos, the role of woman and man in the world, the structure of moral evil, original sin, the redemption of creation by Jesus, grace, the function of the church in the process of salva-

tion, forgiveness and reconciliation, death and the afterlife, and the end of the
world.

In clear and accessible language Ormerod presents an insightful and chal-
lenging theology of the human by enriching the teachings of the Bible and
the church with the insights of contemporary theologians, chief among whom
are Bernard Lonergan, Henri de Lubac, Karl Rahner, Robert Doran, and both
liberationist and feminist theologians. In line with the orientations of
"Theology in Global Perspective," Omerod also brings Christian teachings
into dialogue with those of other religious traditions.

In Ormerod's skillful hands, well-worn traditional themes of Christian
anthropology such as creation, original sin, grace and salvation, and death and
eternal life are rejuvenated and acquire expansive freshness that comes from
his deep knowledge of the Christian tradition and a willingness to bring it
into conversation with the urgent issues of our times. Thus, the biblical
account of creation is discussed in light of the theory of the "Big Bang," the
place of humanity in the cosmos in connection with various cosmogonies, evil
and sin in light of ideologies such as racism and patriarchy, original sin in relation to victimhood and addiction, redemption by Jesus' sacrificial death in
confrontation with René Girard's notion of scapegoating, grace and salvation
in connection with spiritual enlightenment, the church's sacramental function·
in relation to its mission for social justice, forgiveness of individual sins in cor-
relation with national reconciliation and abolition of oppressive social structures, and the end of the world in the context of the Big Crunch theory.

Evident throughout the book are not only Ormerod's precise and imaginative mind as a mathematician (his first doctorate is in mathematics!) but
also, and above all, his profound and unshakable hope for a new heaven and a
new earth, and within them, a new humanity to be re-created by Christ. Tes-
tifying of this are Ormerod's eloquent lines limning the final state of the cosmos: "Only in Jesus do we find the pure and spotless victim (Heb 9:14; 1 Pet
1:18-19), the one who through a voluntary act of solidarity has identified
himself with that which is victim in us all. Through this act of identification
he becomes Abel to our Cain, not in accusation (the role of Satan) but in
mediating forgiveness and reconciliation to the whole of human history. This
is the final judgment of human history, where the voices of the victims are
finally heard, where restorative justice is finally effected, and where a new and
glorious human community can live to the glory of God, in the radiance of
their risen Lord." Here God-talk, Christ-talk, and humanity-talk are harmonized into a beautiful melody.

Preface

Theology likes to ask big questions: Where did the universe come from? Why is there something rather than nothing? Why is there evil in the world? How do we deal with the problem of evil in our lives? What happens when we die? Are there rewards and punishments after death? Creation, sin and grace, redemption, life after death, these are the great questions to which the Christian tradition responds and with which Christian theology struggles. This present book represents my attempt to articulate a response of the Christian tradition and to bring issues into sharp relief for a contemporary reader. It is a big task, but one that I hope readers will agree indicates that Christian theology can make an intellectually respectable contribution to contemporary debates on issues of continuing interest and concern to us all.

And Christian theology deserves nothing less. Bernard Lonergan speaks of the need for theologians to be equal to the level of the times, to be conversant with up-to-date findings across a range of disciplines. This is a goal that is increasingly difficult to attain given the enormous expansion of scientific and scholarly research into all aspects of the universe and human existence. In an introductory text such as this it is possible only to scratch the surface of a number of issues that deserve deeper consideration, but I hope enough clues are present for the interested reader to pursue to his or her future benefit.

Christian theology faces numerous challenges in the contemporary world. Christian doctrines of creation, original sin, and eschatology have often been framed within a prescientific cosmology that is simply no longer credible. Doctrines of sin and grace must face up to challenges from contemporary psychology and cultural studies. And of course Christian beliefs must also come to grips with the emerging multifaith environment of a globalizing world. Certainly the answers from the past cannot simply be repeated—not without a serious engagement with these multiple challenges.

Despite these challenges it is my contention that the broad responses of the Christian tradition to the great questions of life remain meaningful for our present situation. Christian theology has no need to feel on the back foot, for the tradition it draws upon is a rich source of wisdom. However, it is a wisdom that can retain its vitality only through a constant dialogue with the prevailing culture, a dialogue in which it is well both to speak and to listen.

To this end the present book brings into creative dialogue the great figures of the Christian past, particularly the voices of Augustine and Aquinas, and contemporary Christian theologians such as Bernard Lonergan and Robert

Doran and movements such as liberation and feminist theologies; it draws on the insights of modern sciences in relation to our cosmic and human origins and what our future may hold; it finds resonances with the Christian tradition in modern psychological authors and the cultural studies of René Girard; it faces questions from the great religious traditions such as Islam, Buddhism, and Hinduism and responds with its own questions to those traditions. It is a rich mix but one I think necessary if one is to speak at the level of the present time.

The end result is a systematic perspective that affirms the continuing power of the Christian tradition to respond to the challenges faced by contemporary theology. It is a perspective that does not back away from the great Christian doctrines of the past—creation, grace, original sin, redemption, and resurrection; rather it seeks to understand them by bringing to bear the resources of our present culture through constructive and critical dialogue.

One reader of the draft text described the book to me as a strongly "positional" text. I am not simply reporting on the positions of others but adopting and defending a position I have found to be most intellectually consistent and coherent with the Christian tradition. Generally speaking, I have not presented expositions of the work of other theologians, except in summary where I felt it contributed to a better understanding of the issue in question. This means I engage with the presenting issue as thoroughly as an introductory text allows. Thus, I do not expect other theologians necessarily to agree with all the positions I adopt, but I hope those positions are the basis for students and teachers to engage in some spirited debate on the questions I am covering in the text. To this end I have included some discussion questions at the end of each chapter to act as a stimulus for such debate.

In any project such as this there are a number of people to thank. Much of the material in this book arose from various courses taught at the Catholic Institute of Sydney. The response of my students to the ideas helped me refine my understanding and I hope this is reflected in the text. In particular I would like to thank Vince Battaglia, who read and commented on a number of the chapters in their early draft form. Thanks also to my Australian colleagues and friends Anthony Kelly and Anne Hunt, who have also contributed to this series, and to my American friends and colleagues Robert Doran and Cynthia Crysdale, each of whom read and commented on the text. Writing is often a lonely task, and the response of trusted readers is invaluable. Finally, my thanks go to Peter Phan, the editor of this series, and William Burrows, the managing editor of Orbis Books, who together conceived this series and asked me to contribute to it. Their enthusiastic responses to the text, together with their helpful comments, have been a strong encouragement to bring this project to completion.

1

The God of Creation

L ET US BEGIN WITH AN EXERCISE we can perhaps all try. Go out in the evening air on a cloudless night and stare up into the sky. Look up at the moon and the stars—perhaps you can see the Milky Way—and just get lost in the vastness, the immensity of it all. Such activity has been part of our history since the beginning of human culture. People have stared in wonder and awe at the heavens. Over time they have sought out patterns among the stars, patterns with links to their emerging mythologies of the gods, and so they named the constellations. Eventually people identified stars that did not fit into the fixed patterns of the majority of stars, and they called these stars planets, because they wandered the sky (from the Greek, *planaō*, "to wander"). With increasing leisure and intellectual curiosity people developed theories that sought to account for both the fixed patterns of the stars and the erratic wanderings of the planets. The primordial wonder we feel in the face of the immensity of the sky yields to the search for order, for cosmos in the apparent chaos, for some explanation for the movements of stars and planets. Ptolemy (85-165 C.E.) put forward a system whereby the Earth was the center of the universe, with the moon, the sun, the planets, and the stars on fixed spheres that moved around the Earth. Despite its flaws, it dominated the scientific imagination for over a thousand years, until Copernicus (1473-1543) argued the case for a heliocentric system, placing the sun at the center with the Earth just one of a number of planets that circled the sun. With meticulous calculations Johannes Kepler (1571-1630) added further refinements, while Galileo (1564-1642) added the power of both calculation and observation through newly invented telescopes. Finally, the towering genius of Isaac Newton (1643-1727) brought the power of mathematics, his newly discovered calculus, to bear and with a few simple equations was able to provide a basic explanation for the movements of the planets. The basic intelligibility of what we now call the solar system had been laid bare, and we now knew with some certainty that our universe was an ordered system.[1]

---

1. Of course it is always possible to argue that the order we "find" is a projection onto otherwise unordered data, that it is basically a construction of the human mind. This reflects a basically Kantian

Scientific observation and Einstein's theory of general relativity have long since moved beyond even the grand synthesis of Newton to reveal a universe billions of years old, billions of light years across, with hundreds of billions of galaxies, each with hundreds of billions of stars.[2] The universe is far bigger and far older than we could ever have imagined. But one thing that has not changed in the whole process is the movement from wonder and awe to the search for patterns and order. Deep within our search for order is the conviction that the universe has not just been thrown together in some random jumble, but that it is patterned, intelligible, and ordered in ways that we can discover and understand. Inevitably, as our constant desire for intelligibility is fulfilled, we ask the question, Why? Why does the universe display such profound patterns? Are these patterns simply the "creation" of our minds, or do we truly "discover" them, so that they really "belong" to the universe itself? Further, is it reasonable that these patterns emerge by chance, or does the intelligibility of the universe reveal a hidden yet powerful intelligence who is in some sense the source of all that is? In facing such questions, even the most committed scientist may develop the conviction that there must be some source for it all.[3]

We find the same conviction at work in the opening chapter of the Book of Genesis. In mytho-poetic language the author of the first chapter of Genesis puts forward a powerfully religious vision of a universe that finds its source and origin in the divine command: "Let there be light . . . let there be night and day . . . let there be lights in the vault of heaven . . . let the earth produce vegetation . . . let the waters teem with life . . . let the earth produce every living creature . . . let us make human beings in our own image and likeness." God speaks and so it happens. Every pattern, every element of order that we find in the universe, from the "lights of the sky" to the complex interacting patterns of living things, has its source and origin in God's creative work. And this same conviction that the universe finds its origin in God stands behind the fundamental belief in the goodness of that creation: "God saw everything that he had made, and indeed, it was very good" (Gen 1:31).

Biblical scholars tell us, however, that the source of this conviction regarding creation began not with speculation about the cosmos, as we have outlined

---

epistemology that separates knowledge and being. Some would counter, however, by arguing that the intelligibility of reality is the a priori condition for the possibility of science. See Roy Bhaskar, *A Realist Theory of Science* (Atlantic Highlands, N.J.: Humanities Press, 1978).

2. It is perhaps worth noting that it was only in the 1920s with the scientific observations of Edwin Hubble, that we learned there were galaxies other than our own. In cultural terms this is very recent.

3. The best example of this is the physicist and natural philosopher Paul Davies, who has moved from a scientific rationalist position to a broad theism, on the basis that the order of physical reality points to a source for order which transcends that reality.

it above, but with a much more concrete experience, that of the establishment of order in society. What emerges from these scholars' work is the strong connection between cosmogenesis and the "creation/redemption" of Israel as a social body. This interrelationship between the cosmological and social is common among what Eric Voegelin would call "cosmological cultures," in which the individual is ordered to the society and the society is ordered to the rhythms of the cosmos.[4] The creation of Israel as a nation, achieved through the gift of the Law, or Torah—out of the social *chaos* of lawlessness emerges the nation built upon the *order* of the Torah—is the basic model of creation within Hebrew thought forms. It is a reminder of the close connections between creation and redemption within this horizon. The creation of social order is the basic experience of redemption. People who have experienced the breakdown or fragility of the social order, such as the recent devastation in New Orleans, will know what this means. These biblical creation texts are not metaphysically speculative, but historically grounded.[5]

Nor should the Bible be read as providing us with a scientific account of the origins of the universe, in particular of the origins of life. The Bible does not seek to provide us with scientific information about the origins of life, but with a faith conviction that everything finds its origins in the divine command. Ultimately God, through divine wisdom, is the source of order and of life, but the Bible does not seek to tell us how God created these things, or the mechanisms for that creation. To read the Bible literally in this case, as found in so-called creation science, is to fundamentally misunderstand the literary form of the text.[6] Science is free to develop theories such as evolution in order to understand the emergence of life, so long as scientists remain faithful to the empirical data, not to a literal misreading of the biblical text.

CREATION *EX NIHILO*

It is commonly stated that Christian belief holds that God created the universe *ex nihilo*, that is, out of nothing (*Catechism of the Catholic Church* no.

---

4. See Robert M. Doran, *Theology and the Dialectics of History* (Toronto: University of Toronto Press, 1990), 502-13, for an account of cosmological and anthropological cultures. Innuit and other First Nation peoples represent contemporary expressions of cosmological cultures.

5. Richard J. Clifford, "The Hebrew Scriptures and the Theology of Creation," *Theological Studies* 46 (1985): 507-23.

6. Of course Catholics are relatively latecomers to the notion of literary form as a significant factor in reading the Scriptures. The teaching of Pius XII in *Divino Afflante Spiritu* (1942) that Catholic scholars should attend to the literary form of the text was reasserted at Vatican II in *Dei Verbum*, the Dogmatic Constitution on Divine Revelation. More recently the Pontifical Biblical Commission has endorsed the use of historical-critical method by Catholic biblical scholars.

338).[7] When we look at the account in chapter 1 of Genesis, however, we do not find such an account. Rather there is a suggestion that God created the universe out of something preexistent: "the earth was a formless void and darkness covered the face of the deep, while a wind from God swept over the face of the waters" (Gen 1:2).[8] Given what we stated above, that the basic analogue for creation is one of social order out of the chaos of lawlessness, this is not surprising. The view of creation "out of nothing" is very sophisticated—indeed unimaginable—and we should not read it into this early biblical text.

The material in Genesis, however, is only one source for a Christian understanding of creation. The Psalms, wisdom literature, and prophetic literature also provide some interesting material. Of particular interest is the hymn to Wisdom in Proverbs 8:22-31 (also Wis 9:9-12, Sir 24:3-22), which forms the background of New Testament reflection on the divine Word and its role in creation. However, we shall turn attention to the initial emergence of belief in creation *ex nihilo*, a belief that begins in the period of the Maccabean persecutions. Thus, in 2 Maccabees 7:28 we find: "I beg you my child, to look at the heaven and the earth and see everything that is in them, and recognize that God did not make them out of things that existed." What is interesting here is the context of the affirmation that God did not create "out of things that existed." The context is not one of metaphysical speculation, as found in the Greek philosophers. Rather the concern is with the possibility of resurrection from the dead, in the face of a major historical problem faced by the Jewish people. Prophetic literature had always understood the defeats and sufferings of Israel as a punishment for their infidelity to the Law. This was the standard prophetic line, particularly in the Deuteronomistic school of thought.[9] The Maccabean persecution was something different. Now they were suffering precisely because they were being faithful to the Law. The traditional prophetic response no longer worked. One feature of this period is the emergence of apocalyptic works such as the Book of Daniel, which seek to give the people hope that their suffering from persecution will not be too long. Nonetheless, the conviction that God is both creator of all that is, and just, required a better solution than simple perseverance—what about those who

---

7. *Catechism of the Catholic Church,* 2nd ed. (Strathfield, N.S.W.: St Pauls, 2000). Henceforth referred to as *CCC* followed by the number of the article.

8. Claus Westermann notes that "the question, 'Is it *creation ex nihilo* or not?' is not relevant to the text" (*Genesis 1-11: A Commentary* [London: SPCK, 1984], 109).

9. For an example of the judgment of the Deuteronomistic Historian on the fall of Samaria, see 2 Kings 18:9-12. The northern kingdom fell because they violated "all that Moses the servant of Yahweh had laid down."

had died in the persecution? What justice could they expect? The solution was the hope/expectation of resurrection:

> The creator of the world, who shaped the beginning of humankind and devised the origins of all things, will in his mercy give life and breath back to you, since you now forget yourselves for the sake of his laws. (2 Macc 7:23)

This same linking between belief in resurrection and creation *ex nihilo* is found in the New Testament. There Paul speaks of God "who gives life to the dead and calls into existence the things that do not exist" (Rom 4:17). The significance of this runs parallel to what we have already seen in the Old Testament, that the issues of creation and redemption cannot be separated. The God who creates is the God who saves and vice versa. Christian faith resists any attempt to separate the two functions, as found in the Marcionite heresy, which set the God of the Old Testament (the creator) in opposition to the God of the New Testament (the redeemer).[10] The work of salvation, of bringing good out of the evil of sin, is truly an act of creation *ex nihilo*, a fundamentally creative act. We shall have more to say on this when we consider the problem of evil.

Now while the roots of the biblical belief in creation *ex nihilo* lie in the saving power of God, it remains a belief rich in metaphysical meaning. Metaphysically, creation *ex nihilo* means creation without prior conditions or constraints, whether these be the constraint of preexistent matter or of some form of necessity imposed on the divine being. It does not mean creation of matter into empty space at a certain point in time, as we might commonly imagine. Space and time are already things that are themselves created. In this sense creation *ex nihilo* is, strictly speaking, unimaginable. We can form no image of it, since any image we might develop evokes notions of space and time. We can try to understand it in terms of an analogy of personal causation, for example, the creative work of an artist creating a work of art, or an engineer building a bridge. But all our analogies break down because God's creative act is complete and without any prior conditions or constraints, whereas in all our analogies people work with something that already exists and transform it into something new. Moreover, on this account God is not constrained to create; God's creative act is entirely free. There is no cause for creation apart from God's free act, God's loving will. Finally, God is not constrained by the

---

10. Marcion (110-160 C.E.) sought to distinguish between the God of the Old Testament (an evil creator God) and the God revealed by Jesus in the New Testament (a loving redeeming God). To achieve this, however, he had to cut out large slabs of the New Testament, leaving only the Gospel of Luke and the writings of Paul. His position was quickly rejected as heretical by the early church.

limits of some preexistent material that confines the divine options. The freedom of this act is complete and sovereign. This sovereignty is the ultimate
guarantee that creation is good. There are no prior conditions that limit God's
creative act, nothing preexisting that lies beyond God's will or power.[11]

In order to clarify further the significance of creation *ex nihilo* we can compare it with some of the alternatives that others have explored in the history
of religious and philosophical thought.

CREATION *EX DIVINO*

According to such a view, creation is out of the divine substance itself. This
view divinizes the created order and makes the universe the physical manifestation of God, leading to a form of pantheism. Such a view is increasingly
popular among ecologically oriented groups who are seeking to preserve the
natural environment. The claim made is that the created order is sacred in
some sense.

One can argue that this position is rejected in the creation account of Genesis 1, which is at pains to stress the transcendence, or otherness, of God, and
the nondivine nature of the created order.[12] The biblical author was rejecting
the then widespread "pagan" view that failed to distinguish between the divine
and the created. In fact, on this pagan view, creation is no longer "created" as
such; rather it is a manifestation of divine being. Some might even speak of
the divine as the soul of the cosmos, so that the cosmos is the body of God.

Many might find this an attractive position; however, there are questions
to be addressed. Apart from the severe compromising of divine transcendence, one should also ask how this view of creation accounts for the problem of evil. If creation is from the very stuff of God, what "space" is there for
evil? Evil becomes less a moral issue than an epistemological one. It becomes
the failure to acknowledge one's own divine nature. Such positions are becoming more common in various new age belief systems. Some might refer to this
view as neopaganism, as evidenced in an increasing interest in the occult and
witchcraft, found in some popular television programs. In its present form it
can be a reaction to the perceived failures of traditional Christian belief to

---

11. See *CCC* no. 338, "*Nothing exists that does not owe its existence to God the Creator.* The world
began when God's word drew it out of nothingness; all existent beings, all of nature, and all human
history are rooted in this primordial event, the very genesis by which the world was constituted and
time begun."

12. See Westermann, *Genesis 1-11*, 119, who notes that even "heaven in the Old Testament is simply something created; it has no divine character at all."

protect and preserve the natural environment. Most notable has been the critique of Christianity by Lynn White. White argues:

> Especially in its Western form, Christianity is the most anthropocentric religion the world has seen. As early as the 2nd century both Tertullian and Saint Irenaeus of Lyons were insisting that when God shaped Adam he was foreshadowing the image of the incarnate Christ, the Second Adam. Man shares, in great measure, God's transcendence of nature. Christianity, in absolute contrast to ancient paganism and Asia's religions (except, perhaps, Zorastrianism), not only established a dualism of man and nature but also insisted that it is God's will that man exploit nature for his proper ends.[13]

In a sense, Catholic thought is better placed to respond to this criticism because of its sacramental view of reality, which recognizes that the material order may mediate the divine, though without a strict identification that blurs the divine transcendence. The reaction is more in relation to a rationalistic understanding of God and religion that is seen in some forms of Protestant thought that place a greater emphasis on the divine Word received through the preaching of the gospel than on the sacraments as mediating God's grace.

CREATION BY EMANATION

Another alternative to creation *ex nihilo* is found in emanationist accounts of creation. These positions are impressed by the divine transcendence but misconstrue the nature of that transcendence as remoteness. Examples can be found in Neoplatonic and Gnostic sources.[14] In order to protect divine transcendence, creation is conceived as a series of emanations from the divine, a graded hierarchy of emanations, with each grade in the hierarchy giving rise to the next lower grade. In this way the divine creative power is mediated through a series of increasingly degraded beings. Not only did this "protect" the divine transcendence; it also accounted for the "coarse" nature of material creation. The physical world is not directly created by God, but by a lower-order being, sometimes referred to as the demiurge, with more limited power. Often these emanations are construed as "necessary," not the product of

---

13. See http://www.bemidjistate.edu/peoplenv/lynnwhite.htm (accessed July 3, 2006) for a copy of White's 1967 article "The Historical Roots of Our Ecological Crisis."

14. A number of early Christian authors were very influenced by Neoplatonic thought, including Origen, Pseudo-Dionysius, Augustine, and Maximus the Confessor. Of these, Origen, Pseudo-Dionysius, and Maximus reflect something of an emanationist perspective.

God's freely willed activity, in order to protect God from being such a poor creator!

While the strength of this view is its desire to protect the divine transcendence, it does so at the expense of the goodness of creation, which is severely compromised. This approach feels the need to protect God from the "obvious" flaws of the material order. God could not possibly have created such a coarse material reality. Moreover, by misconstruing transcendence as remoteness, the emanationist notion requires an imagined bridge between the remote divine being and the material order of creation. The fault with this image is that given the infinite difference between God and creation, no amount of bridging bridges the infinite gap. The imagined graded hierarchy in fact solves nothing.

Christian belief, on the other hand, implies God's direct creative action with the entirety of creation. Because of divine transcendence God needs no intermediaries to create, and so God is directly and immediately present to the whole of the created order. Transcendence does not imply remoteness, but in fact guarantees divine immanence. Nor do we need to protect God from the coarseness of creation. Creation is good, even in its materiality.

Emanationist accounts emerge wherever people argue that somehow God must create the world. The language is often one of the necessity of God sharing the divine goodness, or of the overflowing of that goodness. This captures the fact that creation has its roots in the divine love and will. But by making creation necessary and not freely willed, in fact these positions eventually compromise the goodness of creation, which is made not because of love alone but because of some necessity—or even need—on the part of God

DUALIST ACCOUNTS OF CREATION

Perhaps the notion of creation that most captures the popular imagination is dualism. This position posits two distinct but opposed creative forces: one good, God; the other evil, usually depicted as Satan or the devil. The beauty of this approach is that it provides a direct and simple theoretical solution to the problem of evil. The fact of evil is traced back not to the creative act of God but to the malevolent act of the anti-God figure of Satan. In this schema, God is the creator of spiritual realities while Satan is the creator of material realities. Spirit (reason, intellect, will) is good; matter (body, sexuality, feeling, etc.) is bad. This approach has many historical manifestations such as Zoroastrianism, Manichaeism, Catharism, and some forms of Gnosticism. Overall, Christianity rejects this type of ontological dualism, while maintaining a moral dualism, that is, the objective distinction between good and evil actions and decisions. Nonetheless, some Christian heterodox sects such as the Cathars and some popular forms of Christian belief tend to fall over into an ontological dualism.[15]

In rejecting ontological dualism, Christian belief asserts the sovereign power of God over all creation, including evil spirits. It rejects any notion that creation is evenly poised between forces of good and evil. The ultimate source of all that exists is the divine will, God's love and wisdom. Because of this we can have ultimate confidence in the triumph of good over evil. However, it does raise questions of theodicy, or justifying God in the face of evil, which we consider later.

Dualism remains common in popular discourse. Whenever someone or something is labeled "pure evil," then a dualistic mind-set is evident. Such language is sometimes used in political rhetoric, for example, in speaking of terrorists. In Christian belief there is no such thing as pure evil. It is self-contradictory to think of pure evil, since everything that exists, inasmuch as it exist, has some goodness. Again, this will be explored further when we raise questions of theodicy.

PROCESS ACCOUNTS OF GOD AND CREATION

A more recent contender for addressing the question of God and creation is found in process theology. Initiated in the writings of Alfred North Whitehead and promoted by Charles Hartshorne and John Cobb, process thought seeks to present an alternative to "classical theism" as found in the Christian tradition.[16] There are serious concerns about process theology's interpretation of Christian tradition, which is read largely through second-rate neoscholastic sources.[17] Nonetheless, process theology presents itself as a serious alternative to the classical Christian belief in creation and God's relationship to creation.

Process thought reconceives the God–creation relationship in terms of mutuality. That is, not only does God effect creation; creation also has a real effect on God. Strictly speaking, God is not a creator in the classical sense, as process thought employs elements of both emanationist and preexisting-

---

15. Many films that have explicitly Christian religious themes border on the dualistic, for example, *Stigmata* and the apocalyptic *End of Days*.

16. For example, Alfred North Whitehead, *Process and Reality: An Essay in Cosmology*, ed. David Griffin and Donald W. Sherburne, corrected ed. (New York: Free Press, 1978); Charles Hartshorne, *Aquinas to Whitehead: Seven Centuries of Metaphysics of Religion* (Milwaukee: Marquette University Publications, 1976).

17. David Burrell, "Does Process Theology Rest on a Mistake?" *Theological Studies* 43 (1982): 125-35.

matter versions of creation. God needs to create, and God is not the source of all that is. Indeed, in some forms of process thought God is not the highest principle; rather, something like "creativity" is the highest principle. Further, because God is affected by creation, God is subject to change and development. Process theology speaks of a dipolar conception of divinity, with antecedent (i.e., apart from creation) and subsequent (i.e., in relation to creation) divine natures.[18] Classical divine attributes and perfections such as being impassible and eternal relate to the antecedent nature, while the subsequent nature is passible, temporal, and so on. Many process thinkers would argue that this account is more in line with the biblical account of God.

Although many find this approach more conducive to modern scientific understandings of creation, one must realize that the process account of the God–creation relationship severely compromises divine transcendence. God is no longer sovereign lord of creation, but is subject to the vicissitudes of creation. In particular, it is not clear how process thought deals with the problem of evil, particularly in an eschatological sense. Because God is not sovereign, there is no secure basis for eschatological hope. In the final analysis, within a process account God could well be overcome by evil.[19]

There is a very difficult question here with which various ancient and modern authors struggle in terms of the doctrine of creation. Since God is sovereign Lord of creation, God's will is efficacious. That is, what God wills to happen, in fact happens. How, then, does one avoid the conclusion that everything is determined? This is an issue not only in relation to free will but also in terms of scientific accounts of the world based on indeterminacy of physical phenomena, as found in quantum mechanics. Process "solves" this problem by a reversion to an account of creation based on preexisting matter, in an effort to restore real "chance" in the universe. It is significant, then, that early Christian belief sought to overcome Greek accounts of creation based on preexisting matter precisely because they believed in a provident God (Matt 6:25-34; Luke 12:6-7). Thus, we find a relationship between Christian notions of creation and divine providence.

PROVIDENCE, CREATION, AND CONTINGENCY

Christian belief in creation *ex nihilo* places God apart from the spatio-temporal-material order. God does not create material being in space and time; God creates space, time, and matter. There is no "before" creation, since

---

18. See John Cobb, *A Christian Natural Theology* (Philadelphia: Westminster Press, 1965).

19. There are other, more philosophical concerns with process thought. See Neil Ormerod, "Chance and Necessity, Providence and God," *Irish Theological Quarterly* 70 (2005): 263-78.

"before" implies time and time is as much a created reality as space and matter. God exists not in time but in an "eternal now." Consequently, God's creative act is one and simultaneous. In one act God creates the whole of the created order, past, present, and future. All is immediately present to God and willed by God in the single divine act of creation. Nonetheless, although the act is one and timeless, the consequences are many and temporal.

A consequence of creation *ex nihilo* is that what God wills necessarily happens. There is no disjunction between God's will and the reality of the event, at least in the divine now, though for us the events created by God are divided among past, present, and future. The problem that then arises is: how can there be room for the contingent (chance) in creation? For example, Aristotle allowed for the contingent by appealing to the existence of preexistent matter, which God did not create. If we remove any notion of preexisting prime matter through belief in creation *ex nihilo*, do we then remove any possibility of contingency?

In fact, the view that a creator God removes any possibility of contingency has become part of the common mind. This is most evident in thinkers such as biologist Richard Dawkins, who argues that because evolution depends on contingent events such as chance mutations, God can have nothing to do with it.[20] The claim is made that real chance is incompatible with divine causation. The clear contention is that a notion of divine creation eliminates chance or contingency and eventually eliminates human freedom itself.

Though expressed in modern form, the problem was not unknown to Thomas Aquinas. In *Summa Contra Gentiles*, Aquinas notes: "You object that providence is necessarily efficacious; I retort that therefore what providence intends to be contingent, will inevitably be contingent" (3, c. 94).

In other words, Aquinas would argue that God can use chance/contingency to achieve a desired outcome, and achieve it inevitably, even while the event remains chance.

Transposing this into a modern context, the question can be rephrased thus: Is there any intelligibility in, or science of, chance events? Aristotle denied that there was a science of the contingent, because prime matter lacked intelligibility. Consequently there was no providence for Aristotle, only fate. Aquinas affirms the reality of providence and the complete intelligibility of the created order. Consequently, the logical conclusion is that there must be a "science" of the contingent. In the modern context we would recognize the

---

20. Dawkins in fact argues that "the Argument from Design, then, has been destroyed as a reason for believing in a God." See his article at http://www.secularhumanism.org/library/fi/dawkins_18_3 .html (accessed October 8, 2004). See more fully Richard Dawkins, *The Blind Watchmaker: Why the Evidence of Evolution Reveals a Universe without Design* (New York: Norton, 1996).

role of statistics in science, for example, in quantum mechanics. Thus, even what appear to be random events occur within a certain statistical pattern or probability. We can even use statistical means to achieve desired outcomes, which will nonetheless remain chance. And if we can, so can God! For example, we know that smoking causes lung cancer, but we cannot know who will develop cancer and who will not. We know that if we reduce smoking we will reduce the incidence of lung cancer, but we cannot point to one person whose life has been saved by reducing the incidence of smoking. In reducing the incidence of smoking we will the particular individual outcomes because we will the general outcomes (i.e., fewer deaths by cancer). In choosing to adopt a statistical causation, we accept the fact that there will be a spread of outcomes, within our desired outcome. The difference between our acting and God's in such a case is that while our willing of the particular is mediated through the general approach, God's is immediate because God is the creator of all. All creation is immediately present to God as its fundamental cause and origin.[21]

To invoke statistical lawfulness with contingency is to invite comparison between necessity and the classical mechanical laws such as those of Newtonian science.[22] These laws seemed to offer the possibility of a completely deterministic universe. For example, mathematician Simon Laplace (1749-1827) boasted that, given the position and velocity of every particle in the universe, the future would be as accessible as the past.[23] On such a view, to invoke statistical laws is always a cloak for ignorance. On the other hand, to invoke the reality of contingency is to recognize the irreducible character of statistical lawfulness. Quantum mechanics and evolution have embedded the notion of statistics into the heart of modern science. The realization of the chance nature of events does not exclude the guiding hand of divine providence, but it does indicate the mode of operation of that providence, through both classical and statistical means. Further, Bernard Lonergan has shown how classical and statistical lawfulness combine to lead to what he calls emergent probability, the development of schemes of recurrence that allow evolutionary

---

21. Bernard Lonergan states it thus: "Such a positive statement is the affirmation that God knows with equal infallibility, he wills with equal irresistibility, he effects with equal efficacy both the necessary and the contingent. For however infallible the knowledge, however irresistible the will, however efficacious the action, what is known, willed, effected is no more than hypothetically necessary. And what is hypothetically necessary, absolutely may be necessary or contingent." Bernard J. F. Lonergan, *Grace and Freedom: Operative Grace in the Thought of St. Thomas Aquinas*, ed. Frederick E. Crowe and Robert M. Doran, Collected Works of Bernard Lonergan 1 (Toronto: University of Toronto Press, 2000), 109.

22. It should be noted that Einstein's theory of general relativity is also deterministic in nature, as are the equations governing "chaos theory."

23. See http://plato.stanford.edu/entries/determinism-causal/ (accessed July 11, 2006).

processes to arise.[24] This transposes Aquinas's categories of necessity and contingence into a modern scientific worldview.

THE PROBLEM OF EVIL AND SUFFERING

So far we have been presenting a classical "strong" understanding of the nature of creation and of divine transcendence and its implications in terms of God's efficacious providence. The big question that hangs over our whole discussion has been, What about evil? How do we account for the "presence" of evil in a creation that has been deemed to be "very good" (Gen 1:31)? Indeed the presence of evil undermines our arguments that the universe is an ordered cosmos, since evil injects a pall of meaninglessness into our human experience that threatens to overcome whatever sense of order we might claim to be present. It is not surprising that people turn to dualist accounts of evil as a way of escaping from the obvious dilemmas posed by classical Christian faith.

The problem of evil is perhaps the most pressing existential issue that we face in proclaiming the gospel. Indeed, it may lead us even to doubt the existence of God. The classical rejection of arguments for the existence of God runs along the following lines: *You say God is all good and all powerful; yet evil exists, and God does nothing to stop it. Therefore either God is all good, but not all powerful; or God is all powerful but not all good. Therefore your concept of God is incoherent and so God does not exist.* My own experience tends to indicate that behind such argumentation lies a more pressing existential context of personal suffering and experience of evil. This leads us to the first important issue. Are we dealing with the problem of evil or the problem of suffering?

Suffering or Evil?

Popular author Scott Peck, when planning *People of the Lie*, his study of the nature of evil, was asked by a friend, "Maybe you will help me understand my son's cerebral palsy?" His response was to say he was writing on evil, not suffering.[25] Is there a difference? Is the problem of suffering the same as the problem of evil?

A similar question arises in relation to Buddhism. Buddhism identifies the

---

24. Bernard J. F. Lonergan, *Insight: A Study of Human Understanding*, ed. Frederick E. Crowe and Robert M. Doran, Collected Works of Bernard Lonergan 3 (Toronto: University of Toronto Press, 1992), 126-61. We shall consider this further in the next chapter.

25. M. Scott Peck, *People of the Lie: The Hope for Healing Human Evil* (New York: Simon & Schuster, 1983), 45. Peck is better known for his book *The Road Less Traveled*.

fundamental problem of human living as one of suffering, or *dukkha*, sometimes now translated as "unsatisfactoriness." The saving message of the Buddha is one of the elimination of suffering through the extinction of desire,
which is viewed as the source of all suffering. Nirvana is the total elimination
of desire, and so the total cessation of suffering. Given the current popularity
of Buddhism in Western countries, this analysis of the human condition
deserves deeper reflection.

The question of suffering and evil requires both delicacy and firmness in
response. The two are related but distinct; however, the existential linkage is
strong. Evil can and does lead to great suffering, but evil may also involve little or no suffering whatsoever. In fact, some evil may even be perpetrated in
the name of reducing suffering, such as in cases of euthanasia, where life is
taken to alleviate suffering. On the other hand, some suffering may be freely
entered into as good, not as a masochistic thing, but like the training of the
athlete who must "break through the pain barrier" in order to achieve success.
Pain is also an important indicator for the presence of harmful activities—if
we did not feel pain, would we pull our hands out of a fire? Pain serves a useful purpose in such cases. Then there is the ultimate pain, the "pain" of death,
involving bodily pain, psychological pain, and the pain of separation from
friends and loved ones.

We shall begin with an "ontological" examination of the question of pain
and suffering. A finite being, such as a human being, will always "suffer" the
impact of other beings upon it; that is, a finite being will be passively affected
by other beings, precisely because it is limited. Because of its limitations there
will be occasions when limits are reached that threaten the existence of a finite
being. Then a finite being faces damage or destruction. When a finite being is
conscious, it will consciously experience the reaching of its limits; this conscious
experience is felt as pain or suffering. It occurs when a conscious finite subject
reaches physical, chemical, biological, and psychic limits, when it is pushed to
these limits by forces in its environment or its own free actions. The suffering
incurred indicates that limits have been reached, and unless we act to protect
ourselves we may incur serious damage. Limits may not be absolute, however,
but relative to a current state of development. In this case we may overcome
our limits through a developmental growth or act of self-transcendence, which
moves us, with some discomfort, beyond our current limits. On the other hand,
other limits are absolute, and we transgress them only at the cost of serious suffering and possible death.

In all these ways we can identify a certain intelligibility to suffering. Suffering has an intrinsic relationship to finitude. The only way to avoid the possibility of suffering is to avoid finitude. It is not suffering *per se* that is a problem,
but suffering that is without any apparent meaning, suffering that is caused by

callous indifference, or malicious intent, suffering that is caused for no good reason. This is meaningless suffering. This is where we find an overlap with the problem of evil.

We have already considered some of the "solutions" to the problem of evil when we considered different approaches to creation. When we consider evil "ontologically," in terms of determining its causes, we have limited options:

1. Evil is caused, and caused by some anti-God being such as the devil—this is dualism.
2. Evil is caused, and caused by God—this seems blasphemous.
3. Evil is uncaused—this is the classical Christian ontology of evil, that evil is privation, the privation of the good (*privatio bonum*).

The fundamental privation involved is a privation in the will, that is, sin. The decisions of the will are meant to be caused by "good reasons." A privation of that causation is where the will is moved by something other than good reasons. This absence of "good reasons" is the basic experience of the meaninglessness of evil. When we look at acts of terror, such as the destruction of the Twin Towers on September 11, 2001, we simply cannot find any "good reason" why anyone would do such a thing. It is evil because it is so pointless. The classical exposition of this in the Christian tradition is found in Augustine's *Confessions*, book 2, where Augustine examines his own childhood motivations for stealing pears from his neighbor. Each possible motivation evaporates on examination, leading him to conclude that his act has no good reason whatsoever. Book 7 of the *Confessions* then gives a more ontological analysis of evil as the privation of the good, of being. Evil has no substance, no being; rather, it is the privation of being, the being of *meaningfulness*.

The complexity here is that suffering can be viewed as a privation too. Suffering is a privation of the fullness of being proper to a conscious being. It indicates a diminishment of our being. However, this is not evil in the proper moral sense of the word. It is sometimes referred to as "physical evil" as distinct from "moral evil." Nonetheless, the ground of so-called physical evil is finitude, and even finitude itself can be considered a privation, the privation of unlimited being—hence the temptation of the serpent, "you will be like God" (Gen 3:5). But to view finite being primarily in terms of privation is to go down the path of various dualistic accounts that are implicitly suspicious of the goodness of finite created realities.

On the other hand, much of what we identify in terms of physical evil—for example, earthquakes and other natural disasters, diseases, malformations, and so on—arise out the real contingency of the universe, because it is constructed on the basis of both deterministic and statistical causation. Because God chooses that there be real contingency, including the most highly valued contingency of human freedom, there will always be a statistical spread of outcomes. What is possible, with however small a probability, becomes inevitable over long periods and for large numbers. The very processes that drive evolutionary development allow for the possibility of genetic deformations and diseases (e.g., Down's syndrome, cystic fibrosis, sickle cell anemia, and so on) with all their painful consequences. In that sense God wills these sufferings because God wills the world to be a world in which such things can and will happen. The fact that people overcome such illnesses and disabilities is a constant reminder that suffering is not the greatest evil, and even in these sufferings meaning can be found. There can be dignity for us even in times of great suffering. To quote Pope John Paul II:

> Suffering as it were contains a special call to the virtue which a human being must exercise on her own part. And this is the virtue of perseverance in bearing whatever disturbs and causes harm. In doing this, the individual unleashes hope which maintains in her the conviction that suffering will not get the better of her, that it will not deprive her of her dignity as a human being, a dignity linked to awareness of the meaning of life. (*Salvifici Doloris* 23)

Sin and Suffering

It is important to acknowledge that there is a strong existential linkage between the problems of suffering and evil. Even in the Christian context we find assertions of the link between sin and death—"Therefore, just as sin came into the world through one man, and death came through sin, and so death spread to all because all have sinned" (Rom 5:12). Adam and Eve were expelled from the garden to face trial, suffering, and death, because they ate the forbidden fruit of the tree of life. Do we in fact believe that "if Adam had not sinned then we would not have suffered and died"?

We know from scientific accounts that death and suffering have been part of the biological order since the very beginning of life. The death of organisms is often the basis for the life of another organism, and the decay of one generation of living beings becomes the fertilizer for the next generation of living things. Surely death is "natural," part of the natural order of things? What difference does sin make in such a situation?

It is difficult to speculate on what human life would be like if there were no sin. Clearly the biological capacity for death and suffering are intrinsic to one's bodily constitution. However, one suggestion we can make is that sin changes the meaning of death and suffering. Because of sin, suffering and death become ambiguous realities, tinged with a sense of loss and even pun-ishment—Why did this happen to me? What did I do to deserve it? Why do we spontaneously link suffering with punishment in this way? Why is suffer-ing only "fair" if it is linked somehow with guilt? Is death a joyous "return to the Father," or does it lead to judgment and the possibility of condemnation?

Questions such as these indicate that suffering and death have taken on a new meaning in the light of sin and evil. Because of this new meaning the reality of suffering and death has changed for us. In this case we can say, "death came through sin" (Rom 5:12), in that the form of death we now expe-rience is a different reality from the nature of death without sin. It has the character of "punishment for sin," which it did not have before. It is now an ambiguous event in our lives, one we face with fear and trepidation, because of the ambiguity of our lives affected by sin.

Why Evil?

Finally, we can ask, why is there evil anyway? Perhaps the most shocking response to the question of "why evil?" is that in fact it has no answer. Why evil occurs is a fundamental mystery, and one that completely lacks an intel-ligent answer. Even God cannot answer the question of why someone sins. No satisfactory response can be found that would provide an intelligent answer to the question. The mystery of sin is a mystery even to God. Lonergan put the matter this way:

> We can know sin as a fact; we cannot place it in intelligible correlation with other things except *per accidens* [accidentally]; that is, one sin can be corre-lated with another, for deficient antecedents have defective consequents; but the metaphysical surd of sin cannot be related explanatorily or causally with the integers that are objective truth; for sin is really irrational, a depar-ture at once from the ordinance of the divine mind and from the dictate of right reason. The rational and the irrational cannot mix, except in fallacious speculation. And this precept is not merely relative to man; it is absolute. The mysteries of faith are mysteries only to us because of their excess of intelligibility; but the *mysterium iniquitatis* [mystery of iniquity] is myste-rious in itself and objectively, because of a defect of intelligibility.[26]

One might weaken the question by asking rather, Why does God allow evil? One immediate response is to state that God does not allow evil—in fact God forbids evil through the moral law: "hate what is evil, hold fast to what is

---

26. Lonergan, *Grace and Freedom*, 115.

good" (Rom 12:9). Further, God offers us divine grace so that we may resist the specious attraction of evil. So God enjoins us to resist sin and empowers us to do so.

One might further weaken the question to, Why doesn't God do something about evil? The presumption is that God is not doing something about it. Even our own moral indignation at evil is itself a movement toward good, which God creates in us. Further, God acts through the life, death, and resurrection of Jesus to offer us forgiveness of our sins, and sends the Spirit to empower us to resist evil. The life of Jesus is an extended parable for how God deals with the problem of evil, namely, through redemptive suffering. The real question is not whether God is doing something, or should be doing more, but whether we are doing enough in response to the actions God has taken. For the problem of evil is a practical problem requiring a practical response. It is not a theoretical problem that we can "think away" or rationalize.

Finally, we might weaken the question even further, Why does God create a world in which evil occurs? Now human freedom is a great good; with freedom certainly comes the possibility of sin. There is a gap, however, between the possibility and the actuality of sinning. Could God have made a universe in which in fact no one ever sinned? Perhaps, but even in a world where sin occurs, responsibility for that sin remains with the sinner, not God. Certainly God could have made a world without freedom, but freedom is among the highest created values, a great good. And the fact of evil, unintelligible though it is, makes possible a new type of good, that of mercy, forgiveness, and redemption. This is not a "reason" for evil, or even for allowing evil. It is God's response to the problem of evil, drawing good out of the evil that arises. In the end all we can really assert is that, despite the presence and fact of evil, this creation is still good—indeed it is very good.[27]

PERSPECTIVES FROM OTHER RELIGIONS

Christians derive their belief in creation from the Scriptures, though Christianity also upholds a strong tradition of natural theology that would argue that these beliefs are congruent with and even derivable in some sense from reason alone (DS 3004).[28] Nonetheless other religions have their own perspectives in

---

27. It is perhaps worth noting here that the argument regarding this world being the "best of all possible worlds" because God creates it as good, is entirely fallacious. It assumes some uniform scale against which all possible worlds can be measured, and it assumes in addition that the scale has an upper bound. Without an upper bound the notion becomes vacuous.

28. H. Denzinger and A. Schönmetzer, eds., *Enchiridion Symbolorum Definitionum et Declarationum de Rebus Fidei et Morum*, 36th ed. (Freiburg im Breisgau: Herder, 1965) (hereafter DS). This

relation to the question of creation and the related issues of providence and evil. We shall now consider two of these.

Buddhism

We have already considered some of the differences between the Christian understanding of the human condition and that of Buddhism. Buddhism focuses attention on the problem of suffering, while Christianity views this as secondary to the problem of evil. This also reflects divergent approaches to the question of creation. For Buddhism there is no real sense of creation as the product of a divine creator. The world simply is, and is eternal. Buddhism has no creation myth, and the Buddha was not interested in metaphysical speculation about the origins of the world. For Buddhists, what "creates" the world is the mind, and this is in some sense an illusion. The materiality of the world is "unreal," an illusion that we create in living our lives. The aim of Buddhism is enlightenment, to see through the illusion of the world and the desires that go with it. When we see through the illusion of creation we can eliminate our desires, and with it the suffering (*dukkha*) that these desires cause. When all desire is finally eliminated, we reach nirvana, or extinction.

We can analyze this position from a Christian perspective in light of some of what we have discussed above. If one assumes that the world has no creator, no origin, but is eternally existing, then it has no fundamental intelligibility grounded in a creative act of a wise and loving God. It comes closer to the view of Aristotle that God creates out of preexistent matter, only without God. Hence, there is not real order in creation, only the order imposed on it by the mind, in a desperate attempt to avoid total chaos. But this order is illusory, and our desperation for order leads us to desire the things of the world and so leads to suffering. In a sense, Buddhism is overwhelmed by the omnipresence of suffering, in which it can find no value or meaning. The only solution can be escape from our suffering and finitude by the elimination of all desire and resultant personal dissolution.

This is very different from the Christian position, which affirms both the reality and the goodness of the material world, grounded in the wise and loving act of God. For Christians the problem of the human condition is not suffering and desire but evil and the distortions of desire that occur in sin. Indeed, Christianity can envisage a positive role for suffering in overcoming evil. Rather than eliminate desire, the redemption that Christianity seeks lib-

---

teaching of Vatican I is repeated in *Dei Verbum* 6, the Second Vatican Council's Dogmatic Constitution on Divine Revelation.

erates our desires to embrace the totality of the good, the Kingdom of God, a kingdom of justice and peace. Christians are actually called to a life of desire, but a desire for all things that are good, each desired in its proper proportion. Death then brings not extinction but the fulfillment of our ordered desire in the vision of God.

Hinduism

Hinduism is a very complex religious phenomenon. It comprises deep mystical elements, profound philosophical thought, together with popular manifestations that strike many Western moderns as bordering on the bizarre. In seeking some point of comparison with Christianity I shall consider a particular school of Hindu thought, Advaita Vedanta, which offers a "nondualist" interpretation of creation.[29] Many interpret Hindu teaching on creation as a form of monism whereby there is in fact only one reality, *Brahman*, the changeless, eternal ground of all being. The world that we experience is mere illusion, an appearance of being. The main "problem" of human existence is ignorance resulting in a dualistic consciousness that fails to see the fundamental oneness of all things. This stress on oneness is not just a philosophical position, but is also affirmed in the experience of Hindu mystics. Redemption is the overcoming of dualist consciousness and the realization that there is only one reality, that the higher self (*atman*) is Brahman. When the illusion of the world is stripped away, all that "remains is the impersonal, perfect *Brahman*-consciousness beyond relation, which is infinite, simple, eternal, joyous self-shining. Nothing remains to compromise the radiance, simplicity, fullness and transcendence of this One."[30]

A Christian response to this would want to say yes and no. On the one hand, terms such as "infinite," "simple," "eternal," and "transcendent" resonate with the Christian understanding of God. On the other hand, the Christian conception is of a personal God who exists in a loving relationship with creation. The Vedantan response to Christian belief is to view Christianity as an inferior religion, caught up in a dualistic understanding whereby "God and the world . . . appear in relation to each other as limited parts of a larger whole."[31]

---

29. I am drawing on Bradley Malkovsky, "Advaita Vedanta and Christian Faith," *Journal of Ecumenical Studies* 36 (1999): 397-422. The work by Francis Xavier Clooney, *Theology after Vedanta: An Experiment in Comparative Theology* (Albany: State University of New York Press, 1993), also provides some useful comparative material with a fuller methodological basis; see esp. 153-208.

30. Malkovsky, "Advaita Vedanta and Christian Faith," 402.

31. Ibid., 404. This criticism from Advaita Vedanta can be directed more to process theology than to classic Christian theology.

To them Christian belief in a personal God is little more than an anthropomorphic projection, particularly when they read biblical stories of God being angry, or destroying nations, or changing his mind.

However, just as we must distinguish popular Hinduism from its more philosophical expressions, so too we must recognize the same distinction in Christianity. While many Christians may take biblical stories at face value, early church fathers were aware of the difficulty in taking such stories literally. Origen warned against anthropomorphism in reading biblical stories about God, and Thomas Aquinas presents an account of God as creator in which few would recognize the God of the biblical narrative. For Aquinas, while the world is really related to God, God is not really related to the world, in the sense that creation cannot change or impact God in any way (*Summa Theologiae* I q. 3 a. 7).[32] God is wholly Other from creation, not limited by it in any way. God is not just another being, but Being itself (*subsistens esse*).

In fact, some have argued that there are striking similarities between these two philosophical accounts of creation. The Vedantan position of the illusory character of the world is similar to the insistence of Aquinas on the radical contingency of creation. Creation is contingent not in terms of the chance and necessity we experience in creation but in terms of the more fundamental contingency of the very being of creation. Only God is necessary being, just as for the Hindu thinkers only Brahman is truly real. The insistence of the Vedantan position that Brahman is impersonal can act as an important corrective to Christians who too easily anthropomorphize God, reducing the reality of God to the same level as ourselves, only bigger!

CONCLUSION

Christian belief in creation, notably in the goodness of creation, is a fundamental base for all our theology of grace, redemption, and eschatology. Nonetheless, it is a belief that has been subject to vigorous questioning in modern times, particularly from process thinkers. As we move into a broader multifaith perspective, it is important to recognize the distinctive features of that belief, especially in relation to Eastern belief systems. Christianity's commitment to the goodness of creation is unequivocal, and it is precisely because of this commitment that it feels with greatest urgency the problem of sin and evil. The Christian story, however, speaks of more than creation and sin; it speaks of grace and redemption. The aberration that is sin is never the last word, for God responds to our human plight with love and forgiveness. These

---

32. Henceforth *ST.*

culminate in an eschatological future, the "resurrection of the dead," which we can scarcely imagine. These issues and concerns, then, set the agenda for the present work, to explore these classical concerns in the light of modern science, contemporary Christian thought, the best of the Catholic tradition, and an increasingly multifaith global context.

QUESTIONS FOR REFLECTION

1. Modern science speaks of the beginning of the universe in terms of a Big Bang. How is this different from the Christian conception of creation *ex nihilo?*
2. Many Christians take Genesis literally. How can we reconcile the biblical account of creation with a scientific account that tells us that the universe is billions of years old?
3. Often we have experiences that appear to be chance but are very meaningful, such as a chance meeting with a friend. Can you illustrate from your own experiences the meaning of "providence"?
4. People often identify the problems of evil and suffering. How would you distinguish them?
5. If the problem of evil is one of a lack of meaning, how do we then work to overcome evil?

SUGGESTIONS FOR FURTHER READING AND STUDY

Burrell, David. "Does Process Theology Rest on a Mistake?" *Theological Studies* 43 (1982): 125-35.

Clifford, Richard J. "The Hebrew Scriptures and the Theology of Creation." *Theological Studies* 46 (1985): 507-23.

John Paul II. *Salvifici Doloris*, at http://www.vatican.va/holy_father/john_paul_ii/apost_letters/documents/hf_jp-ii_apl_11021984_salvificidoloris_en.html.

Malkovsky, Bradley. "Advaita Vedanta and Christian Faith." *Journal of Ecumenical Studies* 36 (1999): 397-422.

Ormerod, Neil. "Chance and Necessity, Providence and God." *Irish Theological Quarterly* 70 (2005): 263-78.

Westermann, Claus. *Genesis 1-11: A Commentary*. London: SPCK, 1984.

Whitehead, Alfred North. *Process and Reality: An Essay in Cosmology*. Edited by David Griffin and Donald W. Sherburne. Corrected ed. New York: Free Press, 1978.

2

Human Beings within God's Creation

IN THE PREVIOUS CHAPTER we considered the issue of creation in general, the creation of an ordered cosmos from an act of sovereign, transcendent, and divine wisdom and freedom. In Genesis 1, special place is given to the creation of human beings. They alone, of all creation, are said to be made "in our image, according to our likeness" (Gen 1:26). It is only after the creation of human beings that God pronounces creation to be "very good." Further, human beings alone are given some mastery over and responsibility for the rest of creation (Gen 1:28; 2:15), while the Psalmist asks:

> What are human beings that you are mindful of them,
>   mortals that you care for them?
> Yet you have made them a little lower than God,
>   and crowned them with glory and honor. (Ps 8:4-5)

It is clear that the Bible considers human beings to be the pinnacle of God's material creation, at least in terms of all the other creatures that God creates.

Two elements of modern science tend to make it more difficult to hold on to this biblical vision of the special place of human beings. The first of these arises from the sheer size of the universe. While an earlier time held that the earth was the center of a fairly limited creation, we now know that the universe is billions of years old, billions of light years across, with billions upon billions of other suns, and in all probability planets, much like our own. What claim to specialness can our own existence have in the face of such immensity? The second element is the theory of evolution, which understands human existence as the chance result of millions of years of random genetic mutations. Human beings become "naked apes," the product of "selfish genes," no more special than chimpanzees or dolphins. How can Christian faith respond to such claims?

THE SPECIALNESS OF LIFE IN THE COSMOS

Let us consider the question of the size and age of the universe in relation to the special place of life. The first thing to note is that the age and size of the universe are directly related to eachother. According to the best contemporary science, the universe began with a massive expansion, commonly called the Big Bang, and that expansion continues to "push" the universe apart. Basically the universe is as big as it is because it is as old as it is. A smaller universe is a younger universe, and an older one is bigger. How does this observation relate to the question of life?

Biological life is the product of complex biochemical processes that depend on the availability and existence of the basic chemical building blocks of life—carbon, oxygen, nitrogen, iron, calcium, and so on. These elements were simply not available in the evolution of the universe until well beyond the initial expansion, after several billion years in fact. In its initial stages, the universe consisted of subatomic particles, which settled down into a vast sea mainly of hydrogen. Under the influence of gravity, clouds of hydrogen collapsed into stars, which began the process of nuclear fusion, leading eventually to the formation of heavier elements than hydrogen, a process called nucleosynthesis. But these elements remained locked into the stars until those stars exploded into supernovae, spreading their material out into the universe to be sucked into other stars, or to form interstellar dust, which would eventually condense into planets. Without this process of nucleosynthesis there would be no planets, no solar systems, and no chemicals from which life could form. All this takes time, billions of years in fact. The answer to the question, Why is the universe so old? is that there would not be anyone around to ask the question if it were not as old as it is. Indeed, we are all "made of stardust" because every higher element within our bodies was at some time forged in the heart of a star.[1] As some have concluded, the universe would have to be as big and as old as it is for there to be life anywhere in the universe. A smaller, younger universe would not have had the time for the necessary processes to take place. Indeed, even if we were the sole intelligent inhabitants of the entire universe, it would still have to be as big and old as it is.[2]

Some have pushed this idea further to argue that the universe is fine-tuned for life, that there are a number of features of the universe that were necessary for life to emerge, some of which were established in the first moments of the Big Bang. For example, the rate of expansion of the universe needs to be very close to exactly what it is: too large a rate and the universe flies apart before stars and galaxies can form; too small, and the universe collapses back in on itself before the process has a chance to develop higher

---

1. See Denis Edwards, *Jesus and the Cosmos* (Homebush: St Paul's Publications, 1991), for a fuller account of this observation.

2. So-called creation science might argue that God created a world that simply looks much older than it actually is. It is unclear why God would act in such a deceptive manner.

chemicals. This has led to an approach called the "anthropic cosmological principle."

The basic observation is that there are a number of physical constants and quantities present in the initial stages of the universe, which, if they are a little bit different, would result in a universe that is actively hostile to the formation of biological life. Sometimes these tolerances are very small; that is, small variations in either direction, bigger or smaller, would result in a lifeless universe. Physicists John Barrow and Frank Tipler formulate the "Weak Anthropic Principle" thus:

> The observed values of all physical and cosmological quantities are not equally probable, but they take on values restricted by the requirement that there exist sites where carbon-based life can evolve and the requirement that the universe be old enough for it to have already done so.[3]

Critics argue that this principle is circular, in the sense that if it did not hold there would be no one around to make the observation. It does not constitute evidence of "design," just that things happen to be a certain way. On the other hand, one cannot but be amazed at the amount of "fine-tuning" for life present in the universe. For many this fine-tuning of the universe for life supports their belief in the existence of a provident God.[4]

THE "MIRACLE" OF WATER[5]

As Barrow and Tipler note, "water is actually one of the strangest substances known to science."[6] Despite the fact that we take it so much for granted, water displays a number of properties that make it the ideal medium for the development of life. The one we shall consider here is the commonly observed phenomenon that frozen water, ice, floats. It is an almost universal phenomenon that the solid form of a material is denser than its liquid form. Consequently the solid form sinks to the bottom of

3. John D. Barrow and Frank J. Tipler, *The Anthropic Cosmological Principle* (Oxford: Oxford University Press, 1988), 16. Apart from the question of the size of the universe, Barrow and Tipler also consider the process of nucleosynthesis, whereby hydrogen nuclei are converted to a helium nucleus, which is dependent on the strong nuclear force, and even the geometry of ice crystals which makes ice less dense than liquid water.

4. This argument for providential "fine-tuning" should not be confused with contemporary debates about "intelligent design." Providential fine-tuning takes its stand on the ways in which the "setup" of the cosmos, in terms of the laws of physics and various initial conditions, is conducive to the emergence of life. So-called intelligent design argues that God actively intervenes at specific times and places to create life or otherwise mold the evolutionary process.

5. Barrow and Tipler, *Anthropic Cosmological Principle*, 524-41.

6. Ibid., 525.

the liquid form. But this is not the case with water. The reason is that the angle between the two hydrogen atoms and the oxygen atom is very close to the ideal tetrahedral angle, so that when water freezes it forms a relatively loosely structured tetrahedral crystal. This loose structure gives ice a lesser density than water, and hence ice floats. Barrow and Tipler go on to note that this property makes water ideally suited to the development of life. "If ice were not less dense than water, it would sink on freezing. The coldest water in a lake or ocean would congregate near the bottom and there freeze. Ice would accumulate at the bottom; the amount would become greater each year as more ice formed during winter and did not melt during summer. Finally, all the lakes and oceans would be entirely frozen."[7] Instead, ice freezes on the top and provides insulation, protecting emerging life below it.

Why is the angle so close to the tetrahedral angle? It depends on a complex interaction of a variety of forces within the water molecule. Slight changes in various factors in these forces would lead to a very different outcome. At one level it is just a coincidence. At another level it makes life as we know it possible.

The consequence of this is that the possibility of the existence of life in the universe is not to be taken for granted. It depends on multiple factors, several of which are finely balanced. Without these multiple balances operating in the universe we would not exist. To put it bluntly, we are only beginning to have any conception of what it takes to make a universe capable of sustaining biological life forms. The complexity of the question is really beyond our present comprehension. Modern science is only now identifying some of these multiple requirements.

An emerging nontheistic response to these observations is to invoke a theory of the multiverse, that is, of a large, if not infinite, number of alternative universes, all causally disconnected, each with vastly different physical laws and conditions.[8] Among this large number of universes, ours happens to be one where life is possible, but there are others where no life evolved. This theory seeks to eliminate any sense of importance about the fact that there is life in our universe. The problem with such an account is that it is scientifically unverifiable, given that the various universes would seem to be causally dis-

---

7. Ibid., 533.

8. See, for example, Martin J. Rees, *Just Six Numbers: The Deep Forces That Shape the Universe* (New York: Basic Books, 2000), 148-61. This scenario has been made popular in various forms of science fiction that invoke notions of a "parallel universe." These often confuse two distinct physical theories, those of the multiverse, in which each "universe" has different physical laws, and the "many worlds" interpretation of quantum mechanics, in which reality branches off into alternate paths and histories.

connected.[9] We simply cannot know of their existence by any empirical means. As such the theory is unscientific.

EVOLUTION AND THE CREATION OF HUMAN BEINGS

The second challenge to the special claims made by Christian faith for human beings arises from the theory of evolution. The formulation of the theory of evolution is one of the most significant cultural events of the last two centuries. Prior to its formulation, the cultural expectation was that things would stay the same, unless some good reason could be found to change them. Following its formulation the expectation is now that things will continue to change, or evolve, and that to stay unchanged demands some rationale. We have moved from a fundamentally static conception of reality to a fundamentally dynamic conception, largely through the influence of the theory of evolution. What began as a theory to explain the diversity and development of new species has become a totalizing worldview for everything—not just biological species, but the cosmos, institutions, cultures, technology, economies, and so on. It has taken on a total explanatory quality and in some settings become clearly ideological.

The evolutionary "cultural revolution" has influenced Christian belief in a number of ways. First, the fact that evolution implies a contingent element in creation has been used by some to claim that there is no design for the universe. It is used to reject any argument "by design" that might lead to belief in a creator God. We have already seen in our consideration of providence and contingency in the previous chapter how misleading such a claim is. Second, evolution has been used to suggest that human beings have no special place in creation. We are just the product of random mutations, not the purpose and peak of creation, as suggested by Christian belief. Third, among the ideological features of evolutionary thought, one prominent element has been social Darwinism, the suggestion that our social order should be one of the "survival of the fittest." Such a suggestion hits at the heart of Christian concern for the poor and help for those most in need. Fourth, for those who identify Christian belief with a literal reading of Genesis, evolution is used to reject Christian belief because of its supposed opposition to scientific thought. As we noted earlier, to read the opening chapters of Genesis literally is basically to misunderstand their significance, and, in the face of modern science, to bring faith into disrepute.

---

9. In some accounts the "other universes" are not in fact causally disconnected; but then they may lose their claim to be "another" universe—they are then just another rather odd part of our own universe.

This is a tangled web to deal with, involving scientific, philosophical, ideological, and theological judgments of varying difficulty. Let us deal with these matters constructively; that is, let us seek out the intelligibility of an evolving system. In this I shall be dependent on Bernard Lonergan's notion of emergent probability. This broadens the point of entry beyond the basic biological idea to the more general notion of "evolution" or emergence within the whole created order. It involves a further specification of what we have already spoken about in the previous chapter on the notion of providence and deterministic and statistical lawfulness.[10]

Let us begin with the notion of causal lawfulness, which is either classical (deterministic) or statistical (contingent):

$$A \to B, \text{ unless something acts to prevent it}$$
OR
$$A \to B \text{ with a certain statistical probability}$$

In both cases a statistical element enters, for "unless something acts to prevent it" will itself be governed by a statistical law. Consider now a causal chain:

$$A \to B \to C \to D \ldots \to Z$$

Then the probability of getting to the end of the chain diminishes dramatically with each added step, for the likelihood of getting to the end of the chain is the product of each of the individual probabilities.[11] Consider instead a causal cycle:

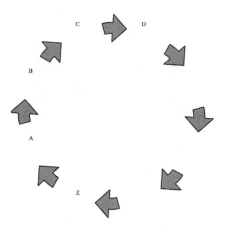

---

10. This draws on material from Bernard J. F. Lonergan, *Insight: A Study of Human Understanding*, ed. Frederick E. Crowe and Robert M. Doran, Collected Works of Bernard Lonergan 3 (Toronto: University of Toronto Press, 1992), 141-51.

11. Astronomer Fred Hoyle once argued that the possibility of life occurring was like the possibility of the Boeing 747 emerging from a hurricane in a junk yard. Part of Hoyle's difficulty was that he thought of the process as a question of causal chains rather than causal cycles.

This shift from a chain of events to a cycle of events dramatically increases the probability of the occurrence of the cycle itself, becoming more like the sum of the individual probabilities. Once such a cycle is established, it can in fact maintain itself. Lonergan calls such a cycle a "scheme of recurrence." Lonergan thus distinguishes between the probability of emergence of the scheme (which might be quite low) and the probability of survival of the scheme (which might be much higher). These two probabilities govern the emergence and survivability of the scheme. Once such a scheme emerges with a high enough probability of survival, it can itself become an element in an even higher scheme of recurrence. We thus have higher-order schemes consisting of schemes within schemes within schemes of recurrence.

The existence and importance of such cycles can be noted in a number of fields, for example, the Krebs cycle in cellular biochemistry,[12] the nitrogen cycle in ecological science,[13] and the Gulf Stream current in oceanography. These are well-known examples, but in fact such schemes are commonplace in most scientific settings if you know what you are looking for. Indeed much of the emerging science of ecology involves the identification of such cycles within the biosphere. What we are learning from ecological science is that the removal of one element in a causal cycle is often enough to destroy the whole scheme. Hence, the destruction of one plant may lead to the elimination of an insect, which is then no longer available for a certain species of bird, and so on, leading to major shifts in a local ecology.

Lonergan's notion of a "scheme of recurrence" removes many of the difficulties associated with the evolutionary cultural revolution. Its basis is an acknowledgment that there are deterministic and statistical laws. These interact to produce the resulting schemes. It thus allows for a "design" argument without falling over into determinism, because in God's providential order large numbers and long time frames have explanatory power for statistical systems. The scheme of recurrence also removes the ideological element because it no longer speaks of "survival of the fittest" but of probabilities of emergence and of survival. When we move to the human realm, these probabilities are also the product of human decision making, not just biological

---

12. The Krebs cycle in biochemistry is the basic cycle of energy production in living cells, breaking down sugars and producing carbon dioxide. It was discovered by Hans Adolf Krebs in 1937, for which he was awarded the Nobel Prize for medicine in 1953. Various Web pages give an animated version of the cycle.

13. The nitrogen cycle is "one of the most important nutrient cycles found in terrestrial ecosystems." It involves the fixation of atmospheric nitrogen in inorganic forms (nitrates and ammonium ions), its transformation into organic forms (amino acids, nucleic acids), and eventual release back into the atmosphere as nitrogen or its various oxides. For more details, see http://www.physicalgeography.net/fundamentals/9s.html (accessed July 11, 2006).

forces. And so we cannot draw the conclusions of social Darwinism that would leave the poor, the sick, and the weak to "fend for themselves." Does it, however, present us with a hierarchically constituted notion of reality? And are humans at the "top" of such a hierarchy? Do human have a special place?

The question of whether being is hierarchically constituted can be answered in the affirmative as long as one is able to resist any temptation to accept a reductionist account of reality. It is easy for the physicist to claim that chemistry is really just a branch of physics; but we still retain separate departments in universities. We train people in very different skills. Chemists and physicists publish in different journals and so on. Is this just academic tribalism, or are we dealing with differing realities? Similar comments could be made about biology and psychology. Do we reduce psychology to biology, biology to chemistry, chemistry to physics, and physics to what? Or do we recognize a hierarchically ordered structure to the physical world that recognizes the reality of increasing complexification? The difference between the reductionist account and the "realist" account adopted here is that the first conceives of reality as constituted by looking—the more intensely we look, the smaller things we can find. The "realist" account conceives of reality as constituted by intelligibility and so recognizes the reality of increasing complexity. Increasing complexity points to new and richer intelligibility and hence new reality.

The question whether human beings occupy some special place in this hierarchy then relates to the question of whether the reality of being human is constituted by defining characteristics that cannot be understood simply as biological or psychological. The traditional answer is to argue that the human soul, understood as the form or intelligibility of a living thing, enjoys a spiritual dimension. This means that, although the soul operates as a higher-level integration of the substratum of physical, chemical, biological, and psychological activities, it is in itself something more than these and relatively independent of its material basis.

SPIRIT AND MATTER

We are probably familiar with language that speaks of "body and soul" or "spirit and matter." Such language can be dualistic, positing two distinct realities, one material, the other spiritual; or it may reflect something of the "duality" of human existence, a duality of distinct but related principles which we speak of as matter and spirit. However, even our discussion above highlights the compact nature of speech about "matter." The material order is itself highly structured, comprising physical, chemical, biological, and psychological orders. Each "layer" of this material order remains open to higher-level integrations, so that the physical is integrated into the chemical, without any violation of physical laws; the chemical is integrated into the biological without any violation of chemical laws, and so on. Is the psyche, with its instinctive drives and conscious responses to pleasure and pain, the highest level of integration to be found in human beings, as suggested by Sigmund Freud and others, or is there something higher within which the psychological is itself integrated? Our response is to speak of the human spirit as a higher level of integration that attains a certain level of independence from its material substratum. What, then, is this human spirit?

Spirit and the Search for Meaning

Rather than begin with a definition, I would like to focus on a basic experience of life as identified by theologian Robert Doran. Doran speaks of our human life project as existential and aesthetic, a dramatic living out of the tension of spirit and matter. He speaks of this project as "the search for direction in the movement of life."[14] We are all caught up in the movement of life, the day-to-day events, the major upheavals, as well as our own feelings in response to these events. In this confluence of inner affect and outer events we seek some sense of direction, of purpose, of meaning to guide our lives. Simply to drift, to be carried along by events, to be overwhelmed by our own feelings, anxieties, fears, or even our exhilarations is to lead a diminished life. We need purpose and direction. That which searches for direction, that which yearns for purpose and meaning, that principle which is within us is the human spirit. Doran would speak of this tension between spirit and matter as a dialectic of transcendence and limitation. To cut off from the transcendence of spirit is to surrender oneself to the rhythms of the psyche, leading to depression and psychosis. To deny the limitation of matter and psyche, to live "like angels," is to invite escape into manic fantasy. In a similar vein Aquinas criticized the Cathars for forgetting their human nature in their rejection of bodiliness (*Summa contra Gentiles* book 3, ch. 119); Aquinas always stressed the need for intellect to "turn to the phantasm [i.e., imagination]" for its proper operation (*ST* I q. 76, a. 2; q. 79 a. 4).

And so we might argue that the human spirit is that which searches, that which explores, and what it searches for are meaning, truth, and value. This is not a search with the eyes—we open our eyes to search the horizon; but this

---

14. Robert M. Doran, *Theology and the Dialectics of History* (Toronto: University of Toronto Press, 1990), 45-49.

is not the type of search we are talking about. This is not an exploration that begins with a single physical step, putting our best foot forward. Rather it begins with questions: What am I to do? Where is my life heading? What am I to make of myself? There is something basic about these questions. German theologian Karl Rahner suggests that we cannot "question the question," in the sense that the question is indubitable, beyond doubt.[15] To question questioning is simply to affirm the reality of questioning by raising yet another question.

But there is something more basic, more primordial than the question. The question is a verbal expression, but behind the question is something more elemental. It is a hunger, a thirst, a wonder, an awe, and a desire. It is a desire for meaning, truth, and value. Simply as desire, it knows no limits. Whenever someone tries to say, "so far but no farther, your search for meaning must end here and now" we can rebel and say, "Why?" Our questioning transcends any arbitrary limits. Inasmuch as our desire bears fruit in finding meaning, truth, and value, it grows in confidence and surety that the cosmos is meaningful, not deceptive, and worthy of our love. Inasmuch as our desire is frustrated in its search we grow more and more anxious, more desperate for meaning, latching onto whatever passing fad catches our attention. Or we may despair of any possibility of meaning, truth, and value. The universe becomes an empty void, meaningless, deceptive, and unlovable.

So we may think of the human spirit as that within us which desires meaning, truth, and value as the sources for direction in the movement of life; it is a desire that potentially encompasses everything and so is not limited by materiality. Still, in practice we often truncate the human spirit's search to the immediate, the commonplace. We remain satisfied with the limited reach of the present and ignore the breadth and depth of our primordial desire. Is this desire within us nothing more than a cosmic joke, a freak of evolutionary nature? Is our unlimited desire for meaning, truth, and value forever to be frustrated in an indifferent or even hostile universe? Or is there something or someone who can fulfill that desire? Is there someone who is so meaning-full, so truth-full, and so full of value that in this one and this one alone our spirit finds its true rest? Indeed, is our spirit simply a pale reflection of that greater Spirit, a dim echo, a sheer potential for what is fully realized in that greater Spirit? And is our desire not simply a plea into the void but in fact a call from that greater Spirit? For then we are not alone in our search, but we are actively engaged by the greater Spirit. We do not just seek that Spirit; that Spirit draws us on, as a partner and friend. This is something of what Aquinas meant when

---

15. Louis Roberts, *The Achievement of Karl Rahner* (New York: Herder & Herder, 1967), 18.

he called the human intellect a "created participation" in the divine intellect (*ST* I q. 84, a. 5).

Do other higher mammals—higher primates or dolphins—also share in this spiritual dimension? People who study animal behavior often point out the similarities between human behaviors and those of other higher mammals. Is this proof of their intelligence or of our animality? Are other animals simply conditioned by instinct and biological drives, or do they also search for meaning and value? While there are some intimations evident in some higher primates in some situations, there is little evidence that such a search is the central concern of their existence, as it is in the case of human beings.

Spirit and Freedom

Human freedom is an important element of our spiritual nature. The search for meaning, truth, and value is not blind or random; rather it is intelligent and responsible. Although the desire is an intrinsic element of our existence, our response to that desire is not automatic. It engages us as free beings, and so we become accountable for the quality of our response to this intrinsic desire. We can engage with energy, dedication, and drive, or we can disengage, lose ourselves in trivialities, or just despair of the possibility of finding meaning, truth, and vlaue.

To conceive of human freedom in this way requires that we question the dominant conception of freedom as "freedom of choice." In our consumer-driven world we tend to think of freedom in terms of the multiple choices that we have, the range of options we can exercise. But when we examine these choices, most of them concern trivialities. Having twenty different types of breakfast cereal does not make us more free. In fact, a multiplicity of trivial choices can distract us from the real task of our freedom, to seek direction in the movement of life. For the object of our decision making is not just the things "out there" that we choose; a more important object of our decision making is ourselves. Freedom is an act of self-constitution, the self as constituting itself through the decisions that it makes. The direction that I seek is one on which I take myself—shall I become more generous, more open, more loving, more responsible? Do I embrace virtue or succumb to vice? Every decision I make shapes me, constitutes me in some way, for better or worse.

Finally, our search for direction, and the freedom that it generates, is never absolute or unconditioned. We live in a world that sets the basic parameters of our search, that structures the options we can choose, prior to anything we might do or hope for. There are a variety of limits and constraints that render the effective reach of our freedom much less than its essentially unlimited intentionality.[16] Our search for direction is always located within a history of other searches from which we can learn, to which we adhere, or which we explicitly reject. We are not just isolated individuals; we are constituted as social and historical beings.

ANGELS?

The question may be raised about the existence of angels and their place in divine creation. The biblical material on angels conceives of them as divine messengers who bridge the gap between divine transcendence and terrestrial existence. The *Catechism of the Catholic Church* speaks of angels as "spiritual creatures" (*CCC* no. 350) and "as intelligent and free creatures, [they] have to journey toward their ultimate destinies by their free choice and preferential love" (no. 311). Further, they "have been present since creation and throughout the history of salvation" (no. 332). There is a significant gap, however, between the metaphysical conception of angels as pure spirits (as found for example in Aquinas) and popular beliefs in the nature and operation of angels. The picture is made more complex by the rise of new age beliefs focusing on angels.

That such purely spiritual beings can exist should not be doubted. The difficulty lies not in such a conception but in how to relate such beings to the material order of human existence. How can we know of their existence? How can their existence be manifest in the material order? Too often imagination takes over in supplying answers to such questions, and we emerge none the wiser.

Belief in the existence of angels can be a corrective to an overinflated sense of human specialness—there are higher orders of being than those, such as ourselves, linked with materiality. On the other hand, excessive interest in and concern with angels can distract us from the here and now of our existence, wherein we must work out our salvation "with fear and trembling" (Phil 2:12).

HUMAN EXISTENCE AS SOCIAL AND HISTORICAL

It is because human existence is spiritual, and not just reducible to the biological and the psychological, that human existence becomes so complex and variable, as is manifested in human history. We do not simply reproduce, hunt for food, eat, and sleep. With great ingenuity we organize ourselves into com-

---

16. See Lonergan, *Insight*, 643-45, on the distinction between essential and effective freedom.

plex social units, extended family groups, tribes, villages, kingdoms, states, and nations with various forms of governance, from tribal chiefs and councils to dictatorships, monarchies, and democracies with various constitutions and structures. With increasing liberation from mere subsistence we free ourselves from the drudgery of labor through art, music, and dance. We begin to speculate about the nature of things, inventing mathematics, science, philosophy, and theology. And so the search for meaning, truth, and value takes on a social, cultural, and historical dimension. It becomes a collaborative effort spanning the centuries.[17]

These social and cultural constructions mean that human existence is never "natural." None of these social and cultural elements can claim to be the "natural" or normative order of human existence. The social order is first and foremost a solution to the problem of people living together in justice and peace, sharing and cooperating, and of course failing in these goals as well. The great variations we witness in social organization in human history are a testament to human creativity. The cultural order is a massive and cumulative effort to make sense of the world, of human living, and of our place in the world, including the social order in which we find ourselves. As such, it can become a major resource in the human search for meaning, truth, and value, though it may equally become a hindrance in that search, as we shall consider in the next chapter. The complexities of human culture, from Aboriginal dreamtime myths to the philosophical writings of Immanuel Kant and Georg Hegel, to the scientific investigations of Albert Einstein and Stephen Hawking, all bear witness to the profundity of the questions and the difficulties in finding conclusive answers.

Concretely, human existence is never without these social and cultural elements; it is always "situated" socially and culturally. Jean-Jacques Rousseau's myth of the "noble savage," freed from all social and cultural accretions, has no basis in fact. Indeed, anthropologist Clifford Geertz has argued that without these accretions we would be worse off than animals, since our instinctive drives are so weak and plastic as to provide no reliable guide for living.[18] For

---

17. Perhaps the best examples of this collaborative process can be found in science and mathematics, which produce enormous cumulative progress through long-term cultural collaboration.

18. Cultural anthropologist Clifford Geertz argues that "the extreme generality, diffuseness, and variability of man's innate (that is, genetically programmed) response capacities mean that without the assistance of cultural patterns [as carriers of meaning, truth, and value], he would be functionally incomplete, not merely a talented ape who had, like some underprivileged child, unfortunately been prevented from realizing his full potentialities, but a kind of formless monster with neither sense of direction nor power of self-control, a chaos of spasmodic impulses and vague emotions" (*The Interpretation of Cultures: Selected Essays* [New York: Basic Books, 1973], 99). Such is the central importance of our orientation to meaning, truth, and value.

good or ill we find ourselves in social and cultural situations not of our making, benefiting from their strengths and suffering from their weaknesses. It
makes a difference to our search whether we are born in Stalinist North
Korea, apartheid South Africa, or Saddam Hussein's Iraq. Our personal story
of freedom, our own search for direction in the movement of life, is but one
element in a larger historical narrative, a narrative of progress, decline, and
redemption. We are both shaped by that narrative and contribute our own
story to it.

The Second Vatican Council captured this aspect of human existence when
it identified human beings as "social by nature":

> The fact that human beings are social by nature indicates that the better-
> ment of the person and the improvement of society depend on each other.
> Insofar as humanity by its very nature stands completely in need of life in
> society, it is and it ought to be the beginning, the subject and the object of
> every social organization. Life in society is not something accessory to
> humanity: through their dealings with others, through mutual service, and
> through fraternal and sororal dialogue, men and women develop all their
> talents and become able to rise to their destiny. (*Gaudium et Spes* 25)

On the other hand, we must always recognize that we are not simply the
products of these social and cultural forces in some deterministic sense. The
same human spirit that creates all our social and cultural orders is not itself
just their product, or there would be no major social and cultural changes. The
human spirit transcends these elements; it goes beyond them, criticizing existing social orders, conceiving of new orders, developing new philosophies, new
sciences, and even new religions. The restlessness of the human spirit cannot
be contained within the straitjackets of any social or cultural construct.

"MALE AND FEMALE GOD CREATED THEM"

A good illustration of the socially and culturally constructed nature of human
existence can be found in the ways in which we understand our existence as
male and female. Genesis 1:28 tells us that our original creation involved our
creation as "male and female." The distinction between the sexes is not some
cosmic error, nor is one gender to be preferred over the other since both have
their origin in the divine creation. Both are equally primordial in the eyes of
the author of Genesis 1. Genesis 2 presents a slightly different account, with
the female being derived from the male, who immediately recognizes his
affinity and relatedness to the one God has created as a helpmate. Nonetheless, this primordial sense of union is disrupted by the emergence of sin, lead-

ing to relationships of domination rather than equality (Gen 3). Already in these first three chapters of Genesis we can grasp something of the complexity of the question of gender in the biblical witness.

The basics of sexual differentiation are, of course, biological. On the level of anatomy, men and women are differentiated by their sexual organs, but there are also a variety of hormones and biological instincts that shape our sexual drives, desires, and orientations. Even at the basic biological level, sexual differentiation is complex and nuanced, as is evident in the variety of sexual responses in the animal world. At this basic biological level, sexual differentiation is fundamental to successful sexual reproduction and the continuance of the species. However, the human story cannot be reduced to mere biology.

In the task of developing social communities, human societies have found it efficient to assign different tasks to men and women in the hunting and gathering of food; the preparation and storage of food; and in the rearing, nurturing, and education of children. Such differentiations of labor are not "natural" or normative; rather, they are a response to recurrent needs within the community that seeks to deal with such needs in a practical and efficient way. This is evident in the wide variety of ways in which different societies in fact differentiate male and female roles. Such a differentiation of roles is based not on the characteristics of individuals but on perceptions of characteristics of the group—men are "generally" stronger than women, and so may be more suited to hunting, which requires physical strength and endurance. Women give birth and are biologically equipped to feed a newborn child, so they are "generally" more suited to child rearing. In such differentiation, if practiced justly, different genders play complementary roles in meeting social needs. Practiced unjustly, differentiation becomes an instrument of constraint that imposes social roles on people that limit their possibilities and establish patterns of domination and power.

Most societies tend to view the particular differentiations of roles within their own social order as "natural." They will express this by pointing to a source of meaning for differentiation that goes beyond the practical, usually to some founding myth. We find vestiges of this in Genesis 2, where the woman is designated as the "helpmate" to the first man. Ideally it is a relationship in which the man esteems the woman as intimately related to himself, "This at last is bone of my bones and flesh of my flesh" (Gen 2:23). However, when sin casts its dark shadow over human beings, the biblical author also recognizes that this relationship can become one of power and domination: "yet your desire shall be for your husband, and he shall rule over you" (Gen 3:16). This distortion of the relationship is not how it was meant to be in the beginning; rather, it arises out of the power of sin entering into human history.

These justifications for the differentiation of gender roles become increasingly elaborate as cultures become more complex and creative. As male power in society becomes entrenched, such justifications become ideological instruments to keep women locked into positions of subjugation and powerlessness, most evident in acts of sexual violence against women.[19] Some within the Christian tradition would view the curse of Eve not as an expression of the distortion that results from sin but as a just punishment from God. Men's "lording it over" women then becomes obedience to the "will of God." Women are the weak ones who seduce men into sin. They are less "spiritual" and more "carnal" than men who possess reason in greater measure and so should rule women just as reason should rule the passions.[20] And so we find some early church fathers discussing whether women actually have rational souls. Augustine denies that women are made "in the image and likeness of God" in the same way men are.

> but when she is referred to separately in her quality as a helpmeet, which regards the woman alone, then she is not the image of God, but as regards the male alone, he is the image of God as fully and completely as when the woman too is joined with him in one. (*De Trinitate* 7.7.10).[21]

Men have the image and likeness in themselves, while women have it inasmuch as they are subject to the man. Further, Aquinas argues, following the biological understanding of the day, that females are deformed males, caused by some corruption of the unborn fetus:

> As regards the individual nature, woman is defective and misbegotten, for the active force in the male seed tends to the production of a perfect likeness in the masculine sex; while the production of woman comes from defect in the active force or from some material indisposition, or even from some external influence; such as that of a south wind, which is moist, as the Philosopher observes. (*De Gener. Animal.* iv, 2)[22]

A very modern and elaborate version of this type of justification of gender roles can be found in the writings of liberation theologian Leonardo Boff. Drawing on the Jungian notion that everyone has within the psyche "mascu-

---

19. Evidence for this can be found in Susan Faludi, *Backlash: The Undeclared War against American Women* (New York: Crown, 1991).

20. For various examples drawn from the history of Christian literature, see Rosemary Radford Ruether, *Sexism and God-Talk: Toward a Feminist Theology*, 10th anniversary ed. (Boston: Beacon Press, 1993), 94-99, 167, 170.

21. Quoted in ibid., 95.

22. Quoted in ibid.

line" (*animus*) and "feminine" (*anima*) characteristics, Boff goes on to identify these in the following terms.

> The feminine—*in every human being, man and woman*—expresses the pole of darkness, mystery, depth, night, death, interiority, earth, feeling, receptivity, generative force, and the vitality of the human. The masculine—in every human being, man and woman—is an expression of the opposite pole: light, sun, time, impulse, surging power, order, exteriority, objectivity, reason.[23]

Reflection on this somewhat confusing cluster of symbols—for example, what links death and vitality, impulse and reason?—would suggest that what Boff is seeking to express is a basic dialectic of transcendence and limitation, the transcendence of the human spirit (present in equal measure in men and women) and the limitations of psyche, bodiliness, and materiality (present in equal measure in men and women). It is possible to argue that women are more in touch with the limitation pole, because of their biological cycles and capacity for childbirth, and that correlatively men are more alienated from this limitation pole, more in denial about the reality of bodies, sex, and death. But these are statements "in general" and may well reflect centuries of social and cultural construction along these lines. It is very difficult to argue that these represent "essential" differences between men and women or that a man is less "masculine" for being well grounded, or a woman less "feminine" for pursuing intellectual goals.

Because of the social and cultural constructions, the decisions and options facing men and women throughout human history have been very different. In particular, women have had very limited options up until the present day, confined largely to the sphere of home and family. The transcending of these options is driven, as we have noted, by the restlessness of the human spirit, which cannot be contained within the straitjackets of any social or cultural construct. That restlessness is not a male characteristic, but is present in both men and women. Because of that restlessness we can witness in the last two hundred years women breaking through the constraints imposed on them, socially, politically, economically, and culturally. Less than one hundred fifty years ago women were denied the vote in Western countries; many could not legally own or inherit property in their own name; and they were denied access to higher education and hence careers in medicine, science, and law. Indeed, many women involved in the early suffragist movement began their

---

23. Leonardo Boff, *The Maternal Face of God: The Feminine and Its Religious Expressions* (San Francisco: Harper & Row, 1987), 54.

political activism in the abolitionist movement. In their efforts to free slaves they noted several similarities between the plight of slaves and their own situation. Now these previous constraints are considered unthinkable in Western countries. Women and men are no longer limited by what may or may not be true of the genders "in general"; rather their decisions are made on the basis of their own individual inclinations, skills, and abilities. Biology is not destiny.

Nonetheless, our identities as male and female are not something we can simply ignore or neglect. As long as human beings engage in reproduction, in the nurturing and raising of children in a family unit, some differentiation of roles is likely to occur. Increasingly such a differentiation need not be made on the basis of gender, but on the abilities and inclinations of partners who must negotiate their own contribution to the life of the family unit. The danger is that the important role of nurturing and raising children, of making a home not just a residence, is devalued because it is viewed as "women's work."

The history of Christian anthropology of gender has gone through two major phases. In the past the Christian tradition adopted a relatively straightforward view that women were inferior to men, morally and spiritually. They could be saved "through childbearing" (1 Tim 2:15). A few exceptional women could "unsex" themselves and become like men, through a commitment to celibacy and other forms of asceticism.[24] In the actual history of Christianity, of course, countless women transcended these constraints, seeking spiritual companionship with other women in the common life of religious communities, often founded by women of exceptional spirituality and vision, such as Teresa of Avila, Angela Merici, Mary Ward, and Mary McKillop. More recently in the church, a second phase has emerged in the writings of John Paul II who has adopted the language of complementarity to describe the mutual relationships of the genders.[25] This is a vast improvement on the teaching of the past, but it can easily fall into the trap of gender essentialism, of viewing one particular social and cultural construct as constituting the "essential" difference between the genders.[26] It is clear that one aspect of this teaching is the concern that work traditionally done by women in the home and family not be neglected or devalued as women move into professional careers. However, while acknowledging the importance of this work, we must also acknowledge that increasingly this is becoming a matter of mutual nego-

---

24. Peter Brown, *The Body and Society: Men, Women, and Sexual Renunciation in Early Christianity* (New York: Columbia University Press, 1988).

25. See, for example, *Mulieris dignitatem* and his *Letter to Women*.

26. For a discussion of the issues of gender essentialism, see Diana Relke, "Is There Life after Difference: Gender Essentialism, Gender Scepticism, and the Ethic of Care (1)," at http://www.usask.ca/wgst/journals/conf1.htm (accessed July 1, 2006).

tiation between men and women. As women have equal access to education, this trend is not likely to decrease. Perhaps we can view the teaching of John Paul II as the first steps in a trajectory whose end point will recognize mutuality not in terms of fixed roles but in the mutual negotiation of roles, which honors the contributions of both "homemakers" and "breadwinners" according to the inclinations and abilities of the individuals involved.

"SUBDUE THE EARTH"

The ambivalence of the biblical witness to the relationships between the sexes can be found also in its account of the relationship between human beings and the natural order, the realm of the earth, plants, animals, and the very soil itself. The author of Genesis 1 gives human beings unique responsibilities and powers in relation to the rest of creation:

> Be fruitful and multiply, and fill the earth and subdue it; and have dominion over the fish of the sea and over the birds of the air and over every living thing that moves upon the earth. (Gen 1:28)

This mastery does not condone mindless exploitation, for God immediately adds:

> See, I have given you every plant yielding seed that is upon the face of all the earth, and every tree with seed in its fruit; you shall have them for food. (Gen 1:29)

Primal human beings were commanded to be vegetarian, not exploiters of animals.[27] The author of Genesis 2 captures the same sense of care and stewardship when he has Yahweh place the first man in the garden "to till it and keep it" (Gen 2:15). The animals are then created so that the man should not be alone.

As with the relationship between the sexes, however, this primal harmony with the natural world is disrupted by the impact of sin. Rather than be fruitful and generous, the soil becomes an enemy to the first man:

> cursed is the ground because of you; in toil you shall eat of it all the days of your life; thorns and thistles it shall bring forth for you; and you shall eat the plants of the field. (Gen 3:17-18)

We can see from this some of the complexity of our relationship to the land and soil. This disruption is in need of healing, of being made whole again. We

---

27. It is only after the Flood, in Gen 9:3, that Noah is given "permission" to eat meat, but not meat with blood in it.

are only just beginning to understand the implications of our brokenness in this regard, through the efforts of the environmental movement.

The first implication is that the Bible clearly views human beings as the pinnacle of God's material creation. Only human beings are made "in the image and likeness of God" and hence are "little lower than the angels" (Ps 8:5). Though God exercises providential care for all creatures, it is only with human beings that God enters into a covenant, to establish mutual rights and responsibilities. Correlatively, it is only human beings who can break the divine covenant, who can sin against God and so can disrupt the order of creation established by God. While the biblical material does not strictly identify what characteristics humans possess that make them "in the image and likeness of God,"[28] Christian tradition reflecting on this theme has identified our spiritual nature as central to our being the peak of God's creation. And this is not an unreasonable position to hold. Whatever intimations there might be among the higher mammals, especially among primates, of the qualities we identify with human intelligence, it is clear that it is only in human beings that meaning, truth, and value have become the central concern of our living. There is simply no evidence that this is the case with other animals.

The second is that while human beings are regarded as the pinnacle of God's creation, this is no license for them to exploit the natural order in an unrestrained fashion. The disruption of our relationship to the natural order is expressed in the third curse of Genesis 3, the cursing of the soil. For the biblical author the disruption is found in the struggle of human beings to live off the soil. This reflects something of the harshness of the Middle Eastern environment and the limited resources of human beings to exploit it. However, in our own context post–Industrial Revolution, this disruption is more evident in the relentless exploitation of the natural world and our harsh treatment of the biosphere, on which we actually depend for our continued existence.

A BRIEF LOOK AT BUDDHIST ANTHROPOLOGY

In our account of the ontological constitution of the human person in terms of bodiliness and spirit, we have defined spirit in terms of the human search for meaning, truth, and value. While human consciousness experiences a multiplicity of desires, it is the desire for meaning, truth, and value that constitutes the core of our personal human identity. This desire constitutes us as "spiritual beings," and any argument for the immortality of the soul takes as its starting

---

28. See Claus Westermann, *Genesis 1–11: A Commentary* (London: SPCK, 1984), 148-55, for the multiple interpretations of this text.

point the transcendent quality of the goals of this desire. In our day-to-day experience this desire may, however, be swamped by other, lesser desires—what we will later call concupiscence. The moral life is, then, a matter of allowing our desire for meaning, truth, and value to be the core that directs all our desiring. Sadly, this is a difficult task, one that is full of failure and disappointments.

Buddhism takes a different stance in relation to these matters. In the previous chapter we noted that Buddhism does not really have a concept of creation, particularly creation by God. The world is in some sense an illusion, and so too there is an illusory element to our sense of personal identity. A major issue here is the role of desire. Our desires attach us to the world, and so attach us to an illusion. Desire thus creates "unsatisfactoriness" (*dukkha*) or suffering. The clinging of desire creates only a larger illusion of permanence and security.

> What creates this dis-ease [i.e., *dukkha*] is desire (*trishna, tanha*), the thirst for being (*bhava tanha*), which grasps for an abiding some-thing to attach itself to in order to find satisfaction and establish lasting security against vulnerability and change. The irony, however, is that clinging to things which are in the final analysis only contingent and perishable—whether in the form of pleasures, possession, position, or belief—actually serves to exacerbate the suffering it intends to quell, creating further and more intense attachments that only perpetuate the wheel of *samsara* (rebirth) by acquiring more and more karma.[29]

For the Buddhist, both the world and the self are contingent, perishable, and ever changing. The order our mind imposes on the world is part of the illusion of self, something that must be eliminated on the path to enlightenment.

In this we can find both similarities and differences from Christian belief. A Christian may accept that many of our desires are in fact disordered attachments, that leave us less than fulfilled while burying us in an illusion of security. Many of our desires are disordered; they manifest what Christian tradition has called concupiscence, leading us to sin and suffering. But the Christian tradition has also recognized a deeper desire, a search for meaning, truth, and value, whose ultimate goal is union with the source of all meaning, truth, and value, that is, God. Although Christians may recognize that there are many false meanings and disordered goods that we project onto the world, they would claim that there is an objective measure of meaning and goodness inherent in the world, against which we often fail to measure up. This mean-

---

29. Thomas Reynolds, "Toward the Other: Christianity and Buddhism on Desire," *Journal of Ecumenical Studies* 39 (2002): 325-40.

ing and goodness are not illusion, but reality. This conviction is grounded in the belief in God as creator of all that is, and hence in the intrinsic meaning-fulness and goodness of creation.

CONCLUSION

These reflections bring us back to the issue we raised in the first chapter. If creation is good, if it is grounded in a source, God, who is meaning-full and loving, why is it that we experience so much evil in the world? In the next chapter we turn our attention more fully to the problem of evil and to the nature of our experience of its disruption of our search for meaning, truth, and value. Only then can we explore the more specific insights of the Christian tradition on the universality of sin and evil (original sin, chapter 4) and how God responds to our human condition in the death and resurrection of Jesus (chapter 5).

QUESTIONS FOR REFLECTION

1. Many people think that the theory of evolution threatens the special place of human beings in creation. How would you argue that humans remain special even within an evolutionary worldview?
2. Some scientists seek to minimize the difference between human beings and other animals. How would you describe the difference between human beings and other animals?
3. Human beings are described in this chapter as "spiritual." What does the word "spiritual" mean for you?
4. Gender essentialism refers to the idea that there are essential differences between males and females. What differences do people sometimes attribute to males and females, and do you think these differences are justified?
5. Buddhists and Christians have a different understanding of the nature of desire. Which corresponds to your own experience of desire?

SUGGESTIONS FOR FURTHER READING AND STUDY

Barrow, John D., and Frank J. Tipler. *The Anthropic Cosmological Principle*. Oxford: Oxford University Press, 1988.

Edwards, Denis. *Jesus and the Cosmos*. Homebush: St Paul's Publications, 1991.

Faludi, Susan. *Backlash: The Undeclared War against American Women*. New York: Crown, 1991.

Geertz, Clifford. *The Interpretation of Cultures: Selected Essays*. New York: Basic Books, 1973.

Rees, Martin J. *Just Six Numbers: The Deep Forces That Shape the Universe*. New York: Basic Books, 2000.

Reynolds, Thomas. "Toward the Other: Christianity and Buddhism on Desire." *Journal of Ecumenical Studies* 39 (2002): 325-40.

Ruether, Rosemary Radford. *Sexism and God-Talk: Toward a Feminist Theology*. 10th anniversary ed. Boston: Beacon Press, 1993.

3

The Structure of Moral Evil

IN CHAPTER 1, WE EXAMINED the problem of evil in relation to Christian belief in the goodness of creation and God's sovereign providence. In this chapter we shall explore more fully the problem of evil. It is important never to underestimate the "problem of evil." Expressed in existential categories, evil is a pervading cancer, eating away at our personal relationships, promoting lies and sin as culturally normative, turning our social institutions into instruments of naked power and personal greed, leaving the poor and starving to fend for themselves as our pollution may destroy the very possibility of biological life on the planet. No aspect of our existence is untouched by the problem of evil. We can attempt to numb its pain from our consciousness through drugs or mindless consumerism; we may deny our responsibility for its cause by pointing the finger at others' faults; we can evade responsibility for its solution by saying "what can one person do?" But in doing so we add to the problem. If we are honest, we recognize that the problem is not simply "out there" but within each one of us, to such an extent that our best efforts at a solution are themselves distorted by the problem itself. Moral effort is, of itself, not enough.

In metaphysical categories, evil is the attempt to undo God's act of creation. In his pithy way Bernard Lonergan summarizes his proof for the existence of God as follows: "If the real is completely intelligible, God exists. But the real is completely intelligible. Therefore, God exists."[1] But evil threatens to cast a pall of meaninglessness over God's meaningful creation; it is an attempt to plunge the order of the cosmos into chaos. For many, the pall of evil is so great as to create doubt about the very existence of God. The problem of evil remains the greatest obstacle to faith: How can a good God allow such appalling evil? And in a sense this is right. If God exists and is good, then God is interested in resolving the problem of evil: "the question really is what God is or has been doing about the fact of evil."[2]

---

1. Bernard J. F. Lonergan, *Insight: A Study of Human Understanding*, ed. Frederick E. Crowe and Robert M. Doran, Collected Works of Bernard Lonergan 3 (Toronto: University of Toronto Press, 1992), 695.
2. Ibid., 707.

Before we can address this question, we shall explore further and in greater depth the nature of the problem of evil and its personal expression in sin. The moral evil of sin has multiple dimensions—personal, social, and cultural—which deserve individual treatment.

EVIL AND PERSONAL SIN

In chapter 1 we introduced the notion of evil as privation and of sin as that privation of the will wherein it acts without "good reason." In chapter 2 the notion of "good reason" was further explored in terms of the search of the human spirit for meaning, truth, and value in the movement of life that we experience. Meaning, truth, and value are the foundations on which "good reasons" are built. When we act out for "good reasons," we expand the field of meaning, truth, and value, not only socially and culturally in the world but just as significantly in ourselves. Meaning, truth, and value find a permanent home within us—in classical language, we embrace the virtues. We add to human flourishing and hence to the building up of God's kingdom. We further described the task of human existence in terms of the aesthetic and dramatic project of living in the tension of transcendence and limitation, of spirit and bodiliness. Virtue lies in the mean, in the ever-moving horizon of the self-transcending subject, committed to the search for meaning, truth, and value, while remaining grounded in the movement of life, of body and affect. Or, as Aristotle says, "Virtue is a state of character concerned with choice, lying in a mean, i.e. the mean relative to us, this being determined by a rational principle, and by that principle by which the person of practical wisdom would determine it."[3] There is no magic formula for determining the right course of action, just a continual commitment to authenticity, of maintaining the taut balance of transcendence and limitation, while committing oneself to the search for meaning. This is an artistic task of making oneself through engagement with the task of making the world.

If virtue lies in a successful engagement with this artistic task, then vice lies in its failure. Morality is usually thought of in terms of sexual morality, the sins and temptations of the flesh, and it is clear that we can fail in our human project by rejecting the search for meaning, by sinking into the world of bodily pleasures, escaping from the demands of the spirit and the responsibilities of freedom. These pleasures need not be sexual; they can equally be the adrenalin rush of dangerous activities, of mindless thrills, drug-induced highs, or

---

3. Aristotle, *Nicomachean Ethics*, trans. W.D. Ross (Oxford: Oxford University Press, 1980), 2.6, 39.

even the pleasures of shopping. None of these pleasures is necessarily evil in itself, but all can be effective strategies for avoiding the ever-pressing demands of the human spirit for meaning, truth, and value. But these are all failures in one direction, in the direction of limitation; hence, they are only one side of the catalogue of vices.

However, we can fail equally in our human project by overreaching, by neglecting the reality of our bodiliness and pretending that we can "live like angels." A morality that fails to attend to this distortion tends toward the idealistic and the dualistic, viewing the body as the source of all sin. Tradition has held, however, that the source of sin lies in pride. This is a failure in the direction not of limitation but of spirit, of transcendence. Pride is the overreaching of the spirit, its attempt to claim more than its proper place. This is the sin of the first humans, succumbing to the temptation, "you will be like God" (Gen 3:5), not being content with the grounded reality of human bodily existence. Such overreaching becomes a *libido dominandi*, a desire to dominate, to control, often resulting in violence against the other. On the other hand, limitation denied will eventually demand recognition. For example, a denial of sexual desire, rationalized by labeling it as dirty and sinful, will eventually lead to an eruption of sexual irresponsibility, for the person simply has no way of controlling what he or she denies.[4] More generally, manic overreaching will be followed by the crashing down of depression, a painful reminder of the unity of spirit and body that constitutes human existence.

Another reminder of this unity is the impact of our moments of failure (sin) upon our own person, in particular on our freedom. Sin captures our freedom, sending us down a spiral of habit and eventual compulsion:

> The truth is that disordered lust springs from a perverted will; when lust is pandered to, a habit is formed; when habit is not checked, it hardens into compulsion. They were like interlinking rings forming what I have described as a chain, and my harsh servitude used it to keep me under duress. (Augustine, *Confessions* 8.10)[5]

In the end the sinner becomes addicted to sin, no longer able to resist its lure. The evil of the will invades our imaginations and awakens biological processes that seek to reproduce the pleasurable impact of the initial sin. Such processes

---

4. Where celibacy is viewed as a denial of sexuality this is inevitably a problem. A person who seeks escape from the reality of their sexual identity through celibacy is a problem waiting to happen. Celibacy should be embraced not because "sex is bad" but because of an overwhelming commitment to work for the Kingdom of God.

5. Augustine, *The Confessions*, trans. Maria Boulding, Vintage Spiritual Classics (New York: Vintage Books, 1998), 192.

can become so habitual that any attempt to resist can produce a physical response of withdrawal.[6] The tradition speaks of this condition as the moral impotence of the sinner, who is *non posse non peccare*, not able not to sin. Sin does not completely destroy freedom but limits it to an ever-tightening circle of possibilities. Each time sinners sin, they sin freely, with the limited and distorted freedom available to them, but they are not free not to sin, not free to break though the cycle of addiction within which they are trapped. They are truly "sold into slavery under sin" (Rom 7:14).

> I do not understand my own actions. For I do not do what I want, but I do the very thing I hate ... Now if I do what I do not want, it is no longer I that do it, but sin that dwells within me ... Wretched man that I am! Who will rescue me from this body of death? (Rom 7:15, 20, 24)

We can witness the compulsive addictive power of sin in the multiple addictions that plague our society. Drugs, pornography, power, violence, greed, sexual promiscuity, and alcohol are the most obvious examples; more subtle are our attachments to consumer products, shopping, entertainment, computer games, mobile phones, and automobiles! Much of modern consumer society is based on the compulsive power of shopping and our attachment to the products that fill our marketplace. Although less destructive than promiscuity, violence, and drugs, the power of these attachments reveals an important area of unfreedom that distorts our relationships with others and trivializes our own life quest. It is not that we want "too much," as some moralizing preachers would suggest, but rather that we think we can be satisfied with so little, with baubles and trinkets, when what our heart truly desires is meaning, truth, and value.

Indeed, in its own way the power of addiction is a hidden reminder of the unlimited intentionality of the human search for meaning and value. Addiction can be thought of as infinite desire of a finite object.[7] To the addict nothing is more important than the object of addiction, nothing more valuable, more valuable indeed than the addict's life or those of his/her own family. Everything can and will be sacrificed on the altar of addiction. The desire of the human heart that is meant to find its fulfillment in God focuses all its energy, all its power on this finite object of addiction. In the very insanity of addiction we can learn the futility of being satisfied by anything less than God. We can also understand why biblical authors often identify sin with

---

6. See Gerald May, *Addiction and Grace* (San Francisco: Harper & Row, 1988), 64-90, on the physiological impact of addictions.

7. May defines addiction in terms of trying "to fulfill our longing for God through objects of attachment ... one could say we displace our longing for God upon other things" (ibid., 92-93).

idolatry. In the grip of the addictive power of sin we truly are worshiping a false god.

The question may arise whether addiction is indeed a "spiritual" problem, a problem of the will, of meaning and value, or is it a "medical" or "psychological" problem? Here we encounter our tendency to compartmentalize and categorize. What we have is, in fact, a single problem with spiritual, psychological, and medical dimensions. The willingness of the addict for the good is weakened; the search for meaning is disrupted, and hence there is a profound spiritual aspect to addiction. However, addicts are also subject to powerful compulsions (psychological) that can even affect them somatically (medical). Again we witness the spiritual-psychological-somatic unity of a human being. That is why serious sin should never be just "spiritualized," as if a "good" confession followed by three Hail Marys will produce lasting effects—this is perhaps apparent in the failure of church authorities to take the problem of clerical sexual abuse with the gravity it deserved. Nor should it be "psychologized," as if the problem simply required counseling and perhaps some pharmaceuticals to lower tensions and anxieties. Addictions distort and eventually break relationships, damaging families and loved ones and further isolating the addict from possible sources of help. For there to be real conversion, the addict needs to take responsibility for his or her actions, to make recompense for past hurts and to apologize for damage done.[8]

The problem of human sinfulness is not just a matter of individual choice and responsibility. Human beings are not isolated monads, cut off from the world of social and cultural forces. Indeed, some of the "addictions" we suffer, such as the overconsumption of material goods, are in fact promoted by free-market capitalism in order to "keep the economy growing." Overconsumption drives the economy, and our "addiction" to shopping is actually promoted by the advertising industry. This is not to deny individual responsibility for actions committed, but it is a reminder that our freedom is always a conditioned freedom, conditioned by our own personal stories and by the social and cultural world in which we live.

SIN AS SOCIAL AND CULTURAL

Much of the focus of traditional accounts of sin has been on the actions of the individual person. However, thanks largely to the efforts of liberation theol-

---

8. We can see such principles at work in Twelve Step programs, which require the addict to make a searching and fearless moral inventory (Step 4), to identify people the addict has harmed (Step 8), and to seek to make amends to them (Step 9). We shall consider Twelve Steps programs again when we discuss grace in chapter 6.

ogy, we are now much more aware of the bigger picture of human sinfulness, not just as a force within the individual locking us into sinful patterns but also as a transpersonal power that distorts our social and cultural world. This world is the product of thousands, indeed millions of individual decisions, over centuries or even millennia. We can trace the origins of our modern democracies from the seeds in Greek city states, through the Roman republic, in the activities of religious congregations, the Magna Carta, the American Revolution, and various civil wars in Europe through to our modern era. Each of these has contributed to our modern political institutions and helped shape our political imaginations. Nonetheless, while our social and cultural world is the product of millennia of decisions, it is also clear that this world in turn becomes the backdrop for all of our individual decisions, not only determining the effective options available to us but also shaping the way we think about those options and the relative value we place on them.

As a thought experiment, place yourself in the situation of a white middle class South African during the era of apartheid. You have grown up in a situation of relative privilege, enjoying a comfortable lifestyle, with good prospects for education, health care, and personal prosperity in the future. Your family has a couple of black servants whom it treats reasonably well, and you are only vaguely aware that the wealth of your nation is built upon the exploitation of black workers in gold and diamond mines across the country. You live in a country that is systematically built on racial injustice in its laws, its political and judicial institutions, and its economy. This injustice is further rationalized by an ideology of racial superiority that claims to draw at least some of its basis from the Bible. You are raised to love your country and respect its laws. The question arises, at which stage do you become responsible for your participation in a system of sin and lies? Is it the committing of a specific act, a decision you actually make, or is it the failure to act, initially on small things but leading eventually to a lifetime of racial hatred? And how do we divide responsibility between the individual and the society in which he or she lives?

Now place yourself on the other side of the social divide. Now you are a poor black youth living in one of the black townships such as Soweto. You have grown up with poverty and violence. Your father works in a mine and is absent for eleven months of the year, while your mother works in the township doing whatever she can to earn money to supplement the family's meager income. Your future has limited possibilities because you are excluded from the basic health and education services that whites in your country take for granted. The only jobs open to you are either menial or dangerous. When you pass a white person on the street you feel ashamed for being black, for being poor and uneducated. You half believe that you are inferior, internalizing the systemic lie of apartheid; yet anger wells up inside you at the thought of the suffering you and your family endure. At times that anger explodes in violence, fueled by testosterone and cheap alcohol. Again the question arises, at which stage do you become responsible for your participation in, or acquiescence to, a system of sin and lies? How do you maintain a sense of self-worth in the face of the constant barrage of lies telling you that you are worthless, yet avoid the mindless violence that damages both you and your people? And how do we divide responsibility between the individual and the society in which he or she lives?

In both cases sin is not just an individual matter. It is a much larger social and cultural force, what Paul might mean when he speaks of "thrones or dominions or rulers or powers" (Col 1:16; also Rom 8:38), those transpersonal forces for evil that manifest themselves in human existence. The power of sin transcends the individual, and in its wake whole nations can be consumed. What is most disturbing about these larger dimensions of sin is how difficult we find it to detect them, because they have become the very air we breathe. It is often only through our attentiveness to the voice of society's victims that we can begin to recognize the very evils we take for granted.[9]

In considering this larger dimension of sin, we can distinguish between the social, organizational elements (what is sometimes referred to as social sin) and the cultural ideational elements (ideologies) that both support and/or create the organizational elements. In our example above, the core of personal sin is racism, hatred of other persons simply on the basis of the color of their skin, the language they speak, or their way of life. Joined with political power and fueled by greed, this attitude leads to distortions of economic rights, to political marginalization, and to the promotion of laws that enshrine a racist stance. All these are concrete instances of social sin; however, there is more at work. Not content with enshrining their economic and political advantage, they must rationalize their position of privilege with a system of thought that justifies their "preeminence." White people have a natural superiority over the blacks, and indeed the black people are cursed by God.[10] Does the ideology drive the social sin, or does the social sin create the need for the ideology? Both are possibilities, and only an examination of concrete historical cases can determine which is which in any particular case.

Yet not all ideologies are as obvious as apartheid. Some are much more pervasive and hidden. Take our modern stance of cognitional and moral rela-

---

9. Whatever the nuances of meaning in its original context, the parable of the good Samaritan remains a powerful story of hearing the voice of the victim.

10. In Gen 9:25 Noah curses the descendants of his son Ham. Ham is then taken as the original ancestor of the African peoples.

tivism. How readily we say, "That might be true for you, but it is not true for me." Or "Each person should just do what they think is best. No one else should judge." We live in a culture where it is becoming impossible to speak for truth, impossible to establish common moral principles, because we no longer believe that these are realizable common outcomes. Truth and moral value have become privatized, something we are allowed to hold as private opinions but which cannot be brought out in polite company. Indeed we find it almost impossible to think any other way, such is the power of this position. The position is advocated in the name of tolerance, which is of course important, but in the end tolerance becomes another name for permissiveness resulting in a communal moral vacuum. At times of social unrest when people begin to look for alternatives it is easy for that vacuum to be filled by those who mouth the platitudes of moral virtue and the slogans of truth and freedom but in fact are ideologues interested only in the brute exercise of power. As Paul warns: "For such boasters are false apostles, deceitful workers, disguising themselves as apostles of Christ. And no wonder! Even Satan disguises himself as an angel of light" (2 Cor 11:13-14).

Much of the growing sensitivity to the social and cultural dimensions of sin among theologians has been through the impact of two groups, liberation theologians and feminist theologians. We shall now consider something of their contribution each in turn.

LIBERATION THEOLOGY AND SOCIAL SIN

The emergence of liberation theology is one of the distinctive features of the twentieth century. What began as a voice of protest against situations of extreme social injustice in Latin America, a prophetic voice against oppression, poverty, and political violence, developed into a theological movement with its own distinctive themes, methods, and concerns. These themes centered on the issue of social analysis, drawing on the methods of the social sciences (in particular, Marxism)[11] in order to give an account of social process, as a starting point for a theological analysis of the concrete situation of oppression. For liberation theologians, theology is defined not as "faith seeking understanding" but as reflection on Christian praxis, something that grows out of orthopraxis (right action) rather than orthodoxy (right teaching).

---

11. It was these Marxist elements that most concerned the Congregation for the Doctrine of the Faith in its *Instruction on Certain Aspects of the Theology of Liberation* (chapter 7, no. 9): "Let us recall the fact that atheism and the denial of the human person, his liberty and rights, are at the core of the Marxist theory. This theory, then, contains errors which directly threaten the truths of the faith regarding the eternal destiny of individual persons."

Theology is something done at sundown when the day's work is done and the members of the Christian community reflect on what has gone on and make decisions about doing things better tomorrow.

> The pastoral activity of the Church does not flow as a conclusion from theological premises. Theology does not produce pastoral activity; rather it reflects upon it. Theology must be able to find in pastoral activity the presence of the Spirit inspiring the action of the Christian community.[12]

This is not to say that liberation theologians are not concerned with right teaching or with theological rigor. But one's right teaching and theology gain their authenticity from orthopraxis rather than vice versa.

For liberation theology, evil is thought of not primarily in terms of personal sin but in terms of social relationships of domination and power. Through their economic power the rich exploit the poor, enforcing their subjugation through judicial, political, and if necessary martial power. Such an analysis is based not on mere theory but on the experience of the poor in Latin American countries. Where the poor sought to better their situation through organizing local community services or the creation of labor unions, they were often met with violent resistance from the economic and political elites in their countries.[13] This analysis of the situation of the poor has parallels in the Marxist notion of class warfare. For liberation theology, class warfare is a reality that people constantly experience when they question their plight and seek to better their situation. The work of liberation theology has led to the new notion of "social sin," sin that is the product not of individual actions but of social structures, institutions, and relationships.

Compared with traditional accounts of sin, the notion of social sin shifts our focus from the perpetrator of sin to the victim of sin. The poor are not poor because they have sinned; they are poor because they have been sinned against. They are the victims of social and economic forces that perpetuate their poverty, while these same forces benefit the rich. In this way liberation theology recaptures an important dimension of the mission of the historical Jesus, whose preaching of the Kingdom offered not just forgiveness of sin but freedom from all the consequences of sin. This is recognized in the encyclical *Redemptoris Missio,* in which John Paul II states:

> The Kingdom is the concern of everyone: individuals, society, and the world. Working for the Kingdom means acknowledging and promoting God's activity, which is present in human history and transforms it. Building the Kingdom means working for liberation from evil in all its forms. In

---

12. Gustavo Gutiérrez, *A Theology of Liberation: History, Politics, and Salvation,* trans. Sister Caridad Inda and John Eagleson (Maryknoll, N.Y.: Orbis Books, 1973), 9.

13. One might think of the Jesuit martyrs of El Salvador, and Archbishop Oscar Romero.

a word, the Kingdom of God is the manifestation and the realization of God's plan of salvation in all its fullness. (no. 15)

Correlated with the notion of social sin, therefore, is a notion of social salvation, or liberation, to use the term favored by liberation theologians. This relationship between liberation and the religious notion of salvation is the central issue in liberation theology.[14] Gustavo Gutiérrez strongly argues that salvation cannot be limited to a "sphere" of life labeled "religious" or "spiritual." Neither is salvation an individualistic notion. Human beings are social by nature, so salvation has a communal dimension. Inasmuch as salvation reaches out into the social and economic dimensions of human existence, it will be experienced as liberation from oppression and poverty. Thus, "we can say that the historical, political liberation event is the growth of the Kingdom and is a salvific event; but it is not the coming of the Kingdom, not all of salvation."[15]

The connection between social liberation and "religious" salvation found in liberation theology has caused intense debate. Some have been concerned that liberation theology undermines traditional eschatology, reducing heaven to a social utopia.[16] Liberation theology is very aware of the Marxist critique of religion and especially of a futurist eschatology that would placate people in present oppression with promises of heaven in a future life. However, liberation theology is also aware of the dangers in identifying any particular liberation movement with the coming of the Kingdom. Every such attempt must be judged by the "eschatological proviso," that the Kingdom is always "not yet." What we are faced with is a steadfast refusal on the part of liberation theology to divorce religion/faith from the real social, political, and economic conditions of peoples' lives.

A central element of liberation theology is the "preferential option for the poor." The option for the poor has two aspects, one practical and the other hermeneutical. The practical aspect is that the poor have first call on the resources of the world. In justice the poor should have access to adequate food, water, health care, and shelter. The scale of poverty in the world is viewed as a scandal to Christian faith, which views the poor as embodying something of the mystery of Christ—"for I was hungry and you gave me food, I was thirsty and you gave me something to drink, I was a stranger and you welcomed me, I was naked and you gave me clothing, I was sick and you took care of me, I was in prison and you visited me" (Matt 25:35-36). Jesus himself identifies with the poor and the oppressed, and so they make a special demand on Christian generosity.

---

14. Gutiérrez, *Theology of Liberation*, 83-105.
15. Ibid., 104.
16. Most notably, the criticisms of the Congregation for the Doctrine of the Faith.

The hermeneutical aspect relates to the privileged position of the poor in grasping the nature of social reality. It is important to hear their voices, to enter into their perspective on social reality because they are the ones who suffer the consequences of that reality. This is not an attempt to absolutize or idealize the perspective of the poor, but to recognize that it is precisely this perspective that is most often ignored by the more powerful elements in society. Thus, the perspective of the poor requires special attention. The poor are not to be treated simply as objects of concern or charity, but as subjects in their own right who have the dignity to shape their own history.[17]

These two aspects together present the preferential option of the poor as a modern transposition of the traditional virtues of charity and almsgiving for the poor. However, while the implementation of these traditional virtues was at times accompanied by condescension and the objectification of the poor, the preferential option for the poor views the poor as the subjects of their own history. The discovery of the poor in history is not new to liberation theology. Indeed, its lineage can be traced back to the early church fathers, through St. Francis of Assisi, St. Vincent de Paul, and a number of religious orders that have dedicated their existence to the service of the poor. But it has been given a new and important impetus through their writings.

The introduction by liberation theology of the notion of social sin represents a major advance on traditional theology, which tended to individualize and privatize sin, and correlatively salvation as well. It also represents a strong resistance to the spiritualization of salvation, which tends to place it in some eschatological future. Human beings are not spirits trapped in their bodies, but embodied spirits, a complete integration of body and soul. Both evil and salvation must take into account the whole person, including the social dimension of human existence. We shall now consider something of the contribution of feminist theology, which focuses more on the ideological or cultural aspects of sin.

FEMINIST THEOLOGY AND THE CRITIQUE OF PATRIARCHY

One of the remarkable features of the twentieth century has been the rise of a feminist consciousness. Even Vatican documents have acknowledged this

---

17. In a homily on June 8, 1999, Pope John Paul II stated: "We must always recall that the country's economic development must take into consideration the greatness, dignity, and vocation of man, who 'was made in the image and likeness of God' (*Gen* 1:26). Development and economic progress must never be at the expense of men and women, hindering the meeting of their fundamental needs. The human person must be the subject of development, that is, its most important point of reference."

emergence as a significant "sign of the times." For example, Pope John XXIII spoke of women "gaining an increasing awareness of their natural dignity" and "demanding both in domestic and in public life the rights and duties which belong to them as human persons."[18] Pope John Paul II spoke of the continuing significance of women's aspirations as identified in feminist thought and the importance of a "new feminism" committed to overcoming exploitation, violence, and discrimination.[19] While the modern origins of feminism may be traced to the abolitionist and suffragist movements of the nineteenth century, the pervasiveness of its impact is evident in the ways in which many of its original demands—equal voting rights, rights for the ownership of property, access to employment, equal pay for equal work, and so on—have been assimilated into the mainstream of our social and cultural life without need for further justification or defense. More contentious has been the claimed right of women to control their fertility through contraception or abortion. The concerns of some feminists have moved beyond those of middle-class and educated women into areas of domestic violence, sexual abuse, and exploitation; the needs of women in third world countries who are often the poorest of the poor; and even the needs of our exploited biosphere.[20]

It would be a mistake, however, to think of feminism as a monolithic movement without its own variations and even conflicts. Rosemary Radford Ruether identifies a number of different versions of feminism:[21]

- **Eschatological feminism.** Based on an "egalitarian counter-trend" in early Christianity, it develops a "realized eschatology" wherein there is no more distinction between male and female. It is found in various mystical and ascetic sects including the Quakers and early Gnosticism.
- **Liberal feminism.** Based on liberal notions of equality of rights, it worked for the vote, equal pay for equal work, access to employment, and so on, within the framework of liberal democratic processes. This form of feminism is not concerned to radically change society; it works to mollify its harmful effects on women through a gradual shift in policies.

---

18. Pope John XXIII, *Pacem in Terris* 41. He spoke of this emerging consciousness among women as one of three "characteristics of the present day."

19. "In transforming culture so that it supports life, women occupy a place, in thought and action, which is unique and decisive. It depends on them to promote a 'new feminism' which rejects the temptation of imitating models of 'male domination,' in order to acknowledge and affirm the true genius of women in every aspect of the life of society, and overcome all discrimination, violence and exploitation" (*Evangelium Vitae* 99).

20. For example, Rosemary Radford Ruether, *Gaia & God: An Ecofeminist Theology of Earth Healing* (San Francisco: HarperSanFrancisco, 1992).

21. Rosemary Radford Ruether, *Sexism and God-Talk: Toward a Feminist Theology*, 10th anniversary ed. (Boston: Beacon Press, 1993), 99-108.

- **Romantic feminism.** This version stresses the differences between men and women and the complementarity of their roles in society and church. It rejects the view of women as essentially "carnal" and views women more in terms of sensitivity, compassion, purity, and the like. The complementarity is often viewed in terms of public-private spheres. Men's engagement in the public sphere leaves them more prone to sin, while women are shielded from these forces and hence less fallen than men.
- **Conservative feminism.** This approach correlates the private sphere of the home with altruism and love while the public sphere is the realm of pride, egoism, and violence. Women are in fact morally superior to men, but only inasmuch as they maintain themselves in the private sphere of the home and help heal men in that sphere.
- **Reformist romanticism.** This accepts the assumptions of conservative feminism, but then argues that women must actively reform the public sphere, raising it to a higher standard. It would argue, for example, that if women ruled there would be no more wars!
- **Radical romanticism.** This accepts the assumptions of conservative feminism, but goes on to argue that only through separation from men can women maintain their moral standing. Men are essentially irredeemable.

The first two of these tend toward an androgynous conception of humanity that ignores the differences between men and women, while the others tend toward an essentializing of the differences. That is, the differences are part of the metaphysical constitution of gender. Such a position is often found in church documents,[22] and also in the theology of Hans Urs von Balthasar.[23] The androgynous conception seeks to concretize an abstraction, abstract human nature as neither male nor female per se, while the second essentialist approach universalizes what is often historically contingent, since conceptions of what constitutes the "essence" of the male/female distinction vary from culture to culture. Often the essentializing tends toward a matter/spirit dichotomy that is basically dualistic.

Central to a feminist account of sin is the notion of sexism. Sexism involves a devaluing of women, a devaluing that has repercussions in the economic, political, and cultural arenas of human existence. Further, the sexism of individual males is a consequence of the broader ideology of patriarchy, which may be defined as "a male pyramid of graded subordinations and exploitations

---

22. For example, *Mulieris Dignitatem* 21; see also John Paul II's "General Audience," February 6, 1980.

23. See, for example, Hans Urs von Balthasar, "Women Priests? A Marian Church in a Fatherless and Motherless Culture," *Communio* 22 (1995): 164-70.

[which specify] women's oppression in terms of the class, race, country, or religion of the men to whom [women] 'belong.'"[24] In her groundbreaking study of feminist theology, Ruether examines the nature of sexism as evil, as part of our human "original sinfulness," and then goes on to examine the process of conversion away from this evil. Indeed, it is only in the experience of conversion that we are able to identify evil as evil. Until the moment of conversion sexism appears simply as normal, as the way things are. Thus, adopting the position of feminism, which involves a conversion away from patriarchy and the rejection of sexism, "represents a fundamental shift in the valuations of good and evil."[25] Such a conversion involves recognition that sin is not just individual, but includes a disruption of human culture and community.

To recognize sexism as sin is not to label men as naturally more evil or immoral than women. This would be the radical feminism option identified above, which Ruether rejects. Both men and women equally have the capacity to sin; however, this recognition should not blind us to the fact that historically men have been more responsible for moral evil in the world.

> The monopolization of power and privilege by ruling class males also means a monopolization of the opportunities for evil. This means not only that men have been the primary decision-makers of history but also that the very modes of relationship set up by this monopoly of power and privilege create violent and oppressive ways of pursuing the "good ends" envisioned by this male ruling class.[26]

Again, such a position does not imply that any individual male should carry the total burden of guilt for patriarchy and sexism. All men and women carry some guilt, either through enjoying the benefits patriarchy bestows on them, or through their acquiescence to its oppression. Sexism so permeates society as to shape our imagination, our consciousness, from our earliest days. "Long before we can even begin to make our own decisions, we are already thoroughly its product."[27]

When sexism is identified as sin, women may experience a deep anger. But this is not necessarily a destructive anger. It can be a righteous anger at an injustice long perpetrated, the type of anger found in the prophetic denunciations of sin. Such an anger is a "liberating grace" that empowers women to break the chains of sexist socialization. Further, women begin to develop a

---

24. Elisabeth Schüssler Fiorenza, *Bread Not Stone: The Challenge of Feminist Biblical Interpretation,* 10th anniversary ed. (Boston: Beacon Press, 1995), xiv.

25. Ruether, *Sexism and God-Talk,* 160.

26. Ibid., 180

27. Ibid., 182.

sense of their own worth, a new sense of pride, a basic self-esteem. Again, this is not the pride condemned by male moralists as the source of all sin, but a basic self-esteem necessary for one's own identity. "Without basic self-esteem one has no self at all, as a base upon which to build an identity or to criticize past mistakes."[28]

Some feminist writers (and others) have extended this type of analysis to embrace not only the oppression of women by patriarchy but also the exploitation and destruction of the natural environment. Patriarchy involves a larger sense of alienation from the natural world, a world that it increasingly commodifies and exploits. Under the force of "economic necessity" we destroy the natural beauty of the Amazon rain forests, we pump toxic wastes into our waterways and oceans, and we fill our atmosphere with gases whose long-tem effects we do not fully understand. The residues of common insecticides such as DDT are found in every living creature, even in mothers' milk for their newborn infants.[29] Human industrial activity is impacting all aspects of the natural world, from the local garbage dump to the common threat of global warming and climate change. We constantly deplete the topsoil of our main grain-growing lands. We continually act as if there are no limits to what we can do to the earth, no limits to the damage we inflict, as we seek to satisfy our created "needs" for more and more consumer goods. In the face of this widespread destruction and damage, we are only just beginning to grasp the sinfulness of environmental vandalism, a sinfulness that did not register in the more traditional accounts of moral theology.

THE DIALECTIC OF TRANSCENDENCE AND LIMITATION

The preceding analysis of the nature of environmental destruction is suggestive of the fact that, just as we have a dialectic of transcendence and limitation operating within the individual person, so too there are other dialectics operating in an analogous fashion. Broadly speaking we might then conceive of evil in terms of the breakdown and distortion of these dialectics. This suggestion has been given substance in the writings of Lonergan scholar Robert Doran. The starting point of Doran's analysis is what Lonergan refers to as a hierarchical scale of values:

> we may distinguish vital, social, cultural, personal and religious values in an ascending order. Vital values, such as health and strength, grace and vigour, normally are preferred to avoiding the work, privations, pains involved in

---

28. Ibid., 186.
29. See http://www.eap.mcgill.ca/MagRack/JPR/JPR_07.htm (accessed July 1, 2006).

acquiring, maintaining, restoring them. Social values, such as the good of order which conditions the vital values of the whole community, have to be preferred to the vital values of individual members of the community. Cultural values do not exist without the underpinning of vital and social values, but none the less they rank higher. Not by bread alone doth man live. Over and above mere living and operating, men have to find meaning and value in their living and operating. It is the function of culture to discover, express, validate, criticize, correct, develop, improve such meaning and value. Personal value is the person in his self-transcendence, as loving and being loved, as originator of value in himself and in his milieu, as an inspiration and invitation to others to do likewise. Religious values, finally, are at the heart of the meaning and value of man's living and man's world.[30]

Doran builds on Lonergan's work by analyzing three interacting dialectics that are present in the personal, cultural, and social levels of value. Since we have already considered personal sin in terms of the dialectic of transcendence and limitation, of spirit and bodiliness, I shall now turn our attention to the social and cultural levels, to shed further light on the concerns of liberation and feminist theologies.

Social Values

Social values are concerned with the good of order, the distribution of political and economic power, the sense of community belonging, and communal identity. Following Lonergan, Doran sees the social level as a dialectic between spontaneous intersubjectivity, that is, our communal sense of belonging, of sharing, which Lonergan understands as the primordial ground of all human community, and practical intelligence, which consists of the economy, our technological development, and the sphere of political activity. While the dialectic tension between intersubjectivity and practical intelligence is maintained, there is a true progress, which allows for increasing economic, technological, and political complexity while respecting the intersubjective needs of human community. To break the tension in favor of communal sense is to opt for economic, technological, and political stagnation, while to break it in favor of practical intelligence is to undermine social cohesion, leading to the formation of dominant groups and what Lonergan calls "group bias" and the "shorter cycle of decline."[31]

---

30. Bernard J. F. Lonergan, *Method in Theology* (London: Darton, Longman & Todd, 1972), 31-32.

31. Lonergan, *Insight*, 237-50; Robert M. Doran, *Theology and the Dialectics of History* (Toronto: University of Toronto Press, 1990), 359-64.

Perhaps the recent history of Eastern Europe is illustrative of this process. Marxism stressed practical intelligence, social and economic planning, to the detriment of a communal sense of belonging. With the marked failures of an overstretched practical intelligence, evidenced in the collapse of the economy and the disintegration of political power, people are reverting to their "tribal groupings," their more basic communal identity. In this way they are seeking both to reclaim what they had lost and at the same time to dominate other competing groups, a process most evident in the Balkans.

At a more local level, in Western societies we see the competing social values of "progress" and "community" in the battles over the construction of freeways, airports, prisons, and other products of "practical intelligence" that threaten local communities, dividing them geographically or in other ways destroying their local community lifestyle. The cry "not in my back-yard" is often not just individual self-interest. It may also be a protest against the destruction of our local communities, which are threatened by economic, technological, and political decisions made in the name of practical intelligence.

From the perspective of liberation theology, the existence of a large number of poor in any society is a clear sign of the breakdown of the dialectic between practical intelligence and communal sense. That we can tolerate an economic underclass signifies that we no longer feel a sense of identity or community with them; we no longer feel connected with them, and so we no longer feel that their fate is of any concern to us. In fact their pleas for justice are now heard as a threat to the status quo, from which we benefit, and so we seek to objectify them and even demonize them, blaming them for their own poverty. The poor represent the limitation pole of the social dialectic, and our neglect of the poor implies a breakdown in the social dialectic.

Cultural Values

Cultural values give us the whys and wherefores of our living. They inform us about the direction that can be found or lost in the movement of life. They are mediated to us by the stories, narratives, myths, and legends of the culture. They are discussed and criticized in philosophies, theologies, and cultural journals. They are expressed in art and popularized in the media. They exercise the critical reflective function in a society. Although we may tend to downplay the importance of this type of activity, we should never ignore the sheer power of ideas. Marx's years in the British Museum shaped the history of the twentieth century. Economic rationalism first won a handful of hearts and minds before it gained political ascendancy in Britain and the United States, and so changed the landscape of Western democracies, for better or worse. Still, the time scale of an idea is measured in decades, even centuries, and commonly we tend to undervalue ideas because they lack immediate impact. This neglect is itself an instance of what Lonergan calls "general bias," a bias against the theoretical, the long-term in favor of the practical and short-term.[32] It is most evident in the omnicompetent self-assurance of the person of practical common sense who views any theoretical discussion with disdain.

Doran understands the cultural level as also constituted by a dialectic of transcendence and limitation.[33] At the limitation pole of culture Doran speaks of cosmologically grounded meanings and values. These view the world as an ordering that moves from the cosmos, through society, and on to the individual. The individual must align himself or herself with the society, and the society with the cosmos. Thus, for Doran:

> Cosmological symbolizations of the experience of life as a movement with a direction that can be found or missed find the paradigm of order in the cosmic rhythms . . . Cosmological constitutive meaning has its roots in the affective biologically based sympathy of the organism with the rhythms and process of non-human nature.[34]

The cultures of many indigenous peoples, such as Australian Aborigines, Native Americans, and Innuits, are cosmological in form, as are more recent agrarian societies. These cultures take their orderings from the rhythms of nature, the seasons, the migrations of animal herds, the cycles of planting, harvesting, birth, and death. Until the Enlightenment, cosmological symbolisms made a significant contribution to European cultures in, for example, institutions such as monarchies, which represented for many a cosmological hierarchical ordering our societies. The Christian liturgical cycle reflects elements of this, with Easter linked to the new life of spring, and Christmas marking the depths of winter, when the days begin to lengthen.

At the transcendent pole of culture there are anthropologically grounded meanings and values. Such a culture identifies the source of meaning and value in a world-transcendent source, God or reason, with which the individual must align himself or herself. Society is then shaped to the needs of such aligned individuals. For an anthropological culture:

> the measure of integrity is recognized as world-transcendent and as providing the standard first for the individual, whose ordered attunement to

---

32. Lonergan, *Insight*, 250-51.

33. Doran, *Theology and the Dialectics of History*, 45 and part 4. Doran draws on the work of Eric Voeglin in this distinction of cosmological and anthropological cultures.

34. Robert M. Doran, "The Analogy of Dialectic and the Systematics of History," in *Religion in Context*, ed. T. Fallon and P. Riley (Lanham, Md: University Press of America, 1988), 54-55.

the world-transcendent measure is itself the measure of the integrity of society . . . Anthropological truth is . . . constitutive of history as the product of human insight, reflection and decision.[35]

Such a cultural breakthrough occurred initially in the Greek philosophical movement and has been part of our Western cultural heritage ever since. It received a major impetus during the Enlightenment and the industrial and scientific revolutions of the modern era. Again, Christianity reflects these meanings and values in its emphasis on personal responsibility in its teachings on free will and sin.

To break the tension in the direction of cosmological values is to abandon humanity to a cosmologically conceived fate, where human beings are unable to take responsibility for human history. Human history is thought of as the plaything of the gods, of spirits, of "principalities, thrones, and dominations." This is not to say that such societies lack practical intelligence or that they do not change. But the power of their creative intelligence may be hidden from them by the cosmological meanings and values that dominate their lives. Where society must conform to the cosmos and the individual to society, there is little room for the recognition of personal initiative and creativity.

To break the tension in the direction of anthropological values is to lose touch with the rhythms of cycles of nature, to neglect basic limitations of human existence and hence to ignore long-term issues of cultural and historical survival. At the same time there is a distortion of the transcendent pole of the dialectic that is then conceived in terms of domination and control. Lonergan refers to this distortion as "general bias," which promotes an apocalyptic "longer cycle of decline." Theoretical intelligence is subsumed under the demands of the practical, of the marketplace, of investment and its need for quick returns. Long-term problems that require theoretical investigation are neglected, and the short-term solutions proposed by practical common sense, while superficially effective in the short run, simply create more problems in the long run. The social surd accumulates to such an extent that attempted solutions become more and more desperate. "A civilization in decline digs its own grave with a relentless consistency."[36]

Much of the feminist critique of patriarchy can be read as a critique of a culture that has distorted the cultural dialectic in the direction of anthropological culture, in the direction of transcendence. It is a culture no longer cognizant of limitation, which rejects any constraint on its activities and suppresses our linkage with the rhythms and cycles of the natural order. It has

---

35. Ibid., 54-55.
36. Lonergan, *Method*, 55.

led to the decimation of indigenous peoples and cultures, to exploitation of the land, and to the marginalization of women.

Our analysis of both liberation and feminist theology in terms of the social and cultural dialectics should alert us to the fact that the dialectic can also be distorted in the other direction, in the direction of limitation. Societies can suppress technological, economic, and political change; they can lock themselves into a cosmological worldview that severely limits the possibilities for the development of human culture. Although this is not a commonly realized possibility, at least in the Western world, it does point to another way in which evil may be manifested in the social and cultural orders of human existence.

OTHER RELIGIOUS TRADITIONS AND THE PROBLEM OF EVIL

It is not possible to give a full-blown comparison of different world religions on the question of evil in the space of this volume. I would like to suggest, however, that such a comparison is a vital element in terms of the work of comparative theologies.[37] The problem of evil is not just one among a number of problems for interfaith dialogue and comparison. Like the question of the existence of God, it remains always central to any discussion. How one analyzes the nature of the problem of evil uncovers fundamental metaphysical and moral commitments. For example, where we blur the distinction between the problem of evil and the problem of suffering, we tend toward a dualistic metaphysics. A dualistic metaphysics leads inevitably to certain moral commitments in terms of our understanding of sexuality and the body. On the other hand, an epistemological account of evil (evil as ignorance) leads to an account of the question of salvation that is very different from an existential account of evil (evil as residing in the will). So our whole understanding of salvation depends on our prior understanding of the nature of evil.

We have already seen, for example, that Buddhism gives an account of the problem of evil that is different from the Christian account. Buddhism seems to identify evil with suffering (*dukkha*), and suffering has its origin in desire. Does this verge on dualism? Further, Buddhism places emphasis on evil as ignorance and salvation as enlightenment. As we shall see in our chapter on grace, this has a significant impact on our relative understandings of the nature of salvation.

The same problem of dualism emerges in other Indian religious traditions,

---

37. On the methodology of comparative theology, see James L. Fredericks, *Faith among Faiths: Christian Theology and Non-Christian Religions* (New York: Paulist Press, 1999).

such as Hinduism and Jainism. These share a common conceptual framework of karma and rebirth. For many people karma provides a satisfying account of the problem of evil and suffering. Evil and suffering are immediately linked through a cosmic process of retribution. Your suffering here and now is the consequence of past sins, either in this life or in previous lives. Through the process of rebirth one can move through to a higher moral perfection by accepting one's karma and carrying out one's duties in this life.[38] Again the dualistic overtones of the notion of death, the transmigration of the soul, and rebirth are evident.

While many Westerners find this basically Hindu conception of existence more attractive than Christian accounts, it is interesting to note that for the Buddhist this cycle of death and rebirth is something from which to escape, through enlightenment. Moreover, the almost mechanical workings of karma, balancing out the good and evil of the universe, leave no room for notions of mercy and forgiveness, so central to the Christian message. In karmic systems there is no need to "solve" the problem of evil, in a practical sense, since one can leave it all to karma to sort out. In Christianity divine mercy and forgiveness present us with a practical solution to the problem of evil, but it is one in which we are called to respond and participate.

CONCLUSION

While the notion of karma has provided Eastern religions with a way of trying to deal with questions of suffering and evil, Christianity has promoted a very different understanding of the connection, through the notion of original sin. Christian faith has linked suffering and sin through the notion of a primal sin, going back to the foundations of the human race, to "Adam and Eve." Nonetheless, this remains a complex and easily misunderstood belief, and so demands a careful treatment. We shall turn our attention to this in the next chapter.

QUESTIONS FOR REFLECTION

1. The text speaks of personal sinfulness in terms of sins of excess transcendence and excess limitation. Can you correlate these with traditional lists of vices or "deadly sins"?

---

38. For a treatment of the strengths and weaknesses of karmic doctrines as a solution to the problem of evil, see Whitley Kaufman, "Karma, Rebirth and the Problem of Evil," *Philosophy East & West* 55 (2005): 15–32.

2. The text above speaks of sin in terms of the problem of addiction. What are some of the addictions our culture actually encourages within us?
3. How does the notion of personal sin differ from the social and cultural aspects of sinfulness?
4. The text above identifies one aspect of social sinfulness in terms of the social problem of poverty and one aspect of cultural sinfulness in terms of patriarchy. What other examples can you give of social and cultural aspects of sinfulness?
5. How do other non-Christian religions that you are familiar with deal with sinfulness and the problem of evil?

SUGGESTIONS FOR FURTHER READING AND STUDY

Augustine. *The Confessions.* Translated by Maria Boulding. Vintage Spiritual Classics. New York: Vintage Books, 1998.

Balthasar, Hans Urs von. "Women Priests? A Marian Church in a Fatherless and Motherless Culture." *Communio* 22 (1995): 164-70.

Doran, Robert M. "The Analogy of Dialectic and the Systematics of History." In *Religion in Context*, edited by T. Fallon and P. Riley, 35-57. Lanham, Md: University Press of America, 1988.

Gutiérrez, Gustavo. *A Theology of Liberation: History, Politics, and Salvation.* Translated by Sister Caridad Inda and John Eagleson. Maryknoll, N.Y.: Orbis Books, 1973.

Kaufman, Whitley. "Karma, Rebirth and the Problem of Evil." *Philosophy East & West* 55 (2005): 15-32.

May, Gerald. *Addiction and Grace.* San Francisco: Harper & Row, 1988.

Ruether, Rosemary Radford. *Gaia & God: An Ecofeminist Theology of Earth Healing.* San Francisco: HarperSanFrancisco, 1992.

4

Original Sin

THE DOCTRINE OF ORIGINAL SIN is a distinctively Christian belief. Indeed, one could argue that it is a distinctively Western Christian belief, based as it is largely on the writings and authority of Augustine and his conflict with Pelagius. Eastern Orthodox Christianity has no formal doctrine of original sin, as that form of Christianity was not shaped by the Pelagian controversy, which proved so decisive in Western self-understanding. However, not only is the doctrine distinctively Christian, but it is also a doctrine subject to serious distortion and misunderstanding. One set of problems with the doctrine arises from its linkage with an outmoded cosmology, apparently tied to a literal reading of the story of Adam and Eve in Genesis 2-3. As modern culture increasingly adopts evolutionary thought, not just in the biological sciences but as a total worldview, any such linkage makes the doctrine seem more and more unlikely. The narratives of Genesis 2-3 simply do not square with modern scientific accounts of the origins of human life. Another set of problems relates to the ways in which the doctrine can be misread as implying the total depravity of human existence apart from grace. While this pessimistic reading of the human condition had its roots in the writings of Augustine, it found more explicit expression during the Reformation, becoming a mainstay of the teachings of Martin Luther and John Calvin.

In this chapter we shall explore something of the history of the doctrine of original sin, in the hope that this review might assist in highlighting difficulties and possible solutions to the problems it poses for the modern mind. Only then shall we present a contemporary approach that I hope is illuminating.

BRIEF HISTORY OF THE DOCTRINE OF ORIGINAL SIN

Any reading of the New Testament should convince us that the fundamental starting point of Christian faith is an experience of salvation brought about through faith in Jesus Christ, through his death and resurrection. The New Testament abounds in metaphors to express the reality of that experience—it is like being sick and then being made whole (the healing *salve* of salvation); it is like being a slave and then having someone pay the redemption money for your release; it is like going to court expecting to be found guilty, yet being declared righteous and freed from your guilt. All these metaphors speak to us of a powerful experience of liberation, of freedom, of deliverance. Clearly the source or power of this experience is mediated to the believer by Jesus Christ, through his death and resurrection, and this became the focus of the early Christian preaching. This same experience is available to all through faith (Gal 3:28-29). It took a bit longer, however, for people to sit back and reflect more systematically on that experience and to subject it to analysis. One question that necessarily arises is, What exactly are we being saved from? The history of the doctrine of original sin is one of seeking to clarify this question.

There are a number of candidates one may identify as "that from which we are saved." For example, sin, death, slavery to Satan, powers and principalities, and so on. Each of these possibilities can claim scriptural warrant. Some early church fathers developed elaborate soteriological narratives, which we shall explore in the next chapter. However, what was needed was a candidate that matched the scope of the gift involved. The redemption Jesus offers is unlimited, not tied to any group of persons. Jesus died for the rich and the poor, the good and the bad, the young and the old. But what was it that the young, especially the very young, needed to be saved from? In particular, why did the church baptize young children, even in infancy?[1]

Both East and West recognized that baptism washed sinners clean from their sins. However, while the Greek fathers recognized a variety of benefits from infant baptism,[2] in the western Latin church the question of infant baptism became a focal point for speaking about a different type of sin, one that was not personal sin, but one that affected all, even newborn infants. In the thought of Augustine the sin of Adam became not just the first sin in a long and sorry history of human sinfulness; it became an originating sin (originating original sin), something that affected all human beings, who are therefore tarnished from birth, born under guilt, the guilt of original sin (originated

---

1. Although there is no unambiguous evidence of infant baptism in the New Testament, there is clear historical evidence in the first generation of Christians. For example, Polycarp (69-155 C.E.) claimed to have been baptized as a child (*Martyrdom of Polycarp* 9.3).

2. John Chrysostom explicitly denied any sin in infants: "Have you seen the number of benefits of baptism? While many believe that its only benefit is the remission of sins, we have counted at least ten honors conferred by it. It is for this reason that we baptize even little children, even though they have no sins, so that they may receive justice, sonship, inheritance, the grace of being brother and members of Christ, and of becoming the Temple of the Holy Spirit" (quoted in Peter C. Phan, *Grace and the Human Condition*, Message of the Fathers of the Church 15 [Wilmington, Del.: Michael Glazier, 1988], 201).

original sin). Augustine took Paul seriously when he said that baptism freed us from our slavery to sin (Rom 6:6). Since infants were not in a position to commit personal sin, baptism must be for a different type of sin, the sin of Adam, or original sin.

Augustine strengthened his position with other arguments. For example, why is there so much suffering in the world? Surely a just God would not allow such suffering, *unless we deserved it.* Indeed, when we are personally struck by some tragic event, one of the first things we say is, "What did I do to deserve this?," as if suffering only makes sense to us as some type of punishment. The universal plight of suffering as part of the human condition was for Augustine a sign of our original sinfulness, a just punishment for the sin of Adam. He also drew attention to our human condition of concupiscence, the disordering of our desires, particularly in the area of sexual libido. Surely such disordering was not part of God's original creation, and so once again it is a sign of our wounding by the primordial sin of Adam. Finally, Augustine drew on material from Romans 5:12-21, where Paul speaks of the impact of Adam's sin on the human condition, in particular how sin entered the world through Adam's sin. Here Augustine was dependent on the Latin translations of Jerome and others. When Augustine turned to his Latin translation of Romans 5:12-21 to develop his theology of original sin, he read the following verse:

> Therefore, just as sin came into the world through one man, and death came through sin, and so death spread to all, *in quo omnes peccaverunt* (in whom all have sinned).

The problem he faced is the significance of *in quo.* Following what he took to be a text from St. Ambrose (which we now know was not written by Ambrose at all but by an unknown author whom tradition has called *Ambrosiaster*), Augustine took *in quo* as a relative conjunction with its antecedent being Adam. Thus Augustine took the text to be saying that "death spread to all, *in whom* [Adam] *all have sinned.*" For Augustine this is a key text for his scriptural argument for the existence of original sin. Here Paul seemed to be saying that all have sinned in Adam's sin; through some mysterious human solidarity, all are caught up in Adam's guilt.

Augustine's arguments won the day against his opponent, Pelagius, who held that the sin of Adam was purely a matter of providing bad example for the rest of us. Thus he rejected any notion of inherited sin. Pelagius accepted that baptism was for the remission of sin in adults, but for infants it was simply the rite of entry into the church. Given the weight of Augustine's arguments at the time, the church rejected the position of Pelagius and adopted its first official teaching on original sin. At the Council of Carthage (418 C.E.)

Pelagius's position was condemned, and the formal link between baptism and original sin was dogmatically established.

Although Augustine's arguments carried the day, they were not without their difficulties. The notion that suffering was a punishment for sin is much less persuasive in the modern era, which thinks along evolutionary lines (though it still has some "existential" appeal in our more spontaneous identification of suffering and punishment). The ancient world knew nothing of the millions of years of life, with its own toll of suffering, death, and even extinction, prior to the emergence of human life. All this suffering could not be laid at the feet of human sinfulness, and in his exploration of concupiscence Augustine blurred the distinction between two differing issues of human existence—sinfulness and finitude. In book 1 of the *Confessions* Augustine understands the cries of a baby for its mother's milk as signifying its inherent sinfulness:

> Who can recall to me the sins I committed as a baby? For in your sight no man is free from sin, not even a child who has lived only one day on earth. Who can show me what my sins were? . . . Was it a sin to cry when I wanted to feed at the breast? I am too old now to feed on mother's milk, but if I were to cry for some kind of food suited to my age, others would rightly laugh me to scorn and remonstrate with me. So then too I deserved a scolding for what I did; but since I could not have understood the scolding, it would have been unreasonable, and most unusual, to rebuke me. (1.7)[3]

Today we would understand such behavior purely in developmental terms. Most importantly, we now know that Augustine's exegesis of Romans 5:12 is unsustainable. Modern translations reject Augustine's translation of *in quo* as "*in whom* all have sinned" and replace it with a simpler explanation: "death has come to all, *because* all have sinned."[4] Perhaps the main element that remains from Augustine's case is the church's practice of baptizing infants.

The Middle Ages witnessed the beginning of a more speculative exploration of the notion of original sin. As we shall see in a later chapter, central to this speculative development was the emergence of a distinction between grace and nature, where grace is "supernatural," beyond what can be achieved

---

3. Augustine, *The Confessions*, trans. Maria Boulding, Vintage Spiritual Classics (New York: Vintage Books, 1998). In a similar vein: "It raises the doubt whether, if the first human beings had not sinned, they would have had children who could use neither tongue, nor hands, nor feet. . . . In like manner God's almighty power was competent to make her children also, as soon as born, grown up at once" (*On Forgiveness of Sins and Baptism* 1.68).

4. Any standard commentary will deal with the exegetical details of this verse. See, for example, Brendan Byrne, *Romans,* Sacra Pagina 6 (Collegeville, Minn.: Liturgical Press, 1996), 173-86.

by "nature" conceived of as a metaphysical principle of being. According to this view, human nature remains substantially constant before and after the fall, for if there were a substantial change in human nature we would simply cease to be human. What differs is not human nature per se but the overall relationship of human beings to God and divine grace. Significantly, the scholastic theologians of the Middle Ages conceived of Adam and Eve as the recipients of a special grace, which they called "original justice," prior to their first sin. This grace ordered their passions to their will and their will to God. Because of this special grace Adam and Eve could do more than nature itself could achieve on its own. After the fall, however, they lost this original justice. Their passions were no longer ordered by their will, and they experienced concupiscence. This position is significantly different from that of Augustine. For Augustine, concupiscence is the disordering of the passions that arises from original sin, and at times is even equated with original sin. For Aquinas, concupiscence is the natural state to which the passions are returned when human beings are deprived of original justice. In a state of pure nature, which "historically" never existed, the desires are not disordered but unordered. The ordering of the passions is the moral task of self-constitution, through the practice of the virtues. The passions can be thought of as disordered only relative to their supernatural ordering in the state of original justice.

This speculative advance allowed Aquinas to solve a problem of Augustine's position. Augustine found it difficult to distinguish between concupiscence and original sin itself, because of his confusion between the problem of finitude and the problem of sin. He thus found it difficult to explain why concupiscence remained after baptism, which in faith he believed removed original sin. Aquinas, on the other hand, spoke of concupiscence as the "material" component of original sin. Its "formal" component, however, is our lack of original justice, caused by the fall of Adam (*ST* I-II q. 82, a. 3). People may suffer to a greater or lesser extent from concupiscence, but in every case the formal component or meaning is the same—it is the absence of original justice (*ST* I-II q. 82, a. 4). Moreover, one may remove the formal component, for example, through baptism, bringing the gift of sanctifying grace; though the material component (concupiscence) remains, it no longer has the same "formal" meaning. Concupiscence is only "disordered" relative to the supernatural gift of grace; otherwise it is simply a lack of order, an order to be imposed through the growth of natural and supernatural virtues, through a process of moral maturation.

This solution to the unresolved dilemma posed by Augustine's position on original sin allowed the church to affirm the goodness of the natural order, and of human nature in particular (Gen 1:31). This goodness could not be erased by the fall, and so humans could still strive to do the good. The drive to search for meaning, truth, and value remains in every human being, though because of concupiscence it may be swamped by other, more powerful drives and desires and so become ineffective in shaping the direction of our lives. However, the solution of the scholastics was not the only way to resolve the dilemma left by Augustine. Another solution was simply to identify finitude with evil, through the identification of concupiscence with original sin. Since concupiscence remains after baptism, the sinner is not truly regenerate but remains a sinner through and through. The person is *simul justus et peccator*, simultaneously just and sinner. Human justice is not ours; rather it is an alien, imputed justice that remains incapable of eradicating our intrinsic orientation to evil. This was the solution posited by Martin Luther, the great initiator of the Reformation. Luther rejected what he understood of the scholastic notion that original sin was merely a lack or privation of original justice. To accept such a position would "give occasion for lukewarmness and a breakdown of the whole concept of penitence, indeed to implant pride and presumptuousness, to eradicate fear of God, to outlaw humility, to make the command of God invalid, and thus condemn it completely."[5] For Luther, original sin is not merely a privation of original justice but more a positive inclination to evil. It is "a propensity towards evil . . . a nausea towards the good, a loathing of light and wisdom, and a delight in error and darkness, a flight from and abomination of all good works, a pursuit of evil."[6] The other great reformer, John Calvin, concurs with Luther on this point:

> Hence, those who have defined original sin as the want of the original righteousness which we ought to have had, though they substantially comprehend the whole case, do not significantly enough express its power and energy. For our nature is not only utterly devoid of goodness, but so prolific in all kinds of evil, that it can never be idle.[7]

For Calvin we are "perverted and corrupted in all the parts of our nature," and "therefore cannot but be odious and abominable to God."[8] There is no escape from such a condition because it has effectively become equated with our creaturely status. It remains even after baptism. The "middle ground" so carefully carved out by the scholastics with their notion of human "nature" has been eradicated so that anything that falls outside the realm of grace is viewed as thoroughly sinful.[9]

---

5. Martin Luther, *Lecture on Romans*, ed. H. Oswald, vol. 25 of *Luther's Works* (St. Louis: Concordia, 1972), 299.

6. Ibid., 300.

7. John Calvin, *The Institutes of Christian Religion*, trans. Henry Beveridge (Edinburgh: Calvin Translation Society, 1845), chap 1.8.

8. Ibid.

9. Logically there is another solution to the dilemma, and that is to supernaturalize the natural, to the point of eliminating any real notion of sin and evil. Some modern authors move in this direction.

Such a pessimistic anthropology has more than a suggestion of dualism to it. It is only avoided by the assertion of the absolute sovereignty of God, to such an extent that God almost becomes the author of human evil. For Luther, God appears to be the author of both salvation and sin:

> Since then God moves and actuates all in all, he necessarily moves and acts also in Satan and ungodly man . . . Here you see that when God works in and through evil men, evil things are done, and yet God cannot act evilly although he does evil through evil men, because one who is himself good cannot act evilly, yet he uses evil instruments that cannot escape the sway and motion of his omnipotence.[10]

This was not a position that the Catholic Church felt it could tolerate. The Council of Trent reaffirmed key elements of the scholastic position. In its decrees on justification and original sin it condemned several aspects of Luther's teaching. It affirmed the real regeneration of the sinner through grace:

> If anyone shall say that men are justified either by the sole imputation of the justice of Christ or by the sole remission of sins, to the exclusion of the grace and the charity that is poured forth in their hearts by the Holy Spirit and remains in them, or also that the grace by which we are justified is only the good will of God—*anathema sit.* (DS 1561; also see DS 1515 below)

The council rejected the identification of original sin with concupiscence:

> If anyone deny that the guilt of original sin is remitted by the grace of our Lord Jesus Christ conferred in baptism or assert that everything that has the true and proper nature of sin is not taken away but is erased or not reckoned—*anathema sit* . . . The Holy Council, however, knows and confesses that there remains in those who have been baptized concupiscence or the inclination to sin . . . of this concupiscence which the Apostle occasionally calls "sin" this Holy Council declares that the Catholic Church has never understood its being called sin in the sense of real and actual sin. . . . (DS 1515)

The council further rejected any notion that God has any responsibility for the sins of the sinner:

> If anyone shall say that it is not in man's power to make his ways evil, but that the works that are evil as well as those that are good God produces,

---

10. *Luther's Works,* ed. Helmut T. Lehman and Jaroslav Pelikan (Philadelphia: Fortress Press, 1955-76), 33:175-76.

not only permissively but *proprie et per se*, so that the treason of Judas is not less his own proper work than the vocation of St Paul—*anathema sit.* (DS 1556)[11]

These two opposing positions became firmly entrenched in post-Reformation polemics. Nonetheless, some Catholic movements, such as Jansenism, adopted elements of Luther's pessimistic anthropology,[12] while some of the reformers, notably the Wesley brothers, rejected Luther's pessimism to acknowledge a real transformation in the life of believers. For example, John Wesley attacked the notion of imputed righteousness as "a blow at the root of all holiness, all true religion . . . for wherever this doctrine is cordially received, it leaves no place for holiness."[13] These variations aside, the Council of Trent established a dogmatic foundation for a Catholic understanding of original sin well into the twentieth century. It took the major cultural upheaval of evolution to bring new questions to the fore. The difficulty with the teaching of the Council of Trent, particularly on original sin, is not so much the questions the council fathers addressed but the unquestioned assumptions from which they operated.

The unquestioned assumptions drawn from a premodern worldview tended to take the opening chapters of Genesis as a literal account of human origins. The teaching of Trent simply assumed such a reading since this was not the object of contention between the Catholic Church and the reformers. There was no reason at this stage why these assumptions should have been questioned. With the emergence of Darwin's theory of evolution, however, and the geological and cosmological evidence that the time scale for the world stretched beyond the thousands of years of the biblical narrative (taken literally) to reach millions and even billions of years, a literal reading of the biblical narrative became increasingly untenable. From an evolutionary perspective it is highly unlikely that human beings all descended from an original first couple (a position referred to as monogenism), or that they enjoyed an idyllic period in a plentiful garden. Genetically, human beings share a common ancestry with primates, and the first recognizably modern humans seem to have emerged from the plains of Africa. Then there was a period of tens of thousands of years before settled agrarian communities emerged and culture

---

11. Translations taken from Josef Neuner and Heinrich Roos, *The Teaching of the Catholic Church*, ed. Karl Rahner, trans. Geoffrey Stevens (Cork: Mercier Press, 1967).

12. Jansenism was a movement founded on the writings of Cornelius Jansen, bishop of Ypres (1510-1576), who, like Luther, sought to revive the more pessimistic aspects of Augustine's anthropology.

13. Alister E. McGrath, *Iustitia Dei: A History of the Christian Doctrine of Justification*, 2 vols. (Cambridge: Cambridge University Press, 1986), 2:52.

became more than rock art and primitive stone tools. The question that Christian theology faces is, Where in all this history of human existence does the traditional understanding of original sin fit?

For many Christians, belief in original sin was so tied to a premodern worldview that they could not see how the two could be separated. They were left with a simple set of alternatives. They could reassert the premodern worldview and reject the emerging insights of science, and hence was born so-called "creation science." This position clings to a literal reading of Genesis, rejects evolution, and takes Genesis 3 as relating "historical" events.[14] Alternatively, they could simply reject the doctrine of original sin altogether as an Augustinian error imposed on Christianity and distorting its true meaning. Such an approach can be found in some works on "creation spirituality," as proposed by Matthew Fox, and among some liberal Protestant theologians.[15]

A number of Christian thinkers have attempted to integrate evolutionary perspectives into their theology, notably Pierre Teilhard de Chardin and Karl Rahner.[16] Church authorities have viewed these attempts with caution, to say the least. In 1909 the Pontifical Biblical Commission reasserted the "historical" nature of the early chapters of Genesis, though the church later moved away from a literal reading of Scripture when it officially endorsed elements of modern biblical historical criticism, notably with the encyclical *Divino Afflante Spiritu* (1943). In 1950 Pius XII issued the encyclical *Humani Generis,* which, among other things, attempted to defend the position of monogenism on the ground that it was a necessary element in the traditional understanding of original sin. Now there seems to be less anxiety about this question, and Pope John Paul II offered cautious acceptance of evolution as a scientific hypothesis of human origins. Indeed, various theologians have adopted non-monogenistic theories of original sin without comment by church authorities.[17]

---

14. It is clear on any reading of creation science literature that the real issue is not the literal reading of Genesis 1-2, but of Genesis 3, because without it there is no original sin, and without a doctrine of original sin there is no Christian account of redemption. For example, see http://www.csm .org.uk/whoweare.php (accessed July 12, 2006): "[Creation science movement] declares that the doctrine of original sin is not based on myth or fable but rather on the solid foundation of the 'lively oracles' of the Lord God. A blurring of this truth affects the wonder of the Atonement by the peerless Son of God which in turn can lead to a shallow commitment to Him." Of course, the argument can go the other way. Those who promote evolution often argue that it eliminates the notion of original sin and hence any rationale for redemption.

15. Matthew Fox, *Original Blessing* (Santa Fe, N.M.: Bear, 1983).

16. Pierre Teilhard de Chardin, *The Phenomenon of Man,* rev. ed. (London: Collins, 1977); Karl Rahner, *Foundations of Christian Faith: An Introduction to the Idea of Christianity* (New York: Crossroad, 1982), 187-93.

17. Siegfried Wiedenhofer, "The Main Forms of Contemporary Theology of Original Sin," *Communio* 18 (1991): 514-29.

CONTEMPORARY REFLECTION ON ORIGINAL SIN

Today most biblical scholars would argue that the literary form of the material in Genesis 2-3 is myth. This is not to say that it is untrue, but this identifies the literary form through which the biblical truth is conveyed. There are clear mythological elements in the story—the tree of life, the tree of knowledge, the serpent, the angel guarding the way back to Eden—that need to be read according to the canons of myth, not legendary or historical narrative. In particular, the story of the fall in Genesis 3 is an etiological myth for the origins of sin and suffering in what we believe to be a good creation. It expresses in mythological terms four important truths:

1. Sin has been part of the human story "from the beginning," however that beginning might be measured. There is no time in human history when we have not suffered from the problem of evil.
2. The origin of sin lies not in God or in some cosmic struggle between good and evil, but in human actions and decision. Seeking to shift the blame onto someone or something else is in fact part of the problem of sin itself.
3. Once sin enters into the human story its effects spread and grow leaving no one untouched by its consequences. "From the beginning" no one can claim exemption or claim to be untouched by sin.
4. Despite the fact of human sinfulness, God has not abandoned human beings to their fate. Rather, God continues to care for them and work for their good (Gen 3:21)

The Genesis account of itself does not necessarily imply any inherited sin or guilt, but it does suggest that the consequences of sin extend well beyond the individual who sins. No precise content can be assigned to the nature of any primal sin, though René Girard has pointed to persistent and widespread mythological accounts of a primal murder, as is narrated in Genesis 4, the story of Cain and Abel.[18]

Similarly, Scripture scholars find little merit in Augustine's interpretation of Romans 5:12 as providing a basis for any notion of inherited sin or guilt. Rather than positing a primal sin in Adam, *in whom* we all sin through some mysterious human solidarity, they tend to see a fairly factual statement that we all sin, and *because* we have all sinned, death has spread to all (on the con-

---

18. René Girard, Jean-Michel Oughourlian, and Guy Lefort, *Things Hidden since the Foundation of the World* (Stanford, Calif.: Stanford University Press, 1987), esp. 105-25. More broadly, see René Girard, *Violence and the Sacred* (Baltimore: Johns Hopkins University Press, 1977). One should also note Sigmund Freud's account of the first murder in the primal horde in Sigmund Freud, "Totem and Taboo," in *The Origins of Religion*, Pelican Freud Library (London: Penguin, 1985).

nection between sin and death, see chapter 8). Further, they emphasize the christological context of Paul's argument, which highlights not the sin of Adam but the overwhelming gift of grace brought about by the obedience of Jesus Christ.[19]

Similarly, systematic theologians have sought to understand the doctrine of original sin in new ways that are not tied to a premodern worldview. We shall consider three approaches before presenting a further refinement on this difficult topic.

Dutch theologian Alfred Vanneste has suggested that we should think of original sin simply in terms of the universality of actual sin.[20] The universality of sin is simply a brute fact that finds no extra explanation in terms of a prior condition or inclination to sin in the person. We need to look for nothing deeper in our understanding of the traditional teaching. Such a position eliminates any specific notion of original sin per se, and it seems difficult to reconcile with church teachings that distinguish original sin from actual sin, particularly those that refer to the baptism of infants.

Karl Rahner, on the other hand, has suggested that we should think of original sin as an existential, that is, a permanent element, of human consciousness, an empirical given that constitutes our concrete human existence. Using his distinction between the transcendental and the historical, Rahner sees original sin in terms of the deprivation of sanctifying grace which was meant to be mediated historically by the "first man," Adam, taken here as representative of the first human beings. This failure in the historical mediation of grace results in a sinful situation, or "sin of the world," into which all human persons are born. This is the way in which original sin is propagated to all human beings. As an existential, original sin should be identified not in terms of a human history of sinfulness but in terms of the impact of that history on human consciousness. Moreover, it is not the only such existential for Rahner, for there is also the supernatural existential, which orients us dynamically to God. The history of humanity is, then, the struggle and conflict between these two existentials.[21]

A fruitful approach, adopted by British theologian Sebastian Moore, has been to explore the impact of the history of sinfulness of human consciousness through the categories of modern psychology.[22] This is the approach I shall be following in the section below.

---

19. See Byrne, *Romans*, 173-82.

20. Alfred Vanneste, *The Dogma of Original Sin*, trans. E. Callens (Louvain: Nauwelaerts, 1975).

21. Karl Rahner, "The Sin of Adam," in *Confrontations*, vol. 11 of *Theological Investigations* (New York: Seabury Press, 1974), 247-62.

22. Moore has written various works that touch on these issues, for example, *Let This Mind Be in You* (London: Darton, Longman & Todd, 1985).

ORIGINAL SIN AS OUR UNIVERSAL VICTIMHOOD

As we have already seen, there are many elements of the doctrine of original sin that have become part of our dogmatic tradition: debates about monogenism versus evolution, propagation versus imitation, notions of original justice, concupiscence, and so on. All these have their place; however, they can tend to obscure the key tension of the doctrine. The doctrine attempts to take a path between a position that understands the human condition as substantially affected by evil, trapped in an ontologically determined fate, a position we could label as Manichean, and a moral individualism that sees us each as the sole creator of our own drama, a position we could label as Pelagian.[23]

In order to mediate between these two unacceptable alternatives I want to focus on the basic elements of the story, the narrative of original sin. At its most basic level, I would state it thus:

1. Adam sinned (however we may understand this). From the beginning of human history sin has been part of our condition.
2. Because of Adam's sin, we all suffer (however this suffering may be conceived). Sin has its consequences, not just for the one who sins but for all those around.

About such a simple restatement there would perhaps be little debate. The question is, what conclusions do we and should we draw? I would like to argue that the simplest and most obvious conclusion would be as follows:

3. We are all the victims of Adam's sin.

The heart of the doctrine of original sin is arguably a statement about the universal victimhood of humankind. It is saying that in one way or another we are all the victims of another's (i.e., Adam's) sin.

I think that simply to state it in these terms is an important shift. The doctrine of original sin says that, prior to sinning, we are first and foremost sinned against. To be sinned against is to be a victim of another's sin. To be sinned against, especially in early childhood, is to enter into a condition of human brokenness, an interior shattering or distortion of consciousness that muddies our search for direction in the movement of life. To be sinned against in this way, to be thus broken, is the prior state that inclines us all to personal sins of our own. It is the weakness that undermines us; it creates what Sebastian Moore calls our inner "wobble," a weakened sense of our own worth, which inclines us, with a statistical inevitability, to sin.[24]

---

23. Stephen J. Duffy, "Original Sin: Our Hearts of Darkness Revisited," *Theological Studies* 49 (1988): 597-622.

24. Moore, *Let This Mind Be in You*, xiii.

Vatican I enjoined theologians to find analogies for the mysteries of faith (DS 3016). On original sin Thomas Aquinas proposed an analogy of the family shame for a criminal forebear (*ST* I-II q. 18, a. 1). Such shame is real and has a real impact on the lives of those who come after. I would propose another analogy, one drawn more from contemporary literature and experience. The simplest analogy to the above interpretation of original sin is the situation of an abused child. The abused child is, first and foremost, sinned against. He or she is the victim of the parent's cruelty, however that may be expressed, physically, sexually, or emotionally. The consequences in the life of the child are frequently—unless there is some loving intervention by an "enlightened witness" (according to therapist Alice Miller)[25]—a life of sin, a repeated compulsion of violence toward, and abuse of, others and/or oneself, or some other of the myriad symptoms of a damaged sense of self-worth.[26] Such sin is propagated from parent to child, to the seventh generation, and even beyond.

REFLECTIONS ON THE "GUILT" OF ORIGINAL SIN

Having linked original sin by analogy with abuse, then the guilt of original sin is related to the guilt felt by victims of abuse. It is the guilt you feel when you haven't done anything wrong:
1. The guilt you feel when you have not done anything wrong is the guilt of the victim.
2. The guilt of original sin is guilt you have when you have not done anything wrong.
3. Therefore the guilt of original sin is the guilt of the victim.

Such guilt is real and damaging. It is also very difficult to get rid of, because you cannot be forgiven for something you have not done. What is needed is not forgiveness but healing.

While the analogy points to relatively extreme (though sadly not necessarily uncommon) events, it is not difficult to recall the myriad minor humiliations and cruelties we have all endured in childhood. Here the various writings of Alice Miller give numerous examples, that, while they lack the overpowering impact of direct abuse, still have a deleterious effect on the

---

25. See, for example, Alice Miller, *Banished Knowledge: Facing Childhood Injuries* (New York: Anchor Books, 1990), 171ff.

26. There is a growing body of literature on which one could draw here. Apart from the profound and disturbing works of Alice Miller, there are a large number of books that outline the impact of such abuse. Perhaps the most outstanding recent work is Judith Herman, *Trauma and Recovery* (New York: Basic Books, 1992).

child's emerging sense of self-esteem. As Sebastian Moore has repeatedly argued, it is this diminished, distorted sense of self that lies at the heart of the mystery of original sin.

It is important here to emphasize that the victimhood that constitutes original sin is contingent, not necessary; it is historical and so not an onto-logical constituent of being human. To argue that it is an ontological con-stituent would be a Manichean position. Rather, it arises from concrete, if varied, historical circumstances. We must abandon the view of original sin as some sort of metaphysical sexually transmitted disease and begin to view it in terms of historical causation. In the language of Bernard Lonergan's *Insight*, original sin is then a statistical, not a classical, law. It is a statistical law, with probability one, so that we may say, "The world breaks everyone" yet "after-ward many are strong in the broken places."[27] The mystery of redemption is about how we might become "strong in the broken places," or, as Paul puts it, "Therefore I am content with weaknesses, insults, hardships, persecutions, and calamities for the sake of Christ; for whenever I am weak, then I am strong" (2 Cor 12:10).

If the doctrine of original sin is about our universal status as victims, the question that arises is, What attitude do we have toward victims? What stance do we take to our own victimhood, and what stance do we take to the vic-timhood of others?

As a starting point, let us consider our own victimhood. One response is to reject our own victimhood altogether. We may deny that we have anything of the victim within us. We alone are responsible for our actions, the authors of our stories. This seems to be the moral high ground, taking full responsibility, not putting the blame onto someone else. Indeed, it recalls the position of Pelagius, whom we should remember was a moralist who saw Augustine's doctrine of grace and original sin as undermining moral effort. While Chris-tianity upholds the importance of moral responsibility, it recognizes in the doctrine of original sin, that this responsibility is not absolute, but compro-mised by our fallen state.

The doctrine of original sin tells us that this denial of our compromised state is not the case. In view of original sin such an attitude is nothing but a perpetuation of the myth of "being in control," built on a false and individu-alistic notion of human autonomy.[28] The end point of such a myth is a mask

---

27. "The world breaks everyone and afterward many are strong in the broken places. But those that will not break it kills. It kills the very good and the very gentle and the very brave impartially. If you are none of these you can be sure it will kill you too but there will be no special hurry" (Ernest Hemingway, *A Farewell to Arms*, 1929).

28. A number of commentators have identified such individualism as at the heart of the modern cultural crisis, e.g., Robert Neelly Bellah et al., *Habits of the Heart: Individualism and Commitment in*

of self-righteousness, a pseudo-holiness, being used to hide what is often a great inner brokenness. It is not without reason that Scott Peck calls extreme cases of such persons "people of the lie," for their lives are based on a lie and the road they travel leads to death.[29] At such an end point their blindness to their own brokenness leads to an intolerance of the brokenness and vulnerability of others, whom they ruthlessly exploit and abuse.

Again, such extreme examples should not blind us to the myriad ways in which we mask our own brokenness from others and sometimes even from ourselves, through our "successes," careers, achievements, power, or acclaim. Similarly there are the many minor ways of showing contempt, particularly for the poor, the uneducated, those with handicaps, those whom society judges as failures or "on the scrap heap."[30] Few would not recognize such tendencies within themselves, and those who do not may be the cause of greater concern (John 9:41)!

Significantly, Alice Miller speaks of the contempt of the narcissistically wounded for the vulnerable:

> Contempt for those who are smaller and weaker thus is the best defense against a breakthrough of one's own feelings of helplessness: it is an expression of this split-off weakness. The strong person, who knows that he too carries this weakness within himself, because he has experienced it, does not need to demonstrate this strength through such contempt.[31]

The social expression of this attitude of contempt is the frequently observed phenomenon of "blaming the victim." Women are blamed for being raped; victims of sexual abuse are claimed to have seduced their perpetrators; indigenous populations are blamed for their cultural degradation; the unemployed are blamed for being out of work. Cultural commentators even speak derogatorily of the "victim industry"[32] and "bleeding hearts." So many of our ideologies are just complex ways of blaming victims for their state of vulnerability and violation. Even the doctrine of original sin can be misunderstood as blaming us for our state of being sinned against when it imputes a real responsibility for our state of original sin. Alternatively, victims are silenced or

American Life (Berkeley: University of California Press, 1985); and also Alasdair MacIntyre, *After Virtue: A Study in Moral Theory*, 2nd ed. (Notre Dame, Ind.: University of Notre Dame Press, 1984).

29. See M. Scott Peck, *People of the Lie: The Hope for Healing Human Evil* (New York: Simon & Schuster, 1983).

30. One could add here the large-scale contempt shown by men for women through sexual violence, domestic violence, and other less explicit expressions of sexism.

31. Alice Miller, *The Drama of the Gifted Child* (New York: Basic Books, 1990), 67.

32. See, for example, the provocative writing of Ofer Zur, who is seeking to nuance discourse on victimhood: "Reflections on a Culture of Victims and How Psychotherapy Fuels the Victim Industry," available at http://www.drozur.com/victimhood.html (accessed July 2, 2006).

ignored, their suffering simply falling on deaf ears. These attitudes to victims are nothing but the rejection of our own victimhood writ large upon society.

ORIGINAL SIN AND CHILD REARING

We have already noted Augustine's attitude to the hungry cries of a newborn child. Imagine for a moment what attitude one would have to a newborn child if one believed that original sin meant the total corruption of human nature. How would one respond to every need, every desire, and every impulse of an infant? All such needs, desires, and impulses can be understood only as arising out of a totally corrupt human nature. From the point of view of the parent, they must be controlled, regulated, and hopefully eliminated from the infant's repertoire of responses. Immediately one is in a conflictual situation with the infant, placing great emphasis on obedience and discipline to control the child. One is engaged in a battle of wills. If all else fails, one might try to "beat the devil out of the child." Even sacramental baptism is ineffective in remediating this corruption.

Alice Miller has documented the outcomes of a childhood raised on these principles. They do not make for happy reading.[33]

Of course the rhetoric of victimhood can be misused. People can claim victimhood as an ontological status, something from which they can never escape. They are eternally victims and so deserve special treatment from everyone else. Because of their status as victims they can never be held responsible for anything. Alternatively, people who are clearly culpable for their actions can seek to claim the status of victim in order to gain some sort of moral sympathy that they do not deserve.

Cultural anthropologist René Girard would argue that this recognition of the moral status of the victim is something specifically introduced into cultures through biblical revelation. Girard's speculations about the primal sin of murder center on what he calls the "scapegoat mechanism," whereby societies focus their communal tension on a chosen, innocent victim, the scapegoat, who is ritually expelled or murdered, to alleviate the social tension within the group. Such expulsion "works" at least in the short term, and so restores some level of social harmony, thus conferring on the victim a magical or divine status. According to Girard, this mechanism works only so long as we hide from

---

33. Alice Miller, *For Your Own Good: Hidden Cruelty in Child-Rearing and the Roots of Violence*, 4th ed. (New York: Farrar, Straus & Giroux, 2002).

ourselves the actual innocence of the victim. What happens in the death of Jesus is the unmasking of the scapegoat mechanism through the revelation of the innocence of its victim, in the death and resurrection of Jesus. In cultures affected by Christian belief it becomes increasingly difficult to maintain the guilt of the scapegoat, while the victim more and more takes on the moral high ground. We shall consider these speculations again in the next chapter.[34]

THE VOICE OF ORIGINAL SIN—THE SATAN

At this stage it might be worth saying something about the role of the Satan in our understanding of original sin. I shall begin by noting that the term "Satan" means "adversary" or "accuser."[35] In legal language the Accuser is the prosecuting attorney, the one who puts before the court the accusation against the accused. In the perspective developed here, the Accuser is the voice within, continually undermining our sense of self, running us down with a multitude of accusations, loading us with guilt for things we have never done. Using this we can attempt to uncover some of the mythology about this figure.

If we turn to the Genesis account we find Adam and Eve listening to the voice of the Accuser. The Satan's temptation "you will be like God" (Gen 3:5) is not only a temptation. It is an implied criticism "you want to be like gods and you should be like gods, *but you're not."* The Accuser is getting under the skin of Adam and Eve, taunting them with their finitude—"There is something wrong with you, something wrong with just being human."

In her description of neurosis, Karen Horney picks up a similar tale. She describes how neurotics are driven by their "shoulds"—"I should do this, I should have done that." At the heart of this drivenness is a self-esteem dominated by guilt. She states:

> But when trying—anxiously—to measure up to [his shoulds] he feels most of the time that he falls pitiably short of fulfilling them. The foremost element in his consciousness is therefore self-criticism, *a feeling of guilt for not being the supreme being.*[36]

---

34. It is interesting to note that in the various hostage incidents in the occupation of Iraq, when Japanese hostages were taken and subsequently released, the hostages publicly apologized to the Japanese people for the inconvenience they had caused by being taken hostage. Such an apology is unthinkable in Western countries.

35. See John L. McKenzie, *Dictionary of the Bible* (London: Geoffrey Chapman, 1968), 774. Much of Christian mythology about Satan arises not from the Bible but from the creative rereading of biblical texts by early church fathers.

36. Karen Horney, *Neurosis and Human Growth: The Struggle toward Self-Realization* (New York: Norton, 1991), 76 (emphasis added).

In this description of neurosis we see the work of the Satan undermining our human identity through a series of baseless accusations. Yet who among us would claim to be free from such an inner voice? Surely such a description as that given by Horney is applicable to us all to a greater or lesser extent? Such a bondage to the Satan is not the type of spectacular phenomenon given in "popular" accounts of "demonic possession." It is much more real, more common, and very dangerous.

We should also consider the Christian myth concerning the origin of the Satan. In Christian mythology the Satan was originally a good angel—Lucifer, or the bearer of light.[37] He was indeed the highest angel of the heavens; however, in pride he overreached himself and so fell from heaven and became the Accuser, the Satan attacking humankind. What can be made of this mythological language?

In psychological terms the light within each of us is our conscience. Vatican II describes conscience as our most secret core, a sanctuary where we can be alone with God (*Gaudium et Spes* 16). The role of the Lucifer can be understood psychologically as that of bearing the light of conscience to illuminate human actions by the timely and accurate pronouncement of accusations. This was indeed a godlike task and involved an intimacy with both God and the human person; however, Lucifer overstepped the boundaries of the task. Not satisfied with a godlike task within conscience, he wanted to be the whole of conscience. He ceased being the Lucifer who illuminated our conscience and became Satan, the Accuser, "who accuses [our comrades] day and night before our God" (Rev 12:10). The Satan is a false conscience which leads to the false consciousness that is sin. Only God can quieten the accusations of such a conscience (1 John 3:19-21). The Satan of false accusation must be cast out by the strong man, who brings not accusation but forgiveness and healing (Mark 3:27).

The problem with the accusations of false conscience is that they always carry a certain amount of plausibility. Whatever good we do, we could always have done something better if only circumstances were a bit different, or if we had stretched ourselves a little or a lot. There are always goods left undone or even undoable, which in turn produces a rich field of possibilities for the accusations of the Satan.

Moralists are generally worried about the type of false conscience which tells us that something is good when it is really bad. While such a problem is not uncommon, the opposite is far more common. Not only is it more com-

---

37. The term "lucifer" arose from the Vulgate translation of "morning star" in Isaiah 14:12. The early fathers took this as a reference to "the prince of demons." However, the text originally referred to the death of a king of Babylon, probably Nebuchadnezzar.

mon; it is far more disorienting in the moral sphere. When we do wrong and it is condoned by a false conscience, it is simply rationalizing what we have already decided to do. However, when we have done nothing wrong, yet find ourselves accused by a false conscience, we are totally undermined. It leads us to doubt ourselves and all our moral judgments. Nothing makes sense any more. Even repentance does not help, since there is really nothing from which to repent. Such a confused state will quickly lead to real moral faults.

Indeed the accusations of the Satan, the feelings of guilt upon which he plays, lead to a serious weakening of our sense of evil. When we are confronted with an evil situation, we already feel guilty about it. We feel as if we may already be compromised by it. Since we feel already compromised, we do not—and, in fact, cannot afford to—see the evil as bad as it really is. We get sucked into its framework or definition of reality—"It's really not so bad." The freer we are from such a pervasive sense of guilt, the more clearly we see evil for what it is. Indeed no one sees evil with as much clarity as Jesus, who sees it in all its ugliness.

Finally, we should note that the Johannine Jesus refers to the Satan as the Father of Lies (John 8:44). The biggest and most damaging lie is that there is something wrong with us, that we are not lovable, that God wants nothing to do with us, that God is angry with us before we have even done anything. Yet these are the lies that the Satan tells us, and we believe him.

To live in the life of grace does not mean that one no longer hears the voice of the Satan. It is always present, hoping to get our attention with some new accusation. The voice does not die. It is, however, drowned out by a stronger voice, the powerful and primal affirmation of "Yes" given by Jesus (2 Cor 1:17-20). In Jesus there is no ambivalent yes and no. Jesus affirms human existence, my existence, completely. Hence Paul can say, even though he never met Jesus, that Jesus "loved *me* and gave himself for *me*" (Gal 2:20). Grace is God's stronger voice saying "you are precious in my sight, and honored, and I love you" (Isa 43:4). Nothing can come between us and such a love from God (Rom 8:38-39), certainly not the voice of the Accuser.

From this perspective it is possible to read Augustine's arguments for original sin in a new light. In particular, I shall consider the arguments on suffering and the nature of concupiscence. Augustine argues that the human experience of suffering points to the reality of original sin. Since God is good and just, human suffering must be a punishment for some original sin in which we all share. While I previously criticized this as being based on a static view of the universe, it would be wrong to ignore the psychological significance of this analysis.

The spontaneous link between suffering and moral evil is very common. People caught in great suffering exclaim "Why me?!", as if their suffering is meant to be a punishment for some unknown wrong. "I don't deserve this," or worse still, "I must deserve this," they say, as if suffering is "just" and hence deserved, only as a punishment. Yet ontologically, as we argued earlier, suffering has no connection with punishment or moral evil per se. All finite being suffers in as much as it comes up against its limits. Suffering is part of any finite existence. In a very real sense there is simply no way to avoid such suffering.

Yet we continue, as did Augustine, spontaneously to make a link between suffering and punishment. It is not difficult to see in this link the work of the Satan, the voice of original sin. In the experience of suffering the accusation arises, "This is your fault; this is a punishment for your wrongdoing." Since my finitude is part of my ontological structure as human, the accusation is saying that there is something wrong with being human, with being finite. It is telling us we should feel guilt about being human.

Augustine's argument concerning concupiscence has a similar structure. From the scholastic viewpoint, concupiscence is part of the ontological structure of human nature. It is part of the structure of human finitude. Yet Augustine evokes in us a sense of guilt about concupiscence. To quote again from Karen Horney, we can develop a real "feeling of guilt for not being the supreme being."[38]

ORIGINAL SIN AND OTHER RELIGIOUS WORLDVIEWS

As we noted at the beginning of this discussion on original sin, the starting point for our Christian belief in original sin is fundamentally an experience of salvation, brought about by the death and resurrection of Jesus Christ. We only really know what we have been saved from (original sin) in the light shone on human experience through the event of salvation. If this is correct, then one would really expect an account of original sin only within Christian belief. Indeed, without some account of original sin the whole account of salvation begins to lose coherence.

If we turn our attention, then, to the two religious worldviews closest to Christianity—those of Judaism and Islam—it should come as no surprise that neither of these religions has a belief in original sin, though both share something of the founding narrative of Genesis 3.

Judaism directly shares the biblical narrative of Genesis 3 with Christianity, but completely rejects any notion that the actions of Adam and Eve constitute a sin whose effects include guilt for the rest of humankind. Judaism is

---

38. Horney, *Neurosis and Human Growth*, 76.

a religion built on the notion of obedience—obedience to the Torah, the will of God proclaimed by the Jewish Law. The doctrine of original sin undermines this central concept by casting doubt on our human ability to fulfill the Law. Original sin appears to teach that each person is born guilty and incapable of pleasing God without some saving "grace" earned for us by Jesus. Judaism recognizes that there are evil inclinations in human beings, but these inclinations do not constitute sin or guilt. There is no sense in Judaism that the promised Messiah will earn forgiveness of sins for other human beings (vicarious satisfaction).

Islam, too, rejects any notion of original sin and correlatively any notion of salvation brought about by Jesus. In Islam each person is responsible for his or her own actions, and each person must seek forgiveness directly from Allah for sins committed. While there are holy persons and teachers in Islam, there is no priesthood, no sense of mediation of the divine, for each believer can directly approach Allah. Muslims tend to read the Christian position on original sin as implying that human beings are basically evil, which is more the Reformed position than the Catholic one. For Muslims, all human beings are essentially good and only need forgiveness for sins they actually commit.

From a Christian perspective both of these positions are structurally similar to each other and to the position of Pelagius. They both stress personal responsibility and a sense of complete freedom of action. They do not seek to shift the blame to someone else, particularly some ancient ancestor. One has to ask, however, whether human freedom can bear the weight of this responsibility? We know, for example, the ways in which freedom can be compromised by addictions, or by a history of abuse. Do these religions allow for a recognition of this compromised freedom? Do they recognize that "the world breaks everyone"? Can they show compassion for human weakness (Heb 4:15)? Or must we bear the full brunt of all our bad decisions?

This is not to say that Christian belief in original sin eliminates any sense of personal responsibility. Indeed, the path of repentance will mean learning to take real responsibility for one's actions, seeking to repair damage done, and to avoid sin in the future. But mixed with this is a realistic recognition that this is no simple task, because the primary damage done is to our freedom itself, which has been weakened, though not destroyed.

CONCLUSION

In this chapter our focus has been on the question, From what are we saved? Heuristically the answer can be given, "original sin." This names the condition that binds us, but to understand the nature of that condition we must explore the impact that human sinfulness, historically mediated, has on each one of us. This has been the aim of the present chapter. However, it is preliminary to our next chapter, which explores the nature of that salvation: How do the death and resurrection of Jesus save us from "original sin"? Again we need to explore some of the traditional responses to this question before we then turn to a more contemporary approach.

QUESTIONS FOR REFLECTION

1. For most of Christian history, belief in original sin has been tied to a fairly literal reading of Genesis 3. Can we still believe in original sin if we reject a literal reading of Genesis 3 and adopt an evolutionary account of human origins? What difference does such a shift make?
2. Do you think it is reasonable to think of new born infants as affected by original sin? Why or why not?
3. What are some of the ways you are aware of that we have for blaming victims for their sufferings?
4. What would be the difficulties in viewing belief in original sin as simply a statement that "all have sinned"?
5. What difference do you think it would make to Christianity not to have a doctrine of original sin?

SUGGESTIONS FOR FURTHER READING AND STUDY

Augustine. *The Confessions*. Translated by Maria Boulding. Vintage Spiritual Classics. New York: Vintage Books, 1998.

Duffy, Stephen J. "Original Sin: Our Hearts of Darkness Revisited." *Theological Studies* 49 (1988): 597-622.

Girard, René, Jean-Michel Oughourlian, and Guy Lefort. *Things Hidden since the Foundation of the World*. Stanford, Calif.: Stanford University Press, 1987.

Herman, Judith. *Trauma and Recovery*. New York: Basic Books, 1992.

Miller, Alice. *Banished Knowledge: Facing Childhood Injuries*. New York: Anchor Books, 1990.

Moore, Sebastian. *Let This Mind Be in You*. London: Darton, Longman & Todd, 1985.

Rahner, Karl. "The Sin of Adam." In *Confrontations*, vol. 11 of *Theological Investigations*, 247-62. New York: Seabury Press, 1974.

Wiedenhofer, Siegfried. "The Main Forms of Contemporary Theology of Original Sin." *Communio* 18 (1991): 514-29.

Wiley, Tatha. *Original Sin: Origins, Developments, Contemporary Meanings*. New York: Paulist Press, 2002.

5

Jesus and the Story of Redemption

I N THE PREVIOUS CHAPTER we explored the notion of original sin, both in its traditional formulations and in a modern reformulation. As we noted, central to the development of the doctrine of original sin is the question, from what are we saved? Christianity began as an experience of salvation. Central to that salvation were the mission, death, and resurrection of Jesus Christ. Those events transformed lives in powerful and unexpected ways, for example, the conversion of Paul. Yet the early church and the subsequent history of reflection on these experiences have found it difficult to give expression to how it is that Jesus' death and resurrection are saving events. Just as the language of original sin draws on mythological thought forms, so too does the language of salvation (soteriology). In this chapter we shall explore the experience and language of salvation, in its biblical, traditional, and more contemporary forms. In doing so we should never sever the connection between the language of salvation and the language of original sin, for they remain always intimately connected.

THE NEW TESTAMENT WITNESS

Let us begin with a simple question: Why did Jesus die? When we turn to the New Testament witness apart from the Gospels, particularly the letters of Paul, we find a variety of symbols and metaphors for trying to understand the death of Jesus. Jesus' death is redemptive, the offering of a ransom, a sacrifice (Eph 5:2; Heb 9:26), a sin offering (Rom 3:25), bringing about a reconciliation with God; it is the result of a struggle with principalities and powers (Eph 6:12), with death itself (1 Cor 15:26), resulting in the restoration of what was lost by Adam, and so on. On the other hand, when we read the Gospels themselves, we find a fairly grubby story of power and politics, of enemies and rivalries, of people who very early in the ministry of Jesus set out to destroy him, discrediting his teaching and his mission (Mark 3:6). These two accounts of Jesus' death, one highly theologized, and the other embedded in a historical narrative, sit side by side, barely making contact in the consciousness of many Christians. One of the challenges of contemporary soteriology is to bring these two accounts into meaningful contact.

Let us begin with a focus on the religious language we associate with the death of Jesus. Rather than attempt a comprehensive account, I shall make use of a summary presented by Hans Urs von Balthasar of five elements that are discernible in the New Testament witness of salvation, and to which any account must relate in some way or other.[1]

1. The work of reconciliation is achieved through the act of the Son "giving himself up," allowing himself to be handed over, to the point of the "shedding of blood." This shedding of blood "is understood as the atoning (Rom 3:25), justifying (Rom 5:9) and purifying factor (1 John 1:7; Rev 7:14) at all levels of the New Testament."

2. This act of "giving himself up" is "for us," *pro nobis*, to the extent of "exchanging places with us," so that Jesus becomes sin (2 Cor 5:21) and a "curse" (Gal 3:13). "On the basis of this exchange of place, we are already 'reconciled to God' (Rom 5:18) in advance of our own consent, 'while we were yet sinners.'" We have died with Christ and are risen with him; we must now become what we are.

3. Reconciliation involves being liberated from something: from slavery to sin (Rom 7; John 8:34); from the devil (John 8:44; 1 John 3:8); from principalities and powers (Col 2:20); from the law (Rom 7:1); from the wrath to come (1 Thess 1:10). This liberation comes at a high cost or ransom, that is, through the blood of Christ (1 Cor 6:20). It is a propitiation producing an eternal redemption (Heb 9:12).

4. However, more is involved than just a liberation or restoration of lost freedom; there is also being drawn into the trinitarian life of God, becoming adopted sons and daughters (Gal 4:6), receiving the gift of the Holy Spirit poured into our hearts (Rom 5:5). We become sharers in the divine nature (2 Pet 1:4).

5. While there are numerous references to "God's anger," the entire reconciliation process is the result of God's merciful love; it is because of the love of the Father (Rom 8:39) and the love of Christ (Rom 8:35) that Christ was given up for us. Everything flows from this one source, divine love.

Three things should be noted from this summary by Balthasar. First, salvation is a rich notion, not something to be reduced to just one of the aspects that he identifies. It is not only salvation "from," but also salvation "for," in partic-

---

1. Hans Urs von Balthasar, *The Action*, vol. 4 of *Theo-Drama: Theological Dramatic Theory*, 5 vols. (San Francisco: Ignatius Press, 1988-98), 240-43.

ular for our participation in the divine life. Second, the source, impulse, and initiative of salvation come from God, who is first and foremost a God of salvation, not condemnation. Finally, despite the power of this summary, it makes almost no contact with the story of Jesus' own life as narrated in the Gospels.

When we turn to the Gospels we find an equally rich account of a life focused on proclaiming the Kingdom of God. Jesus begins his mission with a call to repent and an announcement of the closeness of the Kingdom (Mark 1:15). He manifests the Kingdom through the power of his miracles, restoring people to a fullness of life and participation in the community, and through his symbolic actions such as table fellowship with public sinners (Matt 11:19). The Kingdom of God becomes the defining symbol of Jesus' mission, a kingdom of reconciliation of people with one another and with God. Jesus' preaching about the Kingdom speaks of reaching out to those at the margins, the poor, the sick, the ones who are lost. All are invited to enter the kingdom, so that even tax collectors and prostitutes are "entering the Kingdom" (Matt 21:32). So powerful is the coming of the Kingdom that even the gates of hell cannot hold out against it (Matt 16:18). Hell itself is under siege.[2]

Yet, inexplicably, this message of forgiveness, inclusiveness, and reconciliation almost immediately provokes resistance (Mark 3:6 and parallels). Jesus' preaching, his miracles, and symbolic actions are unsettling the established religious, political, and social world. He preaches with authority, not like the other religious leaders, and his word of command has the power to expel demons (Mark 1:27; 5:1-20), as even his opponents acknowledge (Mark 3:22). As his mission continues, Jesus encounters growing resistance to his message, and he becomes increasingly strident in his condemnation of the religious leaders of the people (Matt 23:1-39). His own fate at their hands becomes increasingly clear to him and poses a major dilemma for the continuation of his mission. Does he avoid conflict, perhaps modify his actions or his preaching, so that he may continue to actively proclaim the Kingdom, if in more muted form? Or does he find a way to incorporate his predictable fate into the very heart of his mission (Mark 8:31-33)? Can Jesus make his otherwise meaningless fate at the hands of the religious and political authorities something that is full of meaning, a manifestation of the Kingdom of God, in all its powerlessness and power, its strength and weakness?

The most significant indication we have that Jesus sought to integrate his fate into the very fabric of his mission is found in the Last Supper narratives. Drawing on themes from the Old Testament, Jesus speaks of his death as ini-

---

2. It is interesting to note how often in popular preaching this image is turned around so that heaven is under siege. But in fact it is the gates of hell that are under siege and cannot hold out against the preaching of the Kingdom.

tiating a new covenant, to be achieved through the spilling of his blood, his imminent death. His death is a death for others, for the forgiveness of sin "for many" (see Mark 14:22-25). In the words and actions of Jesus at the Last Supper we can find the seeds of the meaning placed on Jesus' death by Paul (notably Rom 3:24-5) and the other authors of the New Testament (e.g., Heb 7:26-27). It is in the intent of Jesus that the two sides of our response to the question, Why did Jesus die? find their point of intersection.

EARLY CHURCH IMAGES FOR REDEMPTION

While the historical narrative of Jesus' conflict with authorities and their part in his execution remained available through the canonical Gospels, it is clear that subsequent theological reflection on the nature of Jesus' death was far more interested in the images found in the other writings of the New Testament as a source of inspiration.

Irenaeus (second century C.E.), for example, develops the Pauline notion of recapitulation (see Eph 1:10). Working on a cosmic canvas, Irenaeus creates an account of Jesus as the one who sums up in himself the seemingly irreconcilable contrasts of the cosmos: corruptibility–incorruptibility; mortality–immortality; passibility–impassibility; comprehensibility–incomprehensibility. All these are brought together in Jesus Christ.

> There is therefore, as I have pointed out, one God the Father, and one Christ Jesus, who came by means of the whole dispensational arrangements [connected with Him], and gathered together all things in Himself. But in every respect, too, He is man, the formation of God; and thus He took up man into Himself, the *invisible* becoming *visible*, the *incomprehensible* being made *comprehensible*, the *impassible* becoming *capable of suffering*, and the Word being made man, thus summing up all things in Himself: so that as in super-celestial, spiritual, and invisible things, the Word of God is supreme, so also in things visible and corporeal He might possess the supremacy, and, taking to Himself the pre-eminence, as well as constituting Himself Head of the Church, He might draw all things (*anakephalaioo*—recapitulate) to Himself at the proper time.[3]

Because of his sharing in our nature, we are able to share in his. It is easy to read this as simply accomplished in the incarnation itself, that is, the very fact of the incarnation is sufficient for salvation, without reference to the death of

---

3. Irenaeus, *Adversus Haereses* 3.16.6 (emphasis added) from http://www.ccel.org/s/schaff/anf01/htm/ix.iv.xvii.htm (accessed July 3, 2006).

Jesus. The mechanism of salvation is then a type of *deus ex machina*, the automatic outcome of the incarnation itself. This tends to downplay the important
role of conversion and repentance in redemption. The image of recapitulation,
however, gives a powerful sense of the wholeness that salvation brings. In
Christ all things are made whole; everything is brought together in him. All
the painful divisions we experience, the lack of wholeness that pervades our
lives—all these thing are healed through the saving work of Jesus.

The Latin theologian Tertullian (b. ca. 160) developed a different account
that draws on the New Testament notion of ransom (Mark 10:45). This
account argues that Jesus' death is in some sense a ransom that had to be paid
for sin:

> Oh how unworthy is it of God and His will that you try to redeem with
> mere money a man who has been *ransomed by the Blood of Christ*! God
> spared not His own Son for you, letting Him become a curse for us; for
> "cursed is he who hangs on a tree"; as a sheep He was led to sacrifice, as a
> lamb to the shearer . . . And all this that He might redeem us from our sins
> . . . *hell lost its right to us* and we were enrolled for heaven . . . man, born of
> the earth, destined for hell, was *purchased for heaven . . . Christ ransomed man*
> from the angels who rule the world, from the powers and spirits of wicked-
> ness, from the darkness of this world.[4]

In this scheme Jesus has paid a ransom, the needed price, so that the "rights"
of hell or the angelic powers have been released, or "enrolled" for heaven.
According to Tertullian, the devil has gained certain rights over humanity
because of the sin of Adam, so that we have become "slaves to sin." God must
treat the devil "fairly" and so must pay the price demanded for our release.
And what could be more valuable than the life of his own Son?

Again this image is clearly a powerful symbol of release from the burden
of slavery, and to that extent has significant existential appeal. How often do
we feel "enslaved" by forces beyond our control? How often do we feel as if a
price is being extracted from us for our past failings and the failings of others?
Imagine what it would be like, then, if someone was to "pay the price" for our
release. What love it would reveal and what gratitude it would elicit from us!

Even in the early church, however, people could see that there were problems associated with the image of ransom. Gregory of Nazianzus, one of the
Cappadocian fathers, for example, asks the question, "To whom is the ransom
paid?"

---

4. Tertullian, *Disciplinary, Moral and Ascetical Works*, ed. Hermigild Dressler, trans. Rudolph
Arbesmann, Emily Daly, and Edwin Quain, Fathers of the Church 40 (Washington, D.C.: Catholic
University of America Press, 1977), 299-300 (emphasis added).

If to the Evil One, fie upon the outrage! If the robber receives ransom, not only from God, but a ransom which consists of God Himself, and has such an illustrious payment for his tyranny, a payment for whose sake it would have been right for him to have left us alone altogether. But if to the Father, I ask first, how? For it was not by Him that we were being oppressed; and next, On what principle did the Blood of His Only begotten Son delight the Father, Who would not receive even Isaac, when he was being offered by his father [i.e., Abraham], but changed the sacrifice, putting a ram in the place of the human victim?[5]

Nonetheless, the theme of ransom was taken up with enthusiasm by Gregory of Nyssa, another of the Cappadocians, who expanded the metaphorical language to include discussion of the "deception" of the devil as part of the transaction. The devil is deceived into taking Jesus, not realizing who Jesus is, since his divinity is clothed in his humanity. The devil literally bites off more than he can chew, overreaching himself in claiming what he has no right to. In doing so he forfeits all claims to humanity. In this way Gregory of Nyssa avoids the notion that somehow the devil profits from accepting a ransom from God. Despite its mythic framework, Gregory's insight effectively captures the way in which evil often overreaches itself and so makes itself undone.

Finally, we should consider the image of "sacrifice," which first finds systematic exploitation in the writings of Origen. Origen moved in a world where the notion of sacrifice is "self-explanatory." It was common among both pagans and Jews, who engaged in various forms of sacrifice. The self-explanatory character of the necessity of sacrifice is spelled out in the following:

It may well be that as our Lord and Savior . . . bestowed remission of sins on the whole world, so also the blood of others, holy and righteous men . . . has been shed for the expiation, in some part, of the people . . . Christ is spoken of as a lamb because his willingness and goodness, by which he made God again propitious to man and bestowed pardon for sins, stood as a lamb, a spotless and innocent victim, a victim by which heaven is believed to be reconciled to men . . . *While there are sins there must needs be required sacrificial victims for sins.* Had there been no sin the Son of God would not have been constrained to become a lamb, nor would there have been a need for him to be incarnate and put to death . . . but since sin entered into the world, and *sin of necessity requires propitiation, and propitiation cannot be effected save by a sacrificial victim, such a victim had to be provided for.*[6]

---

5. Gregory of Nazianzus, *Second Paschal Oration*, from http://www.newadvent.org/fathers/310245.htm (accessed July 3, 2006).

6. Origen, *Commentary on Numbers*, quoted in Michael M. Winter, *The Atonement* (Collegeville, Minn.: Liturgical Press, 1995), 45 (emphasis added).

The logic of the situation is clear: sin requires propitiation; propitiation requires sacrifice; and sacrifice requires a victim. This is simply a given in Origen's worldview. Nonetheless, he was well aware of the ambiguity of the language of sacrifice, that the symbol has certain darker tones that do not seem compatible with a Christian understanding of God:

> But in addition, the other sacrifices akin to this sacrifice seem to me to be the shedding of the blood of the noble martyrs. It was not in vain that the disciple John saw them standing beside the heavenly altar ... Now to comprehend, even if to a limited extent, the more spiritual sense of such sacrifices which cleanse those for whom they are offered, one must understand the sense of the sacrifice of the daughter of Jephte who was offered as a holocaust because of the vow of him who conquered the children of Ammon. She who was offered as a holocaust consented to this vow, for, when her father said, "I have opened my mouth to the Lord against you," she said to him, "And if you have opened your mouth to the Lord against me, perform your vow." *Such accounts give an appearance of great cruelty to God to whom such sacrifices are offered for the salvation of men.*[7]

The mention of Jephtha's sacrifice of his daughter (Judg 11) should sound a warning. It is a classic "text of terror," a text of truly terrifying implications.[8] Do we really want to implicate God in this sacrifice of innocent life to mark the occasion of a military victory? Is this really compatible with the God revealed by Jesus?

Indeed, Origen brings the notions of sacrifice and ransom together so that the sacrifice of Jesus becomes an expiation that averts the power of the devil. Frances Young notes:

> Origen's way of explaining the sacrificial death of Christ and the expiatory power of his blood, is in terms of the offering of a ransom to the devil and the analogy with human sacrifices of aversion, examples of which can be found in pagan literature. He is at a loss as to how such sacrifices of aversion work, but basically feels that the sacrificial death of Christ is only explicable in such terms, while recognizing a great degree of difference, for Christ died to save the whole world ... Christ gave his soul as a ransom for many. To whom did he give it? It could not have been God; rather it was to the wicked one who had dominion over us until the [soul] of Jesus was given to him as

---

7. Origen, *Commentary on the Gospel According to John Books 1-10*, ed. Thomas Halton, trans. Roland Heine, Fathers of the Church 80 (Washington, D.C.: Catholic University of America Press, 1989), 243 (emphasis added).

8. Phyllis Trible, *Texts of Terror: Literary-Feminist Readings of Biblical Narratives* (Philadelphia: Fortress Press, 1984).

a ransom for us. But he was deceived; he thought he could master it . . . and did not realize that he could not bear the torture of holding it. So the life offered in sacrifice and the blood shed as an expiation become in the hands of Origen, the ransom price given by God to the devil.[9]

Despite these difficulties, the symbol of Jesus' death as a sacrifice is firmly embedded in Christian consciousness and particularly in Catholic sacramental doctrine of the eucharist. We shall explore this further below and in chapter 7.

As with notions of recapitulation and ransom, the notion of sacrifice has a strong existential appeal. If someone is willing to sacrifice something valuable for our sake, then we must also be valuable in their eyes. Or, as Paul argues:

> For while we were still weak, at the right time Christ died for the ungodly. Indeed, rarely will anyone die for a righteous person—though perhaps for a good person someone might actually dare to die. But God proves his love for us in that while we still were sinners Christ died for us. (Rom 5:6-8)

But again the image is not without its ambiguities, if it is turned into a sacrifice needed to placate an angry God. Then it is no longer something God does for us to reveal the depths of the divine love and compassion for humanity, but something humanity does to try to get God off its back. Underneath such an inversion of roles lies a powerful ambiguity in our human experience about God—so ambiguous in fact that we end up confusing God with Satan, the Accuser.

The purpose of the above collage is not to present a comprehensive account of how the early church fathers understood the mechanism of redemption. It is to indicate something of the variety of approaches as well as the difficulties each presents. Each has a certain existential appeal; each invites us to explore an aspect of salvation. But if and when we switch to a more explanatory mode of thinking, each also resists an easy systematization. The first real attempts at some form of systematization begin to take shape in the Middle Ages.

THE BEGINNINGS OF SYSTEM IN THE MIDDLE AGES

The most famous attempt at a theological systematization of soteriology is that of Anselm in his work *Cur Deus homo?* (Why the God-man?). Anselm makes clear his rejection of any notion that the death of Jesus should be understood as a ransom paid to the devil. Such a notion is abhorrent to him:

---

9. Frances M. Young, *The Use of Sacrificial Ideas in Greek Christian Writers from the New Testament to John Chrysostom* (Cambridge, Mass.: Philadelphia Patristic Foundation, 1979), 183.

I do not see the force of that argument, which we are wont to make use of, that God, in order to save men, was bound, as it were, to try a contest with the devil in justice, before he did in strength, so that, when the devil should put to death that being in whom there was nothing worthy of death, and who was God, he should justly lose his power over sinners; and that, if it were not so, God would have used undue force against the devil, since the devil had a rightful ownership of man, for the devil had not seized man with violence, but man had freely surrendered to him. It is true that this might well enough be said, if the devil or man belonged to any other being than God, or were in the power of any but God. But since neither the devil nor man belong to any but God, and neither can exist without the exertion of Divine power, what cause ought God to try with his own creature, or what should he do but punish his servant, who had seduced his fellow-servant to desert their common Lord and come over to himself. (*Cur Deus homo?* 1.7)[10]

Rather than speak of ransom Anselm introduces the new concept of his emerging soteriology, that of "satisfaction." According to Anselm, every wish of a rational creature should be subject to the will of God, conceived of as a debt or duty:

This is the debt which man and angel owe to God, and no one who pays this debt commits sin; but every one who does not pay it sins. This is justice, or uprightness of will, which makes a being just or upright in heart, that is, in will; and this is the sole and complete debt of honor which we owe to God, and which God requires of us. For it is such a will only, when it can be exercised, that does works pleasing to God; and when this will cannot be exercised, it is pleasing of itself alone, since without it no work is acceptable. He who does not render this honor which is due to God, robs God of his own and dishonors him; and this is sin. Moreover, so long as he does not restore what he has taken away, he remains in fault; and it will not suffice merely to restore what has been taken away, but, *considering the contempt offered*, he ought to restore more than he took away. For as one who imperils another's safety does not enough by merely restoring his safety, without making some compensation for the anguish incurred; so *he who violates another's honor* does not enough by merely rendering honor again, but must, according to the extent of the injury done, *make restoration in some way satisfactory* to the person whom he has dishonored. We must also

---

10. Anselm, *Cur Deus homo?* from http://www.ccel.org/ccel/anselm/basic_works.viii.ii.VII.html (accessed July 3, 2006).

observe that when any one pays what he has unjustly taken away, he ought to give something which could not have been demanded of him, had he not stolen what belonged to another. So then, *every one who sins ought to pay back the honor of which he has robbed God; and this is the satisfaction which every sinner owes to God.* (1.11; emphasis added)

It is the notions of honor and satisfaction due to dishonor that are central to Anselm's argument. After much discussion he comes to his basic conclusion that satisfaction can be made only by one who is both God and human:

Anselm. But this cannot be effected, except the price paid to God for the sin of man be something greater than all the universe besides God.
Boso. So it appears.
Anselm. Moreover, it is necessary that he who can give God anything of his own which is more valuable than all things in the possession of God, must be greater than all else but God himself.
Boso. I cannot deny it.
Anselm. Therefore none but God can make this satisfaction.
Boso. So it appears.
Anselm. But none but a man ought to do this, otherwise man does not make the satisfaction.
Boso. Nothing seems more just.
Anselm. If it be necessary, therefore, as it appears, that the heavenly kingdom be made up of men, and this cannot be effected unless the aforesaid satisfaction be made, which none but God can make and none but man ought to make, it is necessary for the God-man to make it. (2.6)

To his own satisfaction then Anselm has found necessary reasons why the incarnation had to occur, given the fact of human sinfulness. This account has proven remarkably resilient through the subsequent history of Christian thought on the redemption, to such an extent that it was on the point of formal adoption at the First Vatican Council (1869-70).[11]

Modern commentators have been less sympathetic to Anslem's argument. They have identified two major concerns. First, Anselm's account depends very much on a medieval worldview in which codes of honor were central to the way of life. Codes of honor were one of a number of interlocking elements of mutual rights and obligations in medieval society. Take these elements away and the account tends to become less convincing. Anselm's account is more culturally conditioned than he thought and hence less convincing to

---

11. William P. Loewe, *The College Student's Introduction to Christology* (Collegeville, Minn.: Liturgical Press, 1996), 166.

those of a different worldview. Second, it is difficult to square Anselm's account of how God deals with human sin with the account we find operative in the mission of Jesus. As Michael Winter points out,

> Quite simply, in Jesus' own dealings with sinners and in his teaching about forgiveness, compensation is never required as a prior condition for being received back into the love of God. This is true of the parables of forgiveness, the narratives of conversion or reconciliation of individuals or in the plain teaching of Christ. Satisfaction is never required as a condition of their being reconciled with God.[12]

A further difficulty lies in Anselm's methodology. His desire to find "necessary reasons" for the incarnation means that he has narrowed the experience of salvation to one particular aspect, an aspect that may have made some sense in his own culture, but of itself is a truncation of the full reality of redemption. In Aquinas, on the other hand, we find a much more adequate account, in part because he is not seeking "necessary reasons" but simply seeking to give a fuller understanding. Indeed, he rejects the possibility of finding any necessity for the incarnation, "For God with His omnipotent power could have restored human nature in many other ways" (*ST* III q. 1, a. 2). Aquinas is not arguing for the necessity of the incarnation, but for its fittingness. He is not trying to deduce the truths of faith; he is trying to understand them, and the proposed intelligibility is hypothetical, not necessary. He is adding not to our certainty but to our understanding, and hence the account he gives is much fuller than Anselm can even consider. Aquinas then lists ten reasons why the incarnation is necessary, but in the sense of fitting or convenient: five under the heading "for the furtherance of the good," and another five under the heading "for our withdrawal from evil":

> Now this may be viewed with respect to our "furtherance in good." *First*, with regard to faith, which is made more certain by believing God Himself Who speaks; hence Augustine says (De Civ. Dei xi, 2): "In order that man might journey more trustfully toward the truth, the Truth itself, the Son of God, having assumed human nature, established and founded faith." *Secondly*, with regard to hope, which is thereby greatly strengthened; hence Augustine says (De Trin. xiii): "Nothing was so necessary for raising our hope as to show us how deeply God loved us. And what could afford us a stronger proof of this than that the Son of God should become a partner with us of human nature?" *Thirdly*, with regard to charity, which is greatly enkindled by this; hence Augustine says (De Catech. Rudib. iv): "What

---

12. Michael M. Winter, *Atonement* (Collegeville, Minn.: Liturgical Press, 1995), 66.

greater cause is there of the Lord's coming than to show God's love for us?" And he afterwards adds: "If we have been slow to love, at least let us hasten to love in return." *Fourthly*, with regard to well-doing, in which He set us an example; hence Augustine says in a sermon (xxii de Temp.): "Man who might be seen was not to be followed; but God was to be followed, Who could not be seen. And therefore God was made man, that He Who might be seen by man, and Whom man might follow, might be shown to man." *Fifthly*, with regard to the full participation of the Divinity, which is the true bliss of man and end of human life; and this is bestowed upon us by Christ's humanity; for Augustine says in a sermon (xiii de Temp.): "God was made man, that man might be made God."

So also was this useful for our "withdrawal from evil." *First*, because man is taught by it not to prefer the devil to himself, nor to honor him who is the author of sin; hence Augustine says (De Trin. xiii, 17): "Since human nature is so united to God as to become one person, let not these proud spirits dare to prefer themselves to man, because they have no bodies." *Secondly*, because we are thereby taught how great is man's dignity, lest we should sully it with sin; hence Augustine says (De Vera Relig. xvi): "God has proved to us how high a place human nature holds amongst creatures, inasmuch as He appeared to men as a true man." And Pope Leo says in a sermon on the Nativity (xxi): "Learn, O Christian, thy worth; and being made a partner of the Divine nature, refuse to return by evil deeds to your former worthlessness." *Thirdly*, because, "in order to do away with man's presumption, the grace of God is commended in Jesus Christ, though no merits of ours went before," as Augustine says (De Trin. xiii, 17). *Fourthly*, because "man's pride, which is the greatest stumbling-block to our clinging to God, can be convinced and cured by humility so great," as Augustine says in the same place. *Fifthly*, in order to free man from the thraldom of sin, which, as Augustine says (De Trin. xiii, 13), "ought to be done in such a way that the devil should be overcome by the justice of the man Jesus Christ," and this was done by Christ satisfying for us. Now a mere man could not have satisfied for the whole human race, and God was not bound to satisfy; hence it behooved Jesus Christ to be both God and man. (*ST* III q. 1, a. 2)

Aquinas is often portrayed as simply adopting the Anselmian teaching taken up in his fifth point on "withdrawal from evil," the difference being his dropping of the strict necessity of the incarnation. However, we can see from the above that he places the work of the incarnation in a much richer context than the single explanatory concept of "satisfaction." While it is part of his armory, it is not the whole thing. Moreover, his treatment of satisfaction is more nuanced and careful (more specifically in *ST* III q. 1, a. 2, ad 2). It is also worth noting that Aquinas makes no explicit mention of Anselm himself, but draws heavily from Augustine.

The richness of Aquinas's account rivals that of von Balthasar at the beginning of this chapter; however, it has the advantage of being also very concrete. Aquinas is trying to analyze the impact of Jesus' death, conceived of as an act of love from God toward human beings, on those who recognize this divine intent in Jesus' self-offering. He is literally asking, How does the death of Jesus move us who believe in him, and so save us? Nonetheless, it still makes little direct contact with the historical narrative of Jesus' mission as the precursor to his death. In order to make this connection we might turn to the modern anthropology of René Girard.

MODERN ACCOUNTS—THE INSIGHTS OF RENÉ GIRARD

The cultural anthropological work of René Girard has been a source of inspiration for a number of theologians working in soteriology (e.g., Raymund Schwager, James Alison, and Anthony Bartlett, to name a few).[13] Although Girard's position is not without its problems, it remains highly suggestive for those working with notions of sacrifice in the Christian tradition. As we have already noted, the symbol of sacrifice is a major one in the Christian tradition for understanding the death of Jesus.

For Girard, society is built upon a scapegoat mechanism whereby an innocent victim is expelled to ensure the harmony of the group. This is an act of primordial violence (e.g., the story of Cain and Abel in Genesis 4) upon which all culture and social order are built. Further, this act of violence arises from a process of mimetic desire. Girard holds that we "learn" to desire through the desire of others. I desire something through seeing you desire it first, something that is often evident in young children fighting over toys. This places our desires within a field of competition and conflict in their very origins. This conflict would destroy our social relationships if it were not displaced onto a convenient third party, a scapegoat who bears the brunt of our violence (e.g., Lev 16:5-10). The expulsion or destruction of the scapegoat

13. René Girard, *Violence and the Sacred* (Baltimore: Johns Hopkins University Press, 1977); idem, *The Scapegoat* (Baltimore: Johns Hopkins University Press, 1986); idem, *I See Satan Fall like Lightning* (Maryknoll, N.Y.: Orbis Books, 2001); Raymund Schwager, *Jesus in the Drama of Salvation: Toward a Biblical Doctrine of Redemption* (New York: Crossroad, 1999); James Alison, *The Joy of Being Wrong: Original Sin through Easter Eyes* (New York: Crossroad, 1998); James Alison, *Raising Abel: The Recovery of Eschatological Imagination* (New York: Crossroad, 1996); Anthony W. Bartlett, *Cross Purposes: The Violent Grammar of Christian Atonement* (Harrisburg, Pa.: Trinity Press International, 2001).

restores social harmony and thus imbues the scapegoat with magical or divine powers. This is reminiscent of Origen's account of the efficacy of pagan sacrifices. For Girard this mechanism is the beginning of religion and of human culture.

Girard views the religious history of Israel as a progressive release from this structure of sacrifice of the scapegoat, a history of resistance to the scapegoat mechanism. With its emphasis on the poor and marginalized and social justice as the touchstone of righteousness before God, Israel develops a more purified religious observance. The mission of Jesus is the final stage in this process of purification. Because of Jesus' commitment to nonviolence, his violent death exposes the scapegoat mechanism for what it is, the unjustified murder of the innocent. In this way Jesus' mission is one of the subversion of sacrifice, of uncovering the secret violence on which society is built. For the sacrificial community, "Jesus appears as a destructive and subversive force, as a source of contamination that threatens the community."[14] That community must then turn its violence against Jesus, "the most perfect victim that can be imagined, the victim that, for every conceivable reason, violence has the most reason to pick on. Yet at the same time, this victim is the most innocent."[15] Thus, the violence of the scapegoat mechanism is exposed, releasing a powerful force for social and cultural change, whose implications are still being effected in human history.

What violence does not and cannot comprehend is that, in getting rid of Jesus by the usual means, it falls into the trap that could be laid only by innocence of such a kind because it is really not a trap: there is nothing hidden. Violence reveals its own game in such a way that its workings are compromised at their very source; the more it tries to conceal its ridiculous secret from now on, by forcing itself into action, the more it will succeed in revealing itself. We can see here parallels with the notion of the devil overreaching itself and leading to its own downfall.[16]

Girard will in fact personify this violence as the Satan, the Accuser, whose "power is his ability to make false accusations so convincingly that they become unassailable truth of entire communities," whereas Jesus is the Paraclete, "the lawyer for the defense, the defender of victims."[17] For Girard, the passion of Jesus is "a violent process, a demonic expulsion."[18]

Read in this way, Christianity is in fact antisacrificial. The historic mission of Christianity is to expose the scapegoat mechanism for the violence that it

---

14. René Girard and James G. Williams, *The Girard Reader* (New York: Crossroad, 1996), 182.
15. Ibid.
16. Ibid., 183.
17. Ibid., 201.
18. Ibid., 195.

is, and so put an end to all sacrifice—the sacrifice of Jesus is "once and for all" (Heb 7:27). The use of sacrificial language in the Christian tradition is basically mistaken: "There is nothing in the Gospels to suggest that the death of Jesus is a sacrifice . . . The passages that are invoked to justify a sacrificial conception of the passion both can and should be interpreted with no reference to sacrifice in any of the accepted meanings" of the term.[19]

THE TWO DISCOURSES OF SACRIFICE

While this may be overstating the case for rhetorical effect, it is clear that Girard has identified a very important insight. The language of sacrifice has a dual aspect. One more positive aspect is to view sacrifice as a "sacrifice of praise," the handing of one's life over to God's will in obediential love and service. Christian language of sacrifice reflects this aspect (e.g., Rom 12:1; Phil 4:18; Heb 13:15; 1 Pet 2:5). In doing so, however, it tends to mask a more negative aspect of the same symbol. This more negative aspect is the dark underbelly of sacrifice, the disobedience of killing the innocent, a sacrifice for an evil purpose, often masked by a "religious" or ideological justification: "it is better for you to have one man die for the people than to have the whole nation destroyed" (John 11:50). For both genuine obedience and disobedience have the structure of sacrifice. Genuine obedience sacrifices the lower good for the sake of the higher, while disobedience sacrifices the higher for the sake of the lower. Genuine obedience willingly sacrifices its own good for the sake of a higher good. Disobedience sacrifices the other, the unwilling victim, to fulfill its own desires. The work of Girard focuses our attention on the darker aspects of sacrifice, which should have no place in Christian self-understanding. On the other hand, if we lose touch with this darker aspect we are in danger of removing our understanding of Jesus' death from the historical narrative in which is occurs, making it a purely religious drama with no real historical content. We need to bring these two aspects into a real relationship with each other, if we are to understand the death of Jesus as a response to human sinfulness.

It is instructive in attempting to analyze the reality of salvation to return to the question, From what are we being saved? The ways in which we conceive of this "being saved from" will shape our understanding of the mechanism of salvation itself. As we have seen, the biblical language of salvation presents us with a variety of metaphors to express this "being saved from":

---

19. Ibid., 178.

death, sin, the wrath of God, Satan, and so on. Another candidate that emerges from the tradition is original sin. In *ST* III q. 1, a. 4, Aquinas asks whether the point of the incarnation is to free us from actual sin, or from original sin; he answers that it was "principally to take away original sin." I would take this observation as a starting point to suggest that the problem of salvation has two distinct foci. The first regards the problem of actual sin and how that is to be dealt with by God. The second regards the problem of original sin and how that is dealt with. Further, the two discourses of sacrifice correlate with these two foci of salvation.

Much of the traditional language of salvation focuses on the need for redemption from our actual sins. It presents us with the need for judgment, conversion, and forgiveness. Much of the traditional positive language of sacrifice draws on Old Testament expiatory rites as a type of the more perfect sacrifice of Jesus, which deals with sin through the conversion that it symbolizes, the sacrifice of praise which evokes within us the conversion we need in order to turn again to God and to turn away from our sins. In the death of Jesus we see our sin for what it is; we are judged, convicted of sin yet at the same time offered forgiveness from the cross, as Jesus' final act of obedience to the Father's mission of love.

This cannot be the whole story of salvation, however. When we consider the issue of original sin, we need to ask, How can we be judged for what we have not done, forgiven for a sin that is not ours? In this regard much of the traditional language of salvation and sacrifice begins to break down. Indeed, in dealing with the problem of original sin the tradition has tried to force it into the pattern of the problem of actual sin by equating it with some type of primal guilt we all share in, something that we mysteriously have responsibility for "in Adam." We have then understood the mechanism for its resolution in terms of the same patterns adopted for personal sin. Yet, as I have argued in the chapter on original sin, a coherent account of original sin can be formulated as a statement of our universal victimhood, "in Adam." We are all the victim of others' sins, all the way back to that first primal fault. This state of victimhood does not need judgment and forgiveness; it needs healing and compassion.[20] In this perspective, the death of Jesus, his ritual murder, is transformed by Jesus into an act of solidarity, a voluntary identification on the

---

20. As Robert Doran notes, "The victimized dimension of ourselves will not be met ultimately by judgment and condemnation, but by mercy and gentleness. Judgment may be delivered against our freedom, but not against what our freedom has victimized, even in ourselves" (*Theology and the Dialectics of History* [Toronto: University of Toronto Press, 1990], 238).

part of Jesus with the most victimized, and most despised, part of ourselves.[21] Jesus shares our fate, not as sinners but as sinned against. Of course, this death is a consequence of Jesus' fidelity to his mission and the sinful reaction of those who murdered him. However, Jesus transforms this mindless fate into life-giving sacrament through the meaning he gives to his death in his words and actions at the Last Supper.[22]

I would now like to explore some of the things that can go wrong when we fail to recognize that there are two distinct sacrificial discourses. The first and perhaps most common problem is to conflate the two into a single discourse. This leads to multiple confusions between God and Satan, between goodness and sin, between divine providence and evil. Such confusion is evident in the discussion of the early fathers on the ransom model—is the ransom paid to God or to Satan? In a more systematic mode it is, according to Raymund Schwager, to be found in the writings of Karl Barth. According to Schwager, Barth speaks of "Jesus' opponents as the 'instruments' and 'agents' of divine judgment," leading to the conclusion "that Jesus had suddenly stopped being the revealer of God and instead his opponents had been entrusted with his mission."[23] In fact such an approach lays the blame for sin and the dark side of sacrifice at the feet of God.

The second problem is to emphasize the positive aspect of sacrifice, while denying that the darker side sheds any light on the Christian experience. I think this is evident in a modern trend to suppress the language of sacrifice altogether as inappropriate. Consequently the image of sacrifice loses all its dark connotations, to become simply a "sacrifice of praise." The consequence is a romanticized version of Christian faith and life, which never really touches the hard reality of human sin and the suffering of sin's victims. It correlates with a downplaying of the notion of original sin and of the notion of redemption. Such a trend can be found in the writings of Matthew Fox, with his appeal to the notion of "original blessing."[24]

The third problem is to fail to recognize the positive discourse of sacrifice. Then Christianity becomes a parody of itself, becoming yet another form of paganism rather than its subversion and replacement. This is the danger that Girard attacks in his anti-sacrificial reading of Christianity. He fears that the

---

21. This process of voluntary identification is most evident in the apocalyptic judgment scene of Matthew 25:31-46.

22. Central to the meaning given to Jesus' death is the notion of a covenant sealed in his blood; see Matthew 26:28 and parallels. This is an anticipatory act of "meaning making" in the face of impending death.

23. Schwager, *Jesus in the Drama of Salvation*, 163.

24. Matthew Fox, *Original Blessing* (Santa Fe, N.M.: Bear, 1983).

use of sacrificial language can only be a perversion of the truth of Christian faith, and so it would be. What is less clear is whether the Christian tradition has ever really fallen into such a stance.

DO OTHER RELIGIONS HAVE SAVIORS?

The notion of a savior is so entrenched in Christian self-understanding that it can come as a surprise to realize that for other religions there may be no notion of a savior at all. It is quite feasible to ask: How can the good actions of another person enhance my possibility for salvation? Why do I need another person to act on my behalf?

As we noted in our discussion of original sin, neither Islam nor Judaism has a notion of original sin, and hence correlatively neither has a clear place for the notion of a savior. Neither in Judaism nor in Islam is there solidarity in human sinfulness. Each person stands before God, personally responsible for his or her actions. Just as the sin of another cannot be the cause of my damnation, the good deeds of another cannot be the cause of my salvation. Muhammad, for example, is not a savior but a prophet, God's agent for revelation, but not for salvation. Christianity, on the other hand, holds to a solidarity in both damnation and salvation. While I may contribute to my damnation and my salvation, there are a variety of other influences that are beyond my control but that nonetheless shape my personal history. Our solidarity with Adam in original sin is matched by a more powerful solidarity in faith with Jesus Christ (Rom 5:12-21). To have a notion of a universal savior one needs some account of a universal human condition from which we need salvation. This is a significant difference between Christianity and both Islam and Judaism.

Does Buddhism consider the Buddha a savior? In classical Theravada Buddhism, the answer is no. In fact, the Buddha himself denied such a role to himself. In some forms of Buddhism, however, such as Mahayana Buddhism where the Buddha is viewed more as a semi-divine figure, he does become viewed as a savior. As we shall see, the dominant metaphor for salvation is that of enlightenment, with the Buddha as a teacher who leads the follower to the path of insight into the nature of the world. Still, this role could be played by another teacher who could lead us along the same path. However, the more the Buddha is viewed as a semi-divine figure, the more this enlightenment may be viewed as an act of divine graciousness mediated in some sense by the Buddha. In that sense he may be viewed as a saving figure, but not in the more exclusive sense used by Christian faith in relation to Jesus Christ.

CONCLUSION

These reflections lead us in suitable fashion to the theme of our next chapter, grace. The saving work of Jesus must still be realized within each one of us through the interior transformation, repentance, and conversion, of which Christianity speaks in terms of grace. This grace is a mediated transformation of our own personal immediacy. It is undeserved, unmerited, and an act of pure divine sovereignty. How we conceive of this grace and its effects on us will be the topic of our next chapter.

QUESTIONS FOR REFLECTION

1. 1 Peter 2:24 suggests, "by his wounds you have been healed." How is it that a historical event nearly two thousand years ago can be thought of as saving for human beings today?
2. How can we bridge the gap between the religious understanding of the death of Jesus according to Paul and the narrative of Jesus' death given in the Gospels? To what extent can we know the intention of Jesus in facing his death?
3. How can we understand the death of Jesus as an act of scapegoating, as presented by Girard?
4. What are some of the dangers associated with the notion of self-sacrifical love? How can it be used to justify undue submission and suffering?
5. Aquinas completes his account of the saving work of Jesus with the comment, "And there are very many other advantages which accrued, above man's apprehension" (*ST* III q. 1, a. 2). Can you identify some of the other advantages of the saving work of Jesus?

SUGGESTIONS FOR FURTHER READING AND STUDY

Alison, James. *The Joy of Being Wrong: Original Sin through Easter Eyes*. New York: Crossroad, 1998.

Bartlett, Anthony W. *Cross Purposes: The Violent Grammar of Christian Atonement*. Harrisburg, Pa.: Trinity Press International, 2001.

Crysdale, Cynthia S. W. *Embracing Travail: Retrieving the Cross Today*. New York: Continuum, 2001.

Girard, René. *I See Satan Fall Like Lightning*. Maryknoll, N.Y.: Orbis Books, 2001.

———. *The Scapegoat*. Baltimore: Johns Hopkins University Press, 1986.

Schwager, Raymund. *Jesus in the Drama of Salvation: Toward a Biblical Doctrine of Redemption*. New York: Crossroad, 1999.

Winter, Michael M. *The Atonement*. Collegeville, Minn.: Liturgical Press, 1995.

Young, Frances M. *The Use of Sacrificial Ideas in Greek Christian Writers from the New Testament to John Chrysostom*. Cambridge, Mass.: Philadelphia Patristic Foundation, 1979.

6

Grace and the Supernatural

IN CHAPTER 3 WE DISCUSSED the nature of sin and its effects on human existence. These effects are personal, cultural, and social. The cumulative impact of these effects is a crippling of human freedom, rendering an unredeemed humanity "slaves to sin" (see Rom 6:16), trapped in the compulsive cycles of moral impotence. We have also considered in the previous chapter the revelation of divine love evident in the death and resurrection of Jesus, representing God's ultimate response to our human condition—nothing "will be able to separate us from the love of God in Christ Jesus our Lord" (Rom 8:39). However, there is another side of the story of redemption, our personal appropriation of God's love, "poured into our hearts through the Holy Spirit that has been given to us" (Rom 5:5). This is a more interior story, of freedom transformed whereby God removes our hearts of stone and replaces them with hearts of flesh (Ezek 11:19; 36:26). This is the story of grace as the interior component of the divine solution to the problem of human sin and evil. Of course, the effects of grace ripple out into the cultural and social dimensions of human living, as we shall see in the next two chapters, but for the moment we shall focus on the interior effects of grace.

GRACE AS HEALING

If sin distorts and cripples our freedom, then in the first instance the impact of grace is to heal and strengthen our freedom so that we may break out of the compulsive power of sin. Concretely the decisions we make embody the values we hold—not the values we "notionally" hold but the values we actually hold. Our decisions manifest our own personal scale of values, and a freedom that is captured by sin arises out of a heart whose response to value is fundamentally distorted. As we explored in our discussion of original sin, a key element of this distortion is our sense of our own personal value, our spontaneous sense of our own value or self-esteem. It may be that I feel myself to be unlovable, or that I love myself for all the wrong reasons, puffing myself up with a sense of self-righteousness. Decisions emerge either out of my efforts to bolster my sense of my own goodness or to confirm my own sense of worthlessness.

Despite the promises of self-help gurus, there is a sense in which I simply cannot solve this problem on my own. If my own sense of self is the problem, then all my efforts at "self-help" emerge out of the very same self that needs the help. My efforts will suffer from the same distortions and lead to a reproduction of the same problems in the new edition of "me." I can even enlist others into the project through manipulating them into helping me, but this again emerges from the same distorted self and leads to further reproduction of the same problem once again. In addiction literature this is such a common issue that it gains its own label, co-dependency. The co-dependent person seeks to assist the addict, but does so within the horizon of the addict and his or her addiction. Such co-dependency actually makes things worse, under the guise of seeking to help.

If a solution is to be found, it must be entirely "gratuitous," something that comes to us from a source beyond our manipulation, beyond our control. It must come to us from a source that is untouched by the distortions we suffer, a source of goodness greater than our own. Finally, it must be able to love us "as we are," love the real goodness that we have and so heal the distortions present in our self-esteem by grounding us in the reality of our own real goodness, a goodness that is ours as creations of a wise and loving God. This love must be strong enough to be able to break through the distortions we generate and the lies we tell ourselves. It must be able to confront those distortions and lies, yet do so in a way that both demands and empowers a real change of heart within us. This is the meaning of "grace as healing."

A traditional theology speaks of this inbreaking of grace as "operative grace."[1] God operates on the sinner, taking out the heart of stone and replacing it with a heart of flesh. Such an operation is not dependent on the freedom of the sinner—in fact, God operates to restore the freedom of the sinner, freeing it from its slavery to sin. It is not an attack on our freedom; rather it liberates our freedom to be true to its orientation to the good. However, if we conceived of freedom simply as "freedom of choice" then the notion of operative grace will always appear as somehow contrary to the freedom of the sinner, because it "reduces" our "freedom" to sin. On the other hand, if we view freedom as directed toward good, sin represents a distortion of our freedom. In this case operative grace reestablishes us in true freedom by allowing us once again to act toward the truly good.

---

1. For a thorough treatment of the notion of operative grace, see Bernard J. F. Lonergan, *Grace and Freedom: Operative Grace in the Thought of St. Thomas Aquinas*, ed. Frederick E. Crowe and Robert M. Doran, Collected Works of Bernard Lonergan 1 (Toronto: University of Toronto Press, 2000).

In more modern terms, the prime example of such operative grace is what we would call "conversion." Conversion is not something I produce in myself. It comes to me from without, something that acts upon me. Conversion has various modalities, but a key feature of conversion is the radical change of life it produces in the newly converted subject.[2] After conversion everything is different; the world has changed. Fear turns to courage, hatred to love, resentment to forgiveness, despair to hope, and hardness of heart to compassion. Things that were once impossible—for example, the ability to resist temptation—now become easy; things that were part of the routine of my life—for example, engaging my addiction—become repulsive. I am a new person "walking in the light" compared with the old me that "walked in the darkness" (see John 8:12). In this phase Catholic theology will speak of grace as "cooperative," inasmuch as the grace of conversion allows us to cooperate freely in achieving the good.

Perhaps some of the best accounts of this conversion experience come out of literature dealing with the problems of addiction, such as Twelve Step programs. Indeed the first three steps of Alcoholics Anonymous are:

1. We admitted we were powerless over alcohol—that our lives had become unmanageable.
2. We came to believe that a power greater than ourselves could restore us to sanity.
3. We made a decision to turn our will and our lives over to the care of God *as we understood Him*.[3]

These three steps provide a solid summary of a Christian theology of grace: the problem of moral impotence ("we are powerless over alcohol"), the need for operative grace ("a power greater than ourselves"), and the new-found freedom that this grace as cooperative brings to the converted subject ("made a decision to turn our will . . .").

THE GRACE/SIN DIALECTIC

One of the most moving accounts of conversion found in Christian literature is that of Augustine in book 8 of his *Confessions*. In it he recounts his own

---

2. For example, Lonergan speaks of religious, moral, and intellectual conversion; see Bernard J. F. Lonergan, *Method in Theology* (London: Darton, Longman & Todd, 1972), 217. Doran would add psychic conversion; see Robert M. Doran, *Theology and the Dialectics of History* (Toronto: University of Toronto Press, 1990), 8. The main modes we are talking about in the present context are religious and moral.

3. See, for example, http://psychcentral.com/psypsych/12-step_program#The_twelve_steps (accessed July 3, 2006).

struggle with continence or sexual purity. This was the last moral obstacle for him in coming to the Christian faith,[4] and he felt powerless to do anything about his own weakness in this regard. In the end the radical change in his life did not come about through his own efforts at "self-control" but through the power of God's grace, initiated through the reading of a text from Romans. God produces a change in Augustine, and once that change occurred his problems with continence disappeared. It is clear that this pivotal experience shaped Augustine's whole theology of grace, and through him, the theology and doctrine of the Western church.

Augustine's theology of grace focuses on the existential situation of the individual, caught between being either a "slave to sin" or a "slave to God's law" (see Rom 7:25). Faced with such a dialectic of sin and grace Augustine could find no middle ground, no neutral place that was neither sin nor grace. Consequently Augustine could find nothing good in the life of a pagan—the virtues of the pagans are vices in disguise! Indeed, so extreme was this dialectical position that at one point Augustine even denied that pagans could know anything. Though he was later to retract this position (*Retractationum* 1.4), it was the logical outcome of the dialectic position he adopted.

This difficulty points to an unresolved tension in the work of Augustine. On the one hand, his dialectic of grace and sin clearly identifies and highlights the healing qualities of grace. This is a lasting contribution of Augustine's theology of grace. On the other hand, this same dialectical approach paints a black and white account of the human condition. Either one is "all sin" or "all grace." The danger with such an account of the human condition is that it comes close to a form of dualism whereby the finitude of our human state becomes identified with sin itself. We have already seen this type of problem in relation to Augustine's blurring of the distinction between original sin and concupiscence.

Faced with such tensions, theological reflection can move in two distinct directions. One may seek to reinforce the dialectic, making it the fundamental starting point of one's theology. This is the direction taken by Martin Luther and the other reformers. One of the most powerful modern exponents of such a dialectical theology is the great Swiss theologian Karl Barth. For Barth all human reason is suspect, and all human motivation corrupt: "Faith . . . grips reason by the throat and strangles the beast."[5] Human nature of itself has nothing positive to contribute.

---

4. Augustine also had various intellectual hurdles to overcome, as recounted in book 7 of *Confessions*. His account in this chapter is really one of what Lonergan would call "intellectual conversion" from the real as "already out there now" to the real known as true.

5. Karl Barth, *The Epistle to the Romans*, trans. Edwyn Clement Hoskyns (London: Oxford University Press, 1933), 143.

The alternative is to seek to give some account of the "middle ground" between sin and grace, an arena of goodness that is "natural," not sin, but not yet the salvific goodness of divine grace. It is this line of development that led to the classical grace/nature distinction that became the foundation for the Catholic theology of Thomas Aquinas.[6]

THE GRACE/NATURE DISTINCTION

While Aquinas was not the first of the medieval theologians to introduce the grace/nature distinction, his is the most systematic exploitation of its potential to deal with the tensions present in the Augustinian legacy.[7] In *ST* I-II q. 109, a. 1 Aquinas begins his account of grace by focusing on a very precise point of tension in the work of Augustine: Whether one can know any truth without grace. After noting objections to the position drawn from the writings of Augustine, and then noting Augustine's own retraction of those objections, Aquinas seeks his own response. He acknowledges that to know anything at all requires God's help (*divinum auxilium*), but such help should not be equated with a grace that brings salvation:

> We must therefore say that, if a man is to know any truth whatsoever, he needs divine help in order that his intellect may be moved to its act by God. But he does not need a new light added to his natural light in order to know the truth in all things, but only in such things as transcend his natural knowledge.

Thus, there is a "natural light" of intellect proportionate to natural human knowledge, but there is also the possibility of a revealed knowledge that requires something added to this natural light, that is, the light of faith. In this we see the beginnings of the grace/nature distinction.

Aquinas immediately then moves from the intellect to the will: Whether one can will or do any good without grace (*ST* I-II q. 109, a. 2). This lies at the heart of the grace/sin dialectic, at least in its extreme form. In this dialectic there is either sin or grace, and without grace nothing good can be achieved. Aquinas initially responds by distinguishing between nature in its pure state and nature in its fallen state. As in the previous response, "divine help" is needed for any motion of the will, as of the intellect, but the good proportional to nature is possible without grace to human nature prior to the fall. What of "fallen" nature? Here Aquinas departs from Augustine:

---

6. There is a third possibility, that of supernaturalizing the natural order, arguing that "all is grace." The difficulty here lies in eliminating the problem of evil altogether.

7. The distinction goes back to Phillip the Chancellor; see Lonergan, *Grace and Freedom*, 17.

In the state of corrupt nature he falls short of what nature makes possible, so that he cannot by his own power fulfill the whole good that pertains to his nature. Human nature is not so entirely corrupted by sin, however, as to be deprived of natural good altogether. Consequently, even in the state of corrupt nature a man can do some particular good by the power of his own nature, such as build houses . . . But he cannot achieve the whole good natural to him, as if he lacked nothing.

Aquinas is here asserting that even in the fallen state we are capable of some good, always with divine help, but not necessarily grace. He moves on to make a classical assertion about the necessity of grace:

Thus in the state of pure nature man needs a power added to his natural power by grace, for one reason, namely, in order to do and to will supernatural good. But in the state of corrupt nature he needs this for two reasons, in order to be healed, and in order to achieve the meritorious good of supernatural virtue.

By this stage Aquinas has effectively dismantled the grace/sin dialectic through the theoretical construct of human nature. Human nature is good in itself prior to original sin and can attain the good proportionate to it, but not the supernatural good of salvation, which requires God's grace. After the fall, human nature is weakened and can attain the good proportionate to it only in a spasmodic fashion. In this fallen state grace is necessary for two reasons: first, to heal our weakened orientation to the good, and, second, to elevate our nature to a higher end, to be able to attain God in the beatific vision.

The climax of this line of questioning then comes in *ST* I-II q. 109, a. 5: Whether one can merit eternal life without grace. Here the grace/nature distinction comes to the fore:

Now eternal life is an end that exceeds what is commensurate with human nature . . . it follows that a man cannot, by his natural powers produce meritorious works commensurate with eternal life. A higher power is needed for this, namely, the power of grace. Hence a man cannot merit eternal life without grace, although he can perform works which lead to such good as is connatural to him.

In this passage we can see Aquinas's ultimate rejection of Pelagian anthropology. Human nature is here conceived of teleologically, as oriented to certain ends, with its own operations and power to achieve proportionate ends, rather than an empirical conception of human nature, as found in Augustine. Human nature, according to Aquinas, is oriented to an end, the vision of God, which it simply cannot attain through the operations of its own nature. This end is supernatural, completely beyond the capabilities of any finite nature.

Our attaining of this end can come about only through a special gift from God, something that makes us able to attain what we cannot attain through our own powers. This grace/nature distinction, while recognizing that grace is healing, focuses our attention on the elevating activity of grace. Grace is "supernatural."

EXCURSUS ON GRACE AND DIVINIZATION

While the Catholic tradition has adopted a metaphysical approach that speaks of grace in terms of its relation to the natural order—hence grace as supernatural—the Eastern Orthodox tradition has focused more on the implications of 2 Peter 1:4, that we become sharers of the divine nature through grace. For example, Gregory Nazianzus adopts the language of deification or *theōsis*. This is a new creation that is "more god-like and exalted" than the first creation. This deification is realized by Christ in the incarnation and perfected in the economy of salvation by the Holy Spirit, "appropriated individually in baptism as well as in ascetic and philanthropic acts and finally consummated in the future life."[8] *Theōsis* is a reflection of God's light and brightness; it is proximity to, illumination by, and knowledge of God, demanding imitation of Christ and love of neighbor on our part. It is both God's gift and the reward for human effort.

The issue of *theōsis* finds a more theoretical explanation in the doctrine of the "uncreated energies of God." Cyril of Alexandria spoke of the Holy Spirit implanting a "divine form" in us through sanctification.[9] While this does give expression to the notion of divinization, it is fraught with difficulties. What is the divine form that Cyril is talking about? In Aristotelian terms the form is what makes a thing what it is. The divine form is divinity itself, that is, God. How can this be implanted within us without both compromising the divine transcendence and making us something other than human?

A theoretical response to this was proposed by Gregory Palamas (1296-1359), a monk from Mount Athos. Some would place his contribution to the East as high as that of Aquinas in the West. The context of Palamas's contribution was a dispute concerning the monks' practice of Hesychastic prayer.[10] During this prayer the monks claimed to

---

8. Peter C. Phan, *Grace and the Human Condition*, Message of the Fathers of the Church 15 (Wilmington, Del.: Michael Glazier, 1988), 171.

9. Ibid., 151.

10. See James A. Wiseman, *Spirituality and Mysticism: A Global View*, Theology in Global Perspective (Maryknoll, N.Y.: Orbis Books, 2006), 132-35, for an account of Hesychastic prayer.

behold the glory of God, the uncreated light of the divine essence that
had appeared to the disciples during the transfiguration. Some rejected
this claim, arguing that any light they saw must be a created light. Palamas responded by developing the doctrine of the uncreated divine energies, and so developed a distinction between the divine essence, which
is unknowable (God-in-Godself), and the uncreated energies (God-
for-us) that are God in relationship to the created order.[11] This position
is common among Eastern Orthodox theologians today.

For Aquinas, this metaphysical analysis is not without psychological content. In discussing whether it is possible in the state of nature to love God
above all things (*ST* I-II q. 109, a. 3) he says it is, but grace adds "an immediate willingness and joy to the natural love of God." Grace is "God's love
poured into our hearts" (Rom 5:5), but not God loving us, but us loving
God.[12] While God loving us manifests the healing power of grace, it is in us
loving God as God is in Godself that the elevating power of grace is realized.
It is our love response to God that transcends the limits of our natural human
power of love and reveals the supernatural nature of grace.

The introduction of the grace/nature distinction allowed Aquinas to
resolve the unresolved tensions present in the Augustinian theology of grace,
which took as its starting point the grace/sin dialectic. Since then the
grace/nature distinction has found a relatively permanent place in a Catholic
understanding of grace and salvation.[13] However, it is not without some difficulties. In particular it seems to posit two distinct ends for human existence,
a natural end that is attainable through natural powers of human nature, and
a supernatural end, which is attainable only through divine grace. How is this
possible without dividing human beings in two, without introducing a deep
division in the soul? Historically this problem found its focus in the question:
Is there a natural desire to see God?

THE NATURAL DESIRE TO SEE GOD

Perhaps no phrase from Augustine is more well known than his expression of
the restlessness of the human heart: "You have made us for yourself and our

---

11. For more on this topic, see George Maloney, *A Theology of "Uncreated Energies"* (Milwaukee:
Marquette University Press, 1978).

12. Both Augustine and Aquinas read this text as an objective genitive. Modern commentators
prefer to read it as a subjective genitive, that is, as God's love for us. See, for example, Brendan Byrne,
Romans (Collegeville, Minn.: Liturgical Press, 1996), 171.

13. Its permanent value was defended in Pius XII's encyclical *Humani Generis* (no. 26).

heart is restless until it rests in you" (*Confessions* 1.1). It is interesting, then, to learn that in the later part of his life, Augustine became more tentative about making such a statement, particularly in relation to our fallen nature. It seemed to imply a natural ability to move toward God, but Augustine's later, more dialectical approach found that unacceptable.[14] However, once a place is found in theology for introducing the grace/nature distinction, the question then arises, Is our desire for God part of our human nature, or is it a supernatural gift from God? The posing of this question causes a dilemma. If our desire for God is part of our human nature, then, given that the fulfillment of that desire can only be the beatific vision, which is strictly supernatural, it would seem that God created human nature incapable of attaining its end. Apart from grace, human nature would be eternally frustrated. On the other hand, if the desire is supernatural, then theology needs to account for two distinct ends of human existence, one natural, the other supernatural, running the danger of splitting human beings in two.[15] How are these two ends related to each other? Unless a solution can be found to this dilemma, the intellectual coherence of the construct of human nature remains subject to suspicion, and we should return perhaps to the grace/sin dialectic.

Historically, this problem focused on the teaching of Thomas Aquinas that human nature has a natural desire to see God:

> If therefore the human intellect, knowing the essence of some created effect, knows no more of God than that he is; the perfection of that intellect does not yet reach simply the First cause, but there remains in it the natural desire to seek the cause. (*ST* I-II, q. 3, a. 8)

The great Thomist commentator Cajetan (1469-1534) found difficulty with this position of a "natural" desire.[16] If there is a natural desire, then this orientation is an orientation to grace in a human nature that is taken to be self-sufficient and self-enclosed. It threatened the gratuity of grace by creating in human nature an exigence or demand for grace in order for it to achieve its final happiness. If we have such a desire, then God must offer us grace in justice to the desire God has planted within us. His conclusion was that grace was somehow extrinsic to "pure" human nature, conceived of as a self-enclosed

---

14. J. Patout Burns, *The Development of Augustine's Doctrine of Operative Grace* (Paris: Etudes Augustiniennes, 1980), 184-85.

15. The horns of this dilemma arise only as long as the beatific vision is itself strictly supernatural, that is, something finite nature, indeed any finite nature, of itself cannot attain. But this is due to the ontological disparity between finite and infinite being.

16. J. Michael Stebbins, *The Divine Initiative: Grace, World-Order, and Human Freedom in the Early Writings of Bernard Lonergan*, Lonergan Studies (Toronto: University of Toronto Press, 1995), 161-63.

and complete existence. This developed in the "two-storey" theology of grace, which understood the supernatural as an extrinsic superstructure to human nature. This notion of a "pure" human nature was elevated to a necessary theological principle in order to preserve the gratuity of grace. Human nature was conceived of as having two ends, a natural end determined by its nature, within its powers to attain, and a supernatural end, unrelated to its natural end, totally beyond its powers to attain. While grace was "elevating," adding supernatural ends to human existence, it was no longer clear how or even why it could be healing, and so was lost the great Augustinian insight into grace.

With few exceptions, this extrinsicist position of Cajetan became the dominant one in Catholic theology until the twentieth century. In its wake came a fatal separation of grace from nature, the sacred from the profane, the religious from the secular, and the spiritual from the mundane. Eventually it came under increasing pressure in the twentieth century with the recovery of the work of the early church fathers, to whom the scholastic construct of human nature was unknown. This led to a period of bitter dispute and debate around a movement known as the *nouvelle theologie*.[17] We shall briefly consider three responses that emerged during this debate, those of Henri de Lubac, Karl Rahner, and Bernard Lonergan.

De Lubac's position was spelled out in two works, a historical study of the concept and doctrines concerning the supernatural, entitled *Supernaturel*, and a later, more thorough work that sought to respond to some of the criticisms of his earlier work, while restating its main theses, entitled *The Mystery of the Supernatural*.[18]

The first major thesis of de Lubac's theology is that we are all constituted by a natural desire for God, that this desire is constitutive of our human nature, and that we are freely constituted in this way precisely because God has destined us for the beatific vision. God has willed us to be the way we are, to have a certain "nature" precisely because in the providential ordering of creation we are destined to attain God as God is in Godself. God creates us with a certain finality, and that finality is intrinsic to our nature, to what we are. This position preserves the gratuity of grace because God has freely chosen to create us as beings destined for Godself. However, our desire in itself is ineffective, incapable of attaining that which it desires. De Lubac is here rejecting

---

17. For a thorough examination of this debate, see Stephen Duffy, *The Graced Horizon: Nature and Grace in Modern Catholic Thought* (Collegeville, Minn.: Liturgical Press, 1992). However, I do not agree with the options he takes in relation to the two contrasting positions on the nature of our desire for God.

18. Henri de Lubac, *The Mystery of the Supernatural* (London: Geoffrey Chapman, 1967); idem, *Surnaturel: Études historiques* (Paris: Aubier, 1946).

a position that would think of abstract natures as existing apart from the totality of creation itself, with detachable or interchangeable finalities.

The minor thesis that de Lubac draws from this intrinsic account of grace and its gratuity is that, although God freely chooses to create us with a given finality, once that free decision has been made, "God does not renege on completing a tendency freely willed by Godself. The desire is also, therefore, absolutely, unconditioned and unfrustratable on God's part."[19] Therefore, God will not deny the beatific vision to beings so constituted. This was a sticking point for many of de Lubac's contemporaries. Why is this suggestion a problem? The natural desire to see God is so clearly linked with the desire to know (see the text above from Aquinas), and that desire to know is constitutive of us as rational and hence spiritual creatures. Consequently, de Lubac seemed to be concluding that God could not create rational creatures without destining them for the beatific vision. It appears to thus undermine the gratuity of grace. This was a position that was later to be explicitly rejected by Pius XII in his encyclical *Humani Generis*.[20]

The second major thesis of de Lubac's theology is his attack on the concept of pure nature, an attack that is twofold. First, on the historical level he argues that the concept was unknown to the early church fathers, that it is a misinterpretation of Aquinas, and that the uniform position of the early fathers is that human beings have a single end, that is supernatural. Second, at the speculative level de Lubac argues that the hypothesis of pure nature, while invented to preserve the gratuitousness of grace, does nothing of the sort. In the concrete historical order, we are in fact oriented to grace, so a merely hypothetical construct that protects the gratuity of grace in a hypothetical order tells us nothing about the gratuity of grace in this historical order. A hypothetical humanity in an order of pure nature would simply not be the same humanity we currently experience.

The strength of de Lubac's position is his attempt to overcome the static conceptualist worldview that has dominated the standard position since Cajetan. This position viewed natures as preexisting in the mind of God (like Platonic ideas), who then created a world in which to implant these natures. De Lubac reminds us that God created natures always and already embedded in a particular world order. He also restored the Thomistic position regarding the "natural" desire to see God, which had got lost in the standard position of Cajetan. This helped overcome the extrinsicism of the standard position, which denied any element of human experience in regard to the supernatu-

---

19. Duffy, *Graced Horizon*, 68.

20. *Humani Generis* 26: "Others destroy the gratuity of the supernatural order, since God, they say, cannot create intellectual beings without ordering and calling them to the beatific vision."

ral.[21] The weakness was that he pushed his argument too far. While one may agree that it is fitting for God to ordain a supernatural end for all rational creatures, such fittingness is not a demonstration of necessity.

Among those who rejected de Lubac's position was Karl Rahner. Rahner has been without doubt the most influential theologian in the theology of grace.[22] His positions have become a theological commonplace with friend and foe alike. Like de Lubac, Rahner wanted to overcome the extrinsicism of the standard position. However, he was far more determined to maintain the grace/nature distinction, and hence more careful than de Lubac in that regard. The reach of Rahner's theology of grace is extensive and encompasses more than the grace/nature debate, though that debate and the position Rahner develops in light of it are the key to his theology.

Rahner's solution to the problem of extrinsicism is to introduce the notion of what he calls a "supernatural existential." This is a supernatural orientation or desire for God which nonetheless is empirically constitutive of human nature. What this means is that Rahner holds that every human being has a supernatural desire for God. This desire, however, is not essential to human nature as a nature—and so we would still be human without it—but in fact, every concrete human being has such a desire instilled in him or her by God. Rahner argues that just because such a desire is supernatural does not mean it cannot also be universal. Grace need not be rare just because it is gratuitous. While Rahner recognizes a natural orientation to God, this is not sufficient for his purposes. Although it is an openness, it is not an unconditional ordination for grace, for God. Such an ordination is not part of pure nature but is supernatural, even though in this concrete historical order it is a universal element of our concrete human nature. It is present as offer, even when we reject it through sin.

---

21. Extrinsicism refers to the theology of grace that dominated Catholic theology since Trent; it sees grace as extrinsic to human experience, as belonging to some divine, religious realm above and separate from the human. Such an account of grace severely neglected the healing operations of grace. In different ways both Lonergan and Rahner have sought to overcome this extrinsicism without falling into an intrinsicist account, which would see grace as constitutive of human nature and hence not really gratuitous. See Karl Rahner, "Concerning the Relationship between Nature and Grace," in *Theological Investigations,* vol. 1 (London: Darton, Longman & Todd, 1961), 297-317; and Bernard J. F. Lonergan, "The Natural Desire to See God," in *Collection,* ed. Frederick E. Crowe and Robert M. Doran, Collected Works of Bernard Lonergan 4 (Toronto: University of Toronto Press, 1988), 81-91.

22. There are any number of accounts of Rahner's theology of grace, for example, Duffy, *Graced Horizon*; idem, *The Dynamics of Grace: Perspectives in Theological Anthropology* (Collegeville, Minn.: Liturgical Press, 1993); Herbert Vorgrimler, *Understanding Karl Rahner: An Introduction to His Life and Thought* (New York: Crossroad, 1986). Also primary sources such as Rahner, "Concerning the Relationship between Nature and Grace." An excellent summary can be found in J. Colombo, "Rahner and His Critics: Lindbeck and Metz," *Thomist* 56 (1992): 71-96.

On Rahner's notion of the supernatural existential, grace is always and everywhere on offer, in transcendental mode, that is, as offer within human consciousness. This has important consequences, especially in interreligious dialogue. It led Rahner to develop the notion of "anonymous Christians" as a way of speaking about salvation outside the church. However, some have questioned whether this undermines the historical mediation of grace, notably through the church and sacraments. Johannes Baptist Metz, a student of Rahner, has been very strong on this point. For him, Rahner "wins the race without even running it," by avoiding the difficulties raised in the issue of historical mediation.[23] In a sense Rahner's notion of the supernatural existential seeks to develop a mediating principle between grace and nature, by giving the existential qualities of both grace (as supernatural) and nature (as universal). It raises the question of why such a mediating principle is needed.

Finally, we consider the position of Lonergan on our "natural desire to see God."[24] Lonergan begins by distinguishing between two meanings of the word "natural." First, it is used as distinct from supernatural, something that is beyond the powers of nature; second, when we speak of a natural desire, it is used in distinction from an elicited desire, which is an act of desiring some presenting object. A natural desire, then, pertains not to acts of elicited desire (e.g., in faith we may desire the beatific vision) but the potential orientation of the nature that is manifested in its acts. When Lonergan speaks of a natural desire to see God in God's essence, he uses the word "natural" in both senses. To speak of an elicited desire for the beatific vision as a natural desire would be to claim a natural appreciation of a supernatural good, the beatific vision, which would deny the supernaturality of that vision. Similarly, if one concludes from the fact of a natural desire to an exigence for the beatific vision, one again denies the supernatural quality of that vision.

For Lonergan, the evidence for a natural desire is found in our human intellect, or what we have described as the human search for meaning, truth, and value. As soon as we know that there is a God—attainable through the natural light of intellect according to Vatican I (DS 3004)—we seek meaning, "What is God?" But only the beatific vision is a complete response to that question. Such questioning is natural; it reveals a human potency, the intellect, which is a radical tendency to "know everything about everything." Still, while intellect reveals a potential for the beatific vision, the potential is "obediential"; that is, it lies beyond the proportionate means of the intellect to achieve and can only be received "in obedience" as gift. The proportionate end of

---

23. Johannes Baptist Metz, *Faith in History and Society: Toward a Practical Fundamental Theology*, trans. David Smith (New York: Seabury Press, 1980), 161-63.

24. See Stebbins, *Divine Initiative*, 149-82.

human knowledge is the universe of sensible being. Thus Lonergan allows for two ends, one proportionate, the other supernatural, arising from a single desire. These stand in relationship to each other since our "quest for complete knowledge can reach its term only when we know God *per essentiam*."[25] Grace truly perfects and completes nature. Still, a natural perfection and beatitude are possible without the beatific vision. The language that Lonergan later would use to describe the relationship between the proportionate and supernatural ends would be "sublation": "what sublates goes beyond what is sublated, introduces something new and distinct, puts everything on a new basis, yet so far from interfering with the sublated or destroying it, on the contrary needs it, includes it, preserves all its proper features and properties, and carries them forward to a fuller realization within a richer context."[26]

Lonergan contrasts his position with that of Cajetan. For Cajetan, a natural desire must be fulfilled by natural means. Since there is no natural means for attaining the beatific vision, there can be no natural desire to see God. Next, Cajetan argues that there is a natural desire, but its object is to know God as the first cause, as existent, not for knowledge of God in his essence. Finally, he argues that there may be a natural elicited desire to see God, one dependent on divinely revealed effects. Thus, for Cajetan there are two desires, one natural, a potency of the nature but with a natural object; the other natural as elicited but with a supernatural object. Cajetan sought to protect the gratuity of grace but in doing so produced a human being with two desires and two ends "at the price of obscuring the relation between the natural desire to see God and its ultimate fulfillment in the beatific vision."[27]

Finally, in response to the position of de Lubac, Lonergan strongly asserts the possibility of God creating a world order where grace is not available:

> all things are possible to God on condition that no internal contradiction is involved. But a world-order without grace does not involve an internal contradiction. Therefore a world-order without grace is possible to God and so concretely possible.[28]

While Lonergan accepts that it is fitting for rational creatures to have the beatific vision as their end, it is not necessary. On the other hand, he agrees with de Lubac that the notion of pure nature is hardly a central notion in the theology of grace and loses its significance once one abandons the conceptualist assumptions of Cajetan.

---

25. Ibid., 155.
26. Lonergan, *Method*, 241.
27. Stebbins, *Divine Initiative*, 162.
28. Lonergan, "Natural Desire to See God."

As can be seen from the above discussion, the problem of working with the grace/nature distinction raises some very difficult questions that have exercised the minds of some of our greatest theologians. However, some simple insights might help the student approaching this for the first time. Some of the difficulties we create for ourselves arise with the language we use and the images behind that language. We often speak of the "religious" or "sacred" sphere in contrast to the "secular" sphere. But the image of contrasting spheres is not helpful. How do "spheres" relate to one another? Each is self-enclosed and complete. Try instead the image of "dimension," that is, the sacred dimension of things. Rather than splitting reality into disconnected spheres, the language of dimensions implies a unified reality with several distinct attributes or orders. A sacred dimension may be manifest at any time, in any place; a sacred sphere will be cut off and isolated from the nonsacred. Grace and the supernatural are not a distinct reality but a potential dimension of all reality, something Catholic theology recognizes in its approach to the sacraments.

CAN WE EXPERIENCE GRACE?

Given the emphasis we have placed on grace in terms of conversion and its consequences, it may seem a strange question to ask whether we can experience grace. Conversion is a powerful experience, indeed sometimes overpowering, not something one is likely to miss. However, we should also note the following from the *Catechism of the Catholic Church*: "Since it belongs to the supernatural order grace escapes our experience and cannot be known except by faith. We cannot therefore rely on our feelings or our works to conclude that we are justified or saved" (*CCC* no. 2005). There seems to be a suggestion here that grace is not part of our human experience; it is something that "escapes our experience." Should we then cease talking about grace in experiential terms?

It is important to identify the concerns that this teaching reflects. The *Catechism* itself footnotes the teaching of the Council of Trent (DS 1533-34, 1562-63), which was attempting to counter the "brash presumption" of the "heretics" that unless one were certain of being saved, one was not in fact saved. According to the reformers, faith gave one a firm conviction of one's own salvation, and so that conviction or feeling was itself a sure sign of being saved. The council fathers did not accept this position, perhaps fearing the ways in which human self-deception might misuse it:

> If anyone shall say that justifying faith is nothing else but confidence in divine mercy, which remits sins for Christ's sake, or that it is this confidence alone that justifies us—*anathema sit*.

> If anyone shall say that in order to obtain the remission of sins it is nec-
> essary for every man to believe with certainty and without hesitation on
> account of his own weakness and indisposition that his sins are forgiven
> him—*anathema sit.* (DS 1562-3)[29]

Such a conclusions is in itself unexceptional, but coupled with a theology that
thought of grace as extrinsic to human nature, a theology that could not provide an integrated account of human ends deduced from this position of
Trent that grace was completely outside the range of human experience.
While this was not a valid conclusion to draw from that teaching, it became
an entrenched position in Catholic theology. Grace became like a heavenly
bank account, "out there," beyond our mundane existence with little or no
impact on our day-to-day existence. As a consequence, the vital connection
between grace and conversion and the Augustinian insight on the healing
nature of grace were largely lost. Among other things this led to bad pastoral
practice, especially in relation to the sacrament of confession.

It is instructive, then to turn to Aquinas to see how he deals with the question whether one can know that one has grace (*ST* I-II q. 112, a. 5). Aquinas
distinguishes between an absolute certainty, which is simply not possible, and
knowledge "by signs":

> Things are known conjecturally by signs; and thus anyone may know he
> has grace, when he is conscious of delighting in God, and of despising
> worldly things, and inasmuch as a man is not conscious of any mortal sin
> . . . because whoever receives [grace] knows by experiencing a certain
> sweetness, which he who does not receive it, does not experience.

It is clear from this that Aquinas held that we do in fact experience grace, as
a "certain sweetness" or what Augustine would call "delight," and that this
leads to a level of self-knowledge, though not absolute certainty. To some
extent this is acknowledged also in the *Catechism* when it goes on to conclude:

> However, according to the Lord's words—"Thus you will know them by
> their fruits"—reflection on God's blessing in our life and in the lives of
> saints offers us a guarantee that grace is at work in us and spurs us on to
> an ever greater faith and an attitude of trustful poverty. (*CCC* no. 2005)

So we may conclude that we can indeed experience grace, though it always
retains an element of mystery. After an initial conversion experience, it
becomes more and more an undercurrent in our lives, an unseen presence, a

---

29. Translation from Josef Neuner and Heinrich Roos, *The Teaching of the Catholic Church*, ed.
Karl Rahner, trans. Geoffrey Stevens (Cork: Mercier Press, 1967).

consolation in hard times, a delight in the truly good, difficult to pin down as it becomes more and more integrated into the fabric of our life.

PROVIDENCE AND PREDESTINATION

A central element in the Christian tradition of grace is its "gratuitous" nature. Grace is not something we can control, demand, or require. It is pure gift from God. This gratuitous quality is most evident in the experience of conversion, or operative grace. God turns around the life of the sinner, taking out the heart of stone and replacing it with a heart of flesh. "This is the work of the Lord, a marvel to our eyes" (Ps 118:23). But if this is God's work and not a human achievement, then the question obviously arises, why is it so rare? Perhaps we all have our favorite list of people we think need conversion, whether terrorists, politicians, or CEOs of multinational corporations who exploit the poor and devastate the natural environment. Why is it that God does not turn their hearts into hearts of flesh? Put more bluntly, why is it that some are saved, and others, apparently, are not? This is the classical question of predestination.

The language of predestination is taken from the Scriptures, which clearly recognize the problem we have identified (Rom 8:29-30; Eph 1). There the context is one of conversion of the pagans compared with the lack of response to Jesus among the Jews. Why did some respond and others not? Because of God's divine election (see in particular Rom 9-11). Augustine takes up this theme with a vengeance. For Augustine, the mystery of predestination is one hidden in God. Some are chosen, others are not. The number of the predestined is already determined and cannot be changed—only God knows who they are. The predestined are few in number, while the rest of humanity is a *massa damnata*, or damned lump.[30] This theme was also taken up by a number of the reformers who taught double predestination. God predestines some to heaven and others to hell.

The difficulty is that this scriptural theme must also be kept in balance with other scriptural themes that stress God's love and compassion for all, and in particular that God wills the salvation of all (1 Tim 2:4). Augustine was well aware of such verses, but refused to concede to his opponents that the plain meaning of the text was what the text meant![31] If one combined the universal

---

30. See, for example, Augustine, *On Rebuke and Grace,* available at http://www.newadvent.org/fathers/1511.htm (accessed July 3, 2006).

31. See Augustine, *On Rebuke and Grace*, chaps. 44, 45, 47.

salvific will of God with the notion of predestination and operative grace, one might rather conclude that all are in fact saved. Indeed, some have drawn such a conclusion, a point we shall return to when we consider the question of hell. In the meantime I shall make the following points.

What is most disturbing about the notion of predestination is the sense of some arbitrary choice being made by God about who will be saved and who will be damned. We find the arbitrariness of it repugnant—and so we should, for such arbitrariness is a sign of the inauthentic, not the authentic good. So we need to eliminate any sense that God is making some type of arbitrary decision about our salvation. Here it is important to recall the notion of God's universal salvific will. If God in fact wills that all be saved, then God is doing everything possible to work for our salvation. While it may be presumptuous to conclude that all are saved, the teaching of predestination should give us confidence that God is working for our salvation, not against it, and God's will is anything but arbitrary. As Jesus teaches:

> Do not be afraid of those who kill the body but cannot kill the soul. Rather, be afraid of the One who can destroy both soul and body in hell. Are not two sparrows sold for a penny? Yet not one of them will fall to the ground apart from the will of your Father. And even the very hairs of your head are all numbered. So don't be afraid; you are worth more than many sparrows. (Matt 10:28-31)

Second, we may respond to the question, Why is conversion not more common? Perhaps the reason is because it is so difficult to achieve, even for God. If conversion is too abrupt, it may disrupt the psychological identity of the person, leaving him or her incapable of functioning. Through the operation of divine providence God patiently leads the sinner to the point of conversion, a process that may take a lifetime. We must also take into account the resistance of the sinner to God's promptings, which can make the process even more difficult. After conversion there is still the possibility of breakdown, of turning away from God in sin. All this should remind us of the serious nature of sin, of the rupture it causes in our relationship with God and our fellow humans, and of the high price paid for our redemption.

Finally, as indicated in the previous paragraph, any discussion of predestination must occur within the framework of divine providence. In loving wisdom God creates the whole of the created order in a single act. In that sense, God does not *pre*destine anything, since in God's creative act there is no before or after. God creates the whole of creation, from the initial Big Bang to the final cosmic consummation, in a single divine act. This includes all our free acts and their consequences, all the acts of divine graciousness and all our sins.[32] Again we only have a sense of this as arbitrary if we have lost a sense of God's loving wisdom as the source of creation.

In this sense, then, Catholic teaching affirms a doctrine of predestination, a predestination to glory, grounded in the love and grace of God. It does not affirm any predestination to eternal loss. God does not predestine anyone to hell; that is solely the achievement of the damned.

SOME PRACTICAL INSIGHTS INTO THE LIFE OF GRACE

Grace is the beginning of the spiritual life, and our understanding of grace will influence our spirituality. A good theology of grace will lead us in the direction of a healthy spirituality, while a poor theology will have a detrimental effect upon us. We have already noted the detrimental effect of an extrinsicist account of grace. Detrimental effects also flow from a dualistic account of human existence, which tends to overspiritualize the nature of grace. The following questions and responses from Aquinas provide a good example of a sound and realistic theology of grace and a spirituality that emerges from it.

ST II-II q. 25, a. 4: Whether a man ought to love himself out of charity?
Some forms of spirituality seem to present the spiritual life as a conflict between love of God and love of self. They seem to generate almost a sense of self-hatred or destructive self-denial. They forget that Jesus taught us to love God above all things and our neighbor "as ourselves." Healthy self-love is an essential element in the spiritual life. Indeed, we may love ourselves with a supernatural love (charity). Hence Aquinas concludes:

> we may speak of charity in respect of its specific nature, namely as denoting man's friendship with God in the first place and consequently, with the things of God, among which things is man himself who has charity. Hence among these other things which he loves out of charity because they pertain to God, he loves also himself out of charity.

ST II-II q. 25, a. 5: Whether a man ought to love his body out of charity?
Again, some forms of spirituality seem to be directed against the body as if it were the source of evil and temptation. Forms of mortification are used to dis-

---

32. *CCC* no. 600: "To God, all moments of time are present in their immediacy. When therefore he establishes his eternal plan of 'predestination,' he includes in it each person's free response to his grace: 'In this city, in fact, both Herod and Pontius Pilate, with the Gentiles and the peoples of Israel, gathered together against your holy servant Jesus, whom you anointed, to do whatever your hand and your plan had predestined to take place.' For the sake of accomplishing his plan of salvation, God permitted the acts that flowed from their blindness."

cipline the body and punish it for its weakness. Even apart from such spiritualities we can witness various forms of body-hatred in society, through the
problem young women have with body image, culminating in anorexia, to
body piercing, which seems to be a delight in self-mutilation. For Aquinas, on
the other hand, the body is part of God's handiwork and worthy of not only
a natural love, but also a supernatural love:

> Now the nature of our body was created not by an evil force . . . but by God
> . . . Consequently out of the love of charity with which we love God, we
> ought to love our bodies also.

ST II-II q. 26, a. 4: Whether out of charity man ought to love himself more than his neighbor?

It is not uncommon to view the moral life as a struggle between altruism and
egotism. The moral decision is one that puts others' interests before one's own.
Now there is some truth in recognizing that the moral life involves self-transcendence, going beyond the self one is to become a richer fuller self, but this
does not always mean putting others interests before one's own, particularly
where their interests may lack much by way of moral self-transcendence. The
moral life is not about "self versus other" but about a focus on the good and
moral self-transcendence. One of the goods one needs to take into account is
the good of oneself, especially in one's journey toward moral self-transcendence (virtue). Hence Aquinas argues:

> A man, out of charity, ought to love himself more than his neighbor: in
> sign whereof a man ought not to give way to any evil of sin, not even that
> he may free his neighbor from sin.

ST II-II q. 26, a. 6: Whether we ought to love one neighbor more than another?

Finally, there is a tendency in some forms of idealistic spirituality to state that
we should love everyone equally, without any discrimination or favoritism.
Our own family should be no more important to us than the person down the
street, or even the person on the other side of the world. There is something
otherworldly about such spiritualities, and Aquinas will not accept them:

> the affection of charity, which is the inclination of grace, is not less orderly
> than the natural appetite which is the inclination of nature, for both incli-
> nations flow from divine wisdom . . . consequently the inclination also of
> grace which is the effect of charity must needs be proportionate to those
> actions which have to be performed outwardly, so that, to wit, the affection
> of our charity be more intense towards those whom we ought to behave
> with greater kindness.

SOME RECENT ECUMENICAL CONSIDERATIONS

The doctrine of grace and the justification of the sinner have been major sticking points between the Catholic tradition and that of the Reformation. We identified some of the differences between these two traditions in chapter 4 on original sin. Recent ecumenical dialogue between Lutherans and Catholics have sought to overcome these differences through a renewed appreciation of the issues that triggered the Reformation and the underlying theological values proponents of each side of the debate were seeking to uphold. This process of dialogue bore fruit in 1998 when the Lutheran World Federation and the Catholic Church were able to sign a "Joint Declaration on the Doctrine of Justification" (JD),[33] which indicated both common ground and agreement that: "The understanding of the doctrine of justification set forth in this Declaration shows that a consensus in basic truths of the doctrine of justification exists between Lutherans and Catholics" (JD 40). On the basis of this consensus the Lutheran World Federation and the Catholic Church declare together: "The teaching of the Lutheran Churches presented in the Declaration does not fall under the condemnations from the Council of Trent. The condemnations in the Lutheran Confessions do not apply to the teaching of the Roman Catholic Church presented in this Declaration" (JD 41).

The substantial content of agreement was expressed as follows:

> In faith we together hold the conviction that justification is the work of the triune God. The Father sent his Son into the world to save sinners. The foundation and presupposition of justification is the incarnation, death, and resurrection of Christ. Justification thus means that Christ himself is our righteousness, in which we share through the Holy Spirit in accord with the will of the Father. Together we confess: By grace alone, in faith in Christ's saving work and not because of any merit on our part, we are accepted by God and receive the Holy Spirit, who renews our hearts while equipping and calling us to good works. (JD 15)

The key value each sought to uphold in this joint statement was the absolute priority of divine grace in the process of salvation. Salvation is not something we earn or merit through our actions, but fundamentally a gift from God. Nonetheless this gift of God draws from us a grateful response, which calls us "to good works" and equips us for this response. This is central to the Christian understanding of salvation and grace.

---

33. The full text of the declaration, together with an appendix added by the Vatican to clarify certain matters in relation to the declaration, can be found at http://www.vatican.va/roman_curia/pontifical_councils/chrstuni/documents/rc_pc_chrstuni_doc_31101999_cath-luth-joint-declaration_en.html (accessed July 6, 2006).

The document, however, did not just paper over continuing differences between the two traditions. It identified continuing issues on questions such as the role of human cooperation with grace, whether there is a real inner renewal of the sinner through grace, the relative understandings of the nature of concupiscence, whether justification brings assurance of salvation, and the precise place of good works in salvation. Many of these issues have been subject to continued debate between the two traditions. As Avery Dulles has pointed out, much of the difficulty lies in the different languages adopted by the two traditions, one metaphysical (Catholic) and the other more existential (Lutheran). One is the language of explanation, the other of prayer and entreaty before God. While these must at some level be harmonized, their differences in approach make mutual evaluation difficult and a long-term project. In the meantime, mutual respect as Christian believers has grown so that "it now seems appropriate to measure the Lutheran theses against some standard other than the decrees of Trent."[34]

GRACE OR ENLIGHTENMENT?

The language and experience of grace are central to a Christian understanding of the world, of human existence and its relationship to God. In Buddhism, however, we find quite a different language to speak of its central defining experience. Rather than speak of grace, Buddhists speak of enlightenment. Is this talking about the same thing, giving different words to the same underlying reality, or are we talking about two fundamentally different experiences. Put bluntly, is conversion the same as enlightenment?[35]

It is difficult to decide such a question without a direct encounter with both experiences, something few people would ever be able to achieve. So we shall be satisfied with an exploration of the way these terms operate and the implications they hold. Because here we can compare only language, we are not in a position to identify the underlying experience; however, the language each tradition uses to describe its foundational experiences does influence the expectations of their adherents.

The language of enlightenment seems to identify a fundamentally cognitive experience. The one who is enlightened knows things not known by the unenlightened. Clearly, the cognitive component is not trivial or empirical,

---

34. Avery Dulles, "Two Languages of Salvation: The Lutheran-Catholic Joint Declaration," *First Things* 98, (December 1999): 29.

35. A helpful discussion of the similarities and differences between Buddhism and Christianity in this regard can be found in Hans Tschiggerl, "Two Languages of Salvation: Christian-Buddhist Dialogue with Aloysius Pieris, S.J.," *East Asian Pastoral Review* 34 (1997): 225-54.

but has to do with the nature of the world, of suffering, of personal identity and so on. To Western ears at least, enlightenment sounds like an insight, a powerful insight, but an insight nonetheless. As Hans Tschiggerl notes, the "soteriological nucleus, or liberative core-experience is available in Buddhism in a *gnostic* idiom, as liberative knowledge or enlightenment."[36]

Christianity, on the other hand, develops the language of grace which it relates more to the will or heart, a transformation of affectivity or love. "The Christian core-experience is that of a liberating God, expressed in *agapeic* terms of liberative love."[37] This is not to deny that Christianity has a cognitive component. Indeed, the cognitive component of Christianity, its distinctive set of beliefs in God as triune, the divinity of Jesus, and so on, is constitutive of Christian identity. Similarly, it is not being suggested that Buddhism is not concerned with love. However, the language of the core experiences does seem to differ, one having a cognitive focus, the other having an affective and volitional focus.

Perhaps a more important question, however, concerns the Christian understanding of the gratuitous nature of grace. The question that Christians put to Buddhists is thus: Do you understand your core soteriological experience of enlightenment to be an achievement or a gift? If it is understood to be an achievement, and in fact it is an achievement, then there is a significant difference between Christianity and Buddhism. If it is understood to be a gift and it is in fact a gift, then the two religions have some very common ground.

None of this is to suggest that Buddhists do not experience grace, or that there cannot be holy and morally upright Buddhists. It may well be that Buddhists misunderstand the nature of their core experience if they view it as an achievement, when in fact it is a gift. Indeed, it is clear that Buddhism has produced holy and morally upright men and women since its inception. However, some care needs to be exercised lest we think that Christians and Buddhists are just saying the same thing in different ways.

CONCLUSION

Most of the above discussion on grace concerns the impact of grace in the life of the individual human being. Grace is conceived of in terms of conversion, the sovereign act of God in the life of the sinner that turns our lives around and liberates us to do what is truly good. At the same time the impact of grace is such that it provides us with a new and higher context, "God's love . . .

---

36. Ibid., 230.
37. Ibid.

poured into our hearts through the Holy Spirit that has been given to us" (Rom 5:5). This love secures our conversion and prolongs its effects in the long and at times painful journey toward authentic existence.

Just as sin is not merely personal, however, but has transpersonal elements that we have identified as social, institutional, and historical sinfulness, so too grace must be extended into these dimensions of human existence. This social and historical prolongation of grace affects not just individuals but communities and cultures. And so we turn our attention to the work of the church, as the social and historical extension of the life of grace.

QUESTIONS FOR REFLECTION

1. Grace is both healing and elevating. What happens to our understanding of grace if either of these aspects is neglected?
2. What difference would it make to our theology of grace if we begin with either the grace/sin dialectic or the grace/nature distinction as fundamental to our understanding of grace?
3. Classical commentators have taken the text of Romans 5:5—God's love poured into our hearts—to refer to our love of God (objective genitive). Modern biblical exegesis favors the subjective genitive reading, that is, it refers to God's love for us. How might these experiences be different? How might they be related?
4. How might a sound theology of grace assist us in the spiritual life? How might a poor theology of grace distort our spiritual life?
5. Christians speak of grace and Buddhists speak of enlightenment. How can we tell whether they are speaking of the same thing?

SUGGESTIONS FOR FURTHER READING AND STUDY

Colombo, J. "Rahner and His Critics: Lindbeck and Metz." *Thomist* 56 (1992): 71-96.

Duffy, Stephen. *The Dynamics of Grace: Perspectives in Theological Anthropology*. Collegeville, Minn.: Liturgical Press, 1993.

Dulles, Avery. "Two Languages of Salvation: The Lutheran-Catholic Joint Declaration." *First Things* 98, no. December (1999): 25-30.

Lonergan, Bernard J. F. "The Natural Desire to See God." In *Collection*, edited by Frederick E. Crowe and Robert M. Doran, 81-91. Collected Works of Bernard Lonergan 4. Toronto: University of Toronto Press, 1988.

Rahner, Karl. "Concerning the Relationship between Nature and Grace." In *Theological Investigations*, 297-317. London: Darton, Longman & Todd, 1961.

Tschiggerl, Hans. "Two Languages of Salvation: Christian-Buddhist Dialogue with Aloysius Pieris, S.J." *East Asian Pastoral Review* 34 (1997): 225-54.

7

Church and Sacrament

G RACE IS INTENSELY PERSONAL, but it is never private. Just as human beings are constituted as social beings, just as the impact of sin expands to infiltrate our social and historical existence, so too grace manifests itself in the social and historical dimensions of human existence, calling people into community, transforming our cultures, and creating institutional forms whose purpose is the ongoing historical mediation of grace. There is a sense, then, in which the study of the church (ecclesiology) is the prolongation of the theology of grace into human history. This is the focus of the present chapter. We shall explore the various dimensions of the church's life and activities as an expression of its mission as a mediator of grace seeking to continue the mission of Jesus to build the kingdom of God.

CHURCH—THE RELIGIOUS DIMENSION

The church is first and foremost a religious community. It exists in order to initiate, promote, and celebrate faith in the person of Jesus Christ, in the Father whose mission he fulfilled, and in the Spirit that empowered him and promises to empower those who follow him. Such faith is both gift and invitation. It is gift inasmuch as both the mission of Jesus and the ability to grasp its significance find their ground in divine graciousness, whereby human nature is both healed of the effects of sin and elevated to share in the divine life. The church is thus "a sign and instrument of communion with God" (*Lumen Gentium* 1). The recent rise in *communio* ecclesiology is reflective of this aspect of the life of the church.[1] This gift is also invitation, inasmuch as we are invited to do as Jesus did, empowered by his Spirit to overcome evil through participation in his redemptive suffering.[2] Symbolically this invita-

---

1. See Dennis M. Doyle, *Communion Ecclesiology: Vision and Versions* (Maryknoll, N.Y.: Orbis Books, 2000), for a thorough account of contemporary *communio* ecclesiologies.
2. See Robert M. Doran, *Theology and the Dialectics of History* (Toronto: University of Toronto Press, 1990), 121-22.

tion is captured not by *communio* but by *missio Dei*, our sharing in the divine missions of Word and Spirit. Through both *communio* and *missio* we share in the divine life of the Trinity.[3]

What does it mean, however, to say that this community is "religious"? It means that the ground and source of the Christian community, its central meanings and values, the object of its faith transcend our limited human resources. A more-than-human hand is at work in human history, and without that hand human beings would be impotent in the face of evil (*non posse non peccare*). God has entered into human history to deal with the problem of evil through the life, death, and resurrection of Jesus and the outpouring of the Holy Spirit. Through these God reaches out into human history to transform it from within.

As a religious institution the church promotes and engages in prayer, liturgy, mysticism, and the praise of God in all things. Nonetheless, it would be a mistake to see these things simply as ends in themselves. If we were to see human history simply in terms of the human striving for the transcendent, human creativity culminating in moral and religious goals, then our religious dimension would be an end in itself and the culmination of human living. But in the divine dispensation, the religious dimension, which the church actively promotes, is the entry point of healing grace, whose purpose is found in overcoming evil and its effects in human history. Thus, the religious activities of the church are not ends in themselves but are the starting point for the healing transformation of that human history. As Jesus states, "the sabbath was made for humankind, and not humankind for the sabbath" (Mark 2:27 and parallels).[4] When our religious activities become simply ends in themselves; when they are no longer concerned with moral, cultural, and social transformation; when the religious is separated from the rest of life, then the transforming mission of the Church is undermined and distorted. As John Fuellenbach declares,

> the coming Kingdom of God cannot be seen as purely spiritual, universal and eschatological. The historical and political element is an essential part of the notion itself. No Jew could ever envision a purely spiritual Kingdom

---

3. It is worth noting that much *communio* ecclesiology is weak in its examination of the mission of the church. Mission becomes subsumed within communion. One need only consider the index entries on mission in books such as Doyle, *Communion Ecclesiology*; and Michael G. Lawler and Thomas J. Shanahan, *Church: A Spirited Communion* (Collegeville, Minn.: Liturgical Press, 1995), to verify this observation.

4. Ben Meyer notes that "it was remarkable . . . that when [Jesus] referred to the ritual order it was only to assert its ordination to the moral order (Mt 5:24; 23:23; Mk 7:15; par. Mt 15:11)" (*The Early Christians: Their World Mission and Self-Discovery* [Wilmington, Del.: Michael Glazier, 1986], 72).

without expecting as well a complementary historical and political realization on behalf of Israel. Jesus went beyond these physical and material aspects of God's kingdom, but he definitely did not abandon them.[5]

To which Edward Schillebeeckx adds, "a religious attitude can in fact be suspect of being an ideology if it is socially, politically and personally neutral in the ethical sphere."[6] Sadly, such a separation between the "sacred" and the "secular" can be found in the legacy of the extrinsicism that has dominated Catholic theology since Trent.

CHURCH—THE MORAL DIMENSION

From the earliest time the church has not simply concerned itself with matters that could be identified as religious, for example, matters of obedience to the Father, faith in the person of Jesus, and sharing in the power of the Spirit. In the teaching of Jesus and the letters of Paul we find repeated instances of moral teaching, that is, questions concerning our relationships with one another, of behavior and actions that promote the human good or perpetuate evil. Paul exhorts Christians to do good and avoid evil (Rom 12:9), and the good Paul has in mind is usually instanced in terms of proper relationships within families, among fellow Christians (Rom 14:1ff, 1 Thess 5:14-16), and between persons and society, as represented by the Roman state (Rom 13:1-7). Since that time, the moral behavior of Christians has been a constant theme in preaching and Christian literature.

The transformation of human living toward integrity and authenticity is the proximate goal of the healing power of grace as it enters into human history. Here evil is confronted in a most intimate way, for the roots of evil are not "out there" in culture, in society, in this or that group of "criminals" and "sinners." The roots of evil are to be found in the heart of each person, and it is here that the battle between grace and sin is most intense. At its root, sinfulness is not willfulness or self interest or pride, but that peculiar form of human brokenness that the tradition identifies as original sin. As we argued in chapter 4, the root of evil within each of us is not something we have done, but rather something that has been done to us (the sin of Adam). It is a brokenness that first and foremost needs healing, not an evil requiring denunciation. The first movement of grace is thus healing, a *gratia sanans*, which

---

5. John Fuellenbach, *The Kingdom of God: The Message of Jesus Today* (Maryknoll, N.Y.: Orbis Books, 1995), 33.

6. Edward Schillebeeckx, *Christ, the Christian Experience in the Modern World* (London: S.C.M., 1980), 660.

liberates our moral striving, the core of our freedom, to achieve the truly good.

This is why it is so scandalous when members of the church, especially those who represent the public face of the church, are revealed to be criminals and wrongdoers. It is little consolation that, for example, the church's history of dealing with sexual abuse is no worse than that of other comparable institutions or that its incidence is no greater than society at large. If grace is not making a significant difference, if grace does not shift the probabilities of human actions toward moral integrity and away from sin, then the power of grace in overcoming evil is being rendered ineffective. If those in Christian churches have the same rates of domestic violence; of sexual abuse and incest; of addictive behaviors such as drugs, alcohol, sex, and gambling; of financial fraud or political corruption and so on, then the mediation of grace is having no impact of the problem of evil. The church then becomes a stumbling block to faith.[7]

The problem of evil extends beyond the crimes and misdeeds of individual persons and reaches into that realm whereby we reflect on the nature of human living, its goals and purposes, its meanings and values, through philosophy, science, scholarship, theology, and art. Where grace liberates human creativity to strive for meaning, truth, and value, not necessarily as possessions but at least as the intentional goal of human living, sin distorts our search for direction in the movement of life though the production of alienating ideologies that justify sin, truncate our human strivings, and discredit even the possibilities of meaning, truth, and value. As the problem of evil extends beyond the personal, so too the mission of the church extends beyond the personal, though mediated through personal conversion, into the cultural dimension. And so the history of the church is inextricably bound up with the history of Western ethics, philosophy, science, and scholarship. Where would Western philosophy be without the contributions of the great medieval theologians such as Aquinas? And what would be left of Western art if it were stripped of its Christian images and themes? It should be noted also that some, such as Stanley Jaki, have argued that Christian theology provided the necessary philosophical resources to make Western science possible, by understanding the world as the *intelligible* product of divine creation.[8]

---

7. Note especially *Gaudium et Spes* 19. "Believers can have more than a little to do with the rise of atheism. To the extent that they are careless about their instruction in the faith, or present its teaching falsely, or even fail in their religious, moral and social life, they must be said to conceal rather than reveal the true nature of God."

8. A thesis propounded with vigor by Stanley L. Jaki, *Science and Creation: From Eternal Cycles to an Oscillating Universe* (Edinburgh: Scottish Academic Press, 1974); see also, more recently, Rodney Stark, *The Victory of Reason: How Christianity Led to Freedom, Capitalism, and Western Success* (New York: Random House, 2005).

We must distinguish two aspects of the cultural dimension of the church, one relating to its own internal culture and other pertaining to the church's engagement with wider cultural issues. These are distinct but not separate, as there can never be a barrier between the meanings and values constitutive of the church's own identity and those of the culture at large.

The first and most obvious element of the internal cultural dimension of the church is its concern for the well-being of the word of God revealed through the Scriptures and incarnated in the life, death, and resurrection of Jesus Christ. From the earliest time the church was concerned to maintain its identity in God's revelation and so acted to correct false teaching and to exclude those who perverted its faith (1 John 2:18-27; 1 Tim 1:3-11). This same concern was maintained through the period of the great church councils, of Nicaea, Constantinople, Chalcedon, and others, where the gathered bishops sought to exclude error and promote the truth of the gospel in a new cultural setting. It was not enough, however, to proclaim truth and reject error. The human mind sought understanding of its faith, and so there developed theology as faith seeking understanding. Again, the early church fathers led the way in providing rich reflections that assisted believers in grappling with the meaning of their faith. However, it was the profound syntheses of the Middle Ages, particularly those of Aquinas, that brought theological reflection to a new level. More recently the emergence of historical consciousness has added a new element to the theological task, placing the revealed word in its historical context, in an effort to exercise greater fidelity to the original meanings of the text. In all this theologians have sought to promote the well-being of the word of God in the life of the church.

However, these reflections went beyond the content of faith to the wider issue of moral living. While the church promotes moral living, as noted above, it has not always been uniform in its vision of what constitutes that morality. When Paul wants to exemplify moral principles he refers not to the Torah alone but to Hellenistic teachings on family and society, teachings that today sound quaint and a bit old-fashioned.[9] Although at one stage the church tolerated slavery (on its reading of Paul's Letter to Philemon) and torture (since Augustine invoked the use of the secular arm on schismatics to "compel them to come in"),[10] now they are pronounced "intrinsically evil."[11] Taking interest

---

9. As Rudolf Schnackenburg notes, the so called "'household codes' . . . reflect a type of admonition already to be found in Judeo-Hellenistic propaganda and in the popular philosophy of paganism . . . although, of course, enlarged and deepened with Christian motives" (*The Moral Teaching of the New Testament*, trans. J. Holland-Smith and W. J. O'Hara [London: Burns & Oates, 1965], 246).

10. See David Bosch, *Transforming Mission: Paradigm Shifts in Theology of Mission* (Maryknoll, N.Y.: Orbis Books, 1991), 219.

11. Slavery and torture are some of a number of sins identified as "intrinsically evil" by Pope John Paul II's encyclical *Veritatis Splendor* (see no. 80).

on a loan was once denounced as usury, but now the Vatican has its own bank. Such shifts should not be seen as evidence that morality is relative, as if there were no moral absolutes. But they should be seen as evidence that our human grasp of what constitutes morality and human flourishing, even within the church, is not absolute and is subject to social and cultural influences beyond the church itself. What is generated by the church is a tradition of moral reasoning that strives to achieve greater and greater clarity on moral issues, and addresses new issues as they arise, often in tentative and provisional ways.[12] Neither should it be thought that this is the task only of priests and theologians, for all members of the church can contribute to the task of moral reflection. Grace may illuminate the path of moral righteousness, but it does not completely dispel the darkness or provide automatic answers. This tradition of moral reasoning stands as a countersign to the diverse, confusing and generally relativistic moral codes and philosophies present in the current cultural environment.

One of the great products of this tradition of moral reasoning has been the natural law tradition in the church. Yet, as is well known, this tradition contains a certain ambiguity in terms of the basic principles. Some read natural law as conformity to nature, as given in our biological constitution; others, such as Thomas Aquinas, read natural law as conformity to the law of reason.[13] There is a certain tension between these two readings of natural law and it reflects the tension between cosmological and anthropological cultural types (see chapter 3). If this is correct then our grasp of the content of natural law will permanently reflect this tension.

These internal aspects of the cultural dimension of the church have an inevitable impact on the wider cultures in which the church finds itself. In its theological and moral reflections, the church has consistently drawn upon the available cultural resources of the day, be they Platonic or Aristotelian philosophies or Stoic morality. However, it never adopts these resources without some form of critical engagement, often transforming them in light of the gospel. In this way the church fulfills the cultural dimension of its mission by seeking to correct various cultural distortions in the prevailing culture.

Further, one does not need to look far to see a variety of cultural distortions crying out for healing. Contemporary philosophy is a grab bag of contradictions and conflicts, of mind-numbing logical technicalities, of directionless debates on ordinary language, of cognitional, epistemological, metaphysical,

---

12. See the many examples in Sean Fagan, *Does Morality Change?* (Collegeville, Minn.: Liturgical Press, 1997).

13. See, for example, Charles Curran, *Themes in Fundamental Moral Theology* (Notre Dame, Ind.: University of Notre Dame Press, 1977), 27-75.

and moral relativisms, and now of postmodern nihilism. As Lonergan complains, "the hopeless tangle ... of the endlessly multiplied philosophies is not merely a cul-de-sac for human progress; it is also a reign of sin, a despotism of darkness; and men are its slaves."[14] Christian faith must engage this reign of sin. As Lonergan has repeatedly argued, Christian revelation contains the seeds of "intellectual conversion,"[15] that is, a philosophical stance that affirms our human orientations toward the true and the good, that human understanding and moral appreciation are adequate to the real, the true, and the good. The Christian message is most at home in such a realist philosophy, as exemplified in the work of Aquinas, and so it elicits and nurtures an intellectual tradition of realism as part of the cultural healing process.[16]

Science too has been brought into disrepute in recent decades. It has increasingly been seen in instrumentalized terms, in the mode of domination and control of the natural world.[17] Science is pressed into the service of short-term economic goals, which demand quick results and no concern for the long-term consequences. No longer is science guided by the free reign of the detached disinterested desire to know; now it is the attached and very interested economic objectives of corporations and states that determine the direction of scientific research, often with military or commercial goals in mind.[18] In a world facing ecological breakdown, one is forced to ask whether science is more the solution or the cause of the problem. But the problem is not science itself; rather it is the distortion of science that results when its proper object, that is, understanding of the natural world for its own sake, is radically

---

14. Bernard J. F. Lonergan, *Insight: A Study of Human Understanding*, ed. Frederick E. Crowe and Robert M. Doran, Collected Works of Bernard Lonergan 3 (Toronto: University of Toronto Press, 1992), 714.

15. For example, Bernard J. F. Lonergan, *Method in Theology* (London: Darton, Longman & Todd, 1972), 243, and more fully idem, "The Origins of Christian Realism," in *A Second Collection: Papers*, ed. William F. Ryan and Bernard Tyrrell (Philadelphia: Westminster, 1975), 239-62.

16. This position has been forcefully reaffirmed in the encyclical *Fides et Ratio*, by John Paul II, which promotes a philosophical realism in the face of the problems of nihilism, skepticism, historicism, and relativism. As with the encyclical *Aeterni Patris*, by Leo XIII, the preeminence of the work of Aquinas is also promoted.

17. See Jürgen Habermas, *Knowledge and Human Interests*, trans. Jeremy J. Shapiro, 2nd ed. (London: Heinemann Educational, 1978), esp. 81-122.

18. According to "Ethics in Science and Scholarship: The Toronto Resolution," *Accountability in Research* 3 (1994): 69-72, around 20 percent of the world's 2.5 million research scientists and engineers work only on military research and development. If only physicists and engineering scientists are included, the percentage is even greater: over 50 percent of the world's research physicists and engineering scientists are military scientists. Further, in the United States, for 1989, the military research and development budget was 66 percent of the total for defense, NIH (Health), NSF (Science), NASA (Space), Energy and Agriculture; it dropped to 50 percent in 1992, with the same level proposed in the 1993 budget. See http://www.math.yorku.ca/sfp/sfp2.html (accessed April 14, 2006).

truncated by economic and other imperatives. There is an underlying philosophical problem, part of the Kantian inheritance, which denies science its proper role by undermining the link between knowledge and reality. Again, a proper Christian realism is needed to reaffirm confidence in human intellect and its intentionality toward reality.

Within this cultural dimension, the work of theologians makes a significant contribution to the mission of the church. Theologians mediate between a culture and the meanings and values of the religious tradition.[19] Their task requires both fidelity to the tradition and openness to the emerging intellectual currents of the present day. There needs to be an ongoing dialogue between theologians and the broader culture, on philosophical, ethical, scientific, and artistic matters. The modern emergence of the social, political, cultural, and psychological sciences raises particular questions for theology. Each of these disciplines, including theology, makes the human its specific field of study, each from its own perspective. If truth is one, if our human reality is meaningful at least to the extent that sin does not undermine it, then the human sciences and theology must become partners in the study of the human, each learning to recognize the expertise and the limitations of the other. Ongoing dialogue is an urgent cultural task if the mission of the church is to embrace this modern development.[20]

All this is not to imply that the church has not itself suffered from these same problems. There are those within the church who have promoted intellectual and moral relativism, not as the problem but as the solution to our current plight. For example, some are embracing postmodern relativism with a passion. Often such a stance is a reaction to the dogmatism of the past, in which "the mantle of religious authority [was spread] over the opinions of ignorant men."[21] Clearly we need to be emancipated from such distortions, but not at the price of intellectual, moral, and religious relativism. There has to be a *via media* between dogmatism and relativism, between mindless conservatism and irresponsible rejection of the past. These are not matters of indifference to a church whose mission includes the cultural dimension of the divinely originated solution to the problem of evil.

---

19. Lonergan, *Method*, xi.

20. One of the limitations of the encyclical *Fides et Ratio* is its framing of the question of the relationship between faith and reason as simply a problem of the relationship between faith and philosophy to the neglect of historical reason and reason in the human and physical sciences. See Neil Ormerod, "A Dialectic Engagement with the Social Sciences in an Ecclesiological Context," *Theological Studies* 66 (2005): 815-40, for a thorough analysis of the relationship between theology and the social sciences.

21. Matthew L. Lamb, *Solidarity with Victims* (New York: Crossroad, 1982), 130, quoting an unpublished paper by Lonergan.

CHURCH—THE SOCIAL DIMENSION

The fragmentation of communities, poverty in the midst of wealth, the break-down in community services, faceless bureaucracies making life-and-death decisions about other people's lives, a faltering economy lurching through cycles of boom and bust and fueled by greed, political instability as a result of a lust for power, these are all symptoms of sin and evil reaching into the social fabric of our human communities. While the origins of these problems may lie in the human heart and they may be rationalized by ideologies that attempt to make them appear "natural"—so much so that we cannot even imagine things being different—still they represent a problem in their own right, one that demands a practical solution in the realm of our social life and organization.

In investigating the social dimension of the church we must again distinguish between the internal social constitution of the church and its interactions with and mission toward the social constitution of the larger society.

Now, if the internal cultural life of the church is mediated through personal transformation (grace and conversion) toward religious, moral, and intellectual integrity by the power of grace, it is even further removed when it comes to the level of social organization. In its own social organization, the church has adopted a variety of social forms: in the Constantinian era it adopted the social forms of the Roman empire; in the Middle Ages it adapted itself to a more feudal model; in an age of absolutism the papacy became the very model of absolute monarchism; in the modern era centralized bureaucratization and models of management have become the norm in the church.[22] And in its own history the church has accommodated itself to a variety of political and economic systems, from totalitarian military regimes with economies of patronage, to liberal democratic capitalist societies: feudal, monarchist, republican, democratic, dictatorial—the church has lived with them all at various times. Now we find the church resisting calls to a greater democratization of its life while simultaneously promoting democracy as a positive value for society as a whole.[23] What are we to make of such flexibility?

The first observation is that there is no divine blueprint spelling out every detail of how the church should organize its own life. History makes a lie of

---

22. A point also made by Edward Schillebeeckx, *Church: The Human Story of God*, trans. John Bowden (New York: Crossroad, 1990), 187-88.

23. See, for example, John Paul II, *Centisimus Annus* 46: "The Church values the democratic system inasmuch as it ensures the participation of citizens in making political choices, guarantees to the governed the possibility both of electing and holding accountable those who govern them, and of replacing them through peaceful means where appropriate."

any such claim. Since the mission of the church is to promote the mediation of grace as the solution to the problem of evil, the social dimension of the church is very likely to reflect the social organization of the prevailing society but transforms it by perhaps removing or at least mitigating its harsher features, or by promoting aspects that the current society neglects, or by providing alternative models for future development that are relatively attainable, and so on. This in fact is a not-inaccurate account of its history. The varieties of forms of socio-politico-economic organization found in human history are both a creative product of human intelligence and a distorted product of human sin. The church should seek to heal distortion and promote creativity, as a model in its own structures and through symbolic activities in the larger community.

These same observations pertain when we consider the church in relation to the organization of society at large. It would seem that there is no single, permanent form of social organization, with fixed political, economic, technological, and communal dimensions which alone is the solution to the problem of people living together in justice and peace. Indeed, technological changes can produce massive upheavals in the possible forms of social organization, and such changes are in principle unpredictable. Types of social organization also depend on factors such as the overall level of wealth, the availability of education and health services and so on, all of which vary over historical time frames. Although we may agree that democracy is better than dictatorship, still there are many forms of democracy, from republican to constitutional monarchies with elected governments, with many different electoral methods from first-past-the-post to preferential voting. Each has its own strengths and weaknesses; each can be improved. But more importantly, none is impervious to the intrusions of evil. Each can be manipulated and distorted to satisfy not the common good but a lust for power and wealth. The church has no detailed blueprint for itself or for the larger society, because there is no unique solution to the problems of social organization.[24]

However, the church does have a special role in relation to those who are victims of the existing social order, those whose rights are denied, who suffer from a systematic exclusion from political power and economic benefits of the social order, or who through contingent circumstances simply cannot cope through illness or other forms of disadvantage. Apart from its commitment

---

24. E. F. Schumacher notes: "Gandhi used to talk disparagingly of 'dreaming of systems so perfect that no one will need to be good'" (*Small Is Beautiful: Economics as if People Mattered* [New York: Harper & Row, 1973], 11). The point is well made. Social ordering of itself cannot solve the problem of evil. On the other hand, severe social disorder shifts the probabilities away from good and toward evil.

to the dignity of every person, the church views the plight of such persons as a barometer of social well-being. These persons measure the success and failure of the social order to achieve its purpose, of living together in justice and peace. In some times and some places all that might be possible is the piecemeal distribution of food or other basic goods. In other times and places the church might take on a prophetic role to speak for these people and promote a more just social order. In one way or another, the church's stance to people in such a plight is a litmus test of its fidelity to its mission.[25]

Clearly the church is most visible at the level of its social organization. The structures of parish and diocese, of schools and hospitals, of social welfare bodies and charities manifest the life of the church at its most evident, visible, and effective. For most Christians, local parish communities are their first and most influential exposure to the Christian message. With the support of these communities, as a social extension of their family life, they strive to grow in grace and wisdom in the sight of the Lord. They are baptized and confirmed, celebrate the eucharist, and often are married and buried within the life of a parish community. Still, while participation in the life of the local parish community is the starting point for most of their Christian life, the goal of that life terminates not in such participation but in sharing the mission of Jesus by overcoming evil through redemptive suffering. That goal may be achieved through a substantial commitment to the ongoing ordering of the life of the community, as is found in ordained ministry, but in general that goal transcends churchly commitments and moves out into the world, into the world of politics and economics, of education and academy, and the moral struggles attendant on family, work, and life commitments. Indeed, Vatican II and more recently Pope John Paul II have identified this "secular" realm as "properly and particularly that of the lay faithful" (*Christfideles Laici* 15; *Lumen Gentium* 32).

CHURCH AND EUCHARIST

Cultural anthropologists have long identified the prevalence of ritual among so-called primitive peoples of the world. Ritual is an essential element of such cultures, giving shape and meaning to life, marking out the key transitions of birth, puberty, marriage, and death, placing the life of the tribe within a larger cosmic significance. Philosopher Ernst Cassirer refers to human beings as

---

25. One could note the number of saints and founders of religious orders who have had a special commitment to the poor, e.g., St. Francis of Assisi, St. John Baptist de la Salle, Edmund Rice, Blessed Mary McKillop, and Blessed Mother Teresa of Calcutta. This same commitment is evident today in various missionaries in Latin American, Africa, and Asia.

"symbolic animals"[26] for despite the rise of modern science and technology, we still need ritual and symbol to help us give meaning to our lives, to situate the key events of our lives within a larger account of human existence. Often our modern use of ritual and symbol is more attenuated, more self-conscious, less assured than that of simpler cultures. But the need for ritual and symbol is intrinsically human.

Our need for symbol and ritual is not just a primitive leftover from an earlier age. Rather, it reflects the fact that we are not pure intellects, nor are we mindless animals. We are embodied souls, an underlying unity of body and soul, searching for direction in the movement of life. Symbols that have a significant imaginative component are also involved in mediating both meaning and feeling into our consciousness. As theologian Bernard Lonergan puts it, "It is through symbols that mind and body, mind and heart, heart and body communicate." This internal communication of body, mind, and heart, of image, meaning, and feeling, has a liberating potential that can help us enter into a new horizon, a new world of meanings and values. Symbols help mediate, create, and sustain that new world of meanings and values. On an individual basis, this is the foundation of psychoanalysis with its focus on the personal symbols that emerge in our dreams. On a communal and social basis, our symbols and rituals tend more to be grounded in our common history; the symbols and rituals seek to ground a common identity, a common set of meanings and values that identify who we are, which then shapes our allegiances.

According to a Catholic worldview, our understanding of the sacraments is an extension of this human need for symbol and ritual. Augustine defined a sacrament as a "visible sign of an invisible grace." "Visible sign" we can take as shorthand for the importance of symbol and ritual in our human living. And it is not just the "visibility" but the audibility, the taste, the aroma, and the physical sensations that impinge on our senses. As the Psalmist says, "taste and see that the Lord is good" (Ps 34:8). The visibility of the sacrament encompasses all our senses and initiates the internal communication of which Lonergan speaks. Similarly, the notion of "invisible grace" can be taken as shorthand for the new world of meanings and values that the sacrament seeks to mediate. These meanings and values are an invitation to enter into a world where God's love is the primary reality of our lives; they help shape our thoughts and feelings around that reality so that it reaches to every aspect of our lives; they sustain us in this new world and strengthen our commitment to it. This is most evident in our Sunday liturgy where we place our sacramen-

---

26. See http://plato.stanford.edu/entries/cassirer/ (accessed April 14, 2006).

tal celebration of the eucharist within a framework of prayer, Scripture reading, and preaching, which mutually reinforce the new world of meaning and value that God is seeking to create in our midst.

The Second Vatican Council described the eucharist as the source and summit of the life of the church (*Sacrosanctum Concilium* 10). The celebration of the eucharistic liturgy is the most visible and constant act of the ecclesial community, whereby the members of the church are brought together in a common expression of their true identity as believers and followers of Jesus Christ. It should not therefore be surprising to find the various dimensions of the church identified above reflected in the liturgical celebration of the eucharist.

RELIGIOUS AND MORAL DIMENSION[27]

We have already discussed the death of Jesus under the rubric of "sacrifice" and noted the ambiguity of this form of language. Drawing on the insights of René Girard, we identified a dual language of sacrifice, whereby Jesus is both the victim of human sinfulness and the one offering himself in obedience to the Father as completion of his mission of love. Here I would like to suggest that the religious language of sacrifice is an effective way of capturing the religious and moral dimensions of the eucharistic celebration.

Let us begin, then, with the Last Supper. It is clear that by the time of that final meal Jesus knew that his fate was sealed and that his final confrontation with evil was imminent. There was no escaping the compulsive sacrificial violence at the hands of his enemies if he was to remain faithful to his mission from the Father. In light of the mindless violence that threatened to overtake and consume him Jesus sought a way to give meaning to what would otherwise appear a meaningless death. Summing up his whole mission to the lost sheep of Israel (Matt 15:24), his mission of healing and preaching of forgiveness, of turning the other cheek (Matt 5:39; Luke 6:29), of forgiving not seven times but seventy-seven times (Matt 18:22), of going the extra mile (Matt 5:41), of loving and praying for one's enemies (Matt 5:44; Luke 6:27), he took bread and wine and made of them a symbolic prophetic action of his life and impending death. Through that sacrament he revealed to the disciples the meaning he gave to his life and, more particularly, to his death, the meaning of sacrificial love made in the face of sacrificial violence. In doing so Jesus enacted and revealed God's response to sin and evil in human history. God's

---

27. Material in this section has appeared in modified form in Neil Ormerod, "Eucharist as Sacrifice," in *The Eucharist: Faith and Worship*, ed. Margaret Press (Homebush: St Pauls, 2001), 42-55.

solution to evil is not that it be destroyed or overcome through greater violence or power. Rather, it is transformed through self-sacrificing love into a gracious moment of forgiveness and conversion—"Father, forgive them; for they do not know what they are doing" (Luke 23:34). The violence of evil is exposed and the possibility of its healing is graciously outpoured.

So Jesus is both victim and priest (DS 1739-41). As victim he suffers grievously at the hands of his executioners. Moreover, as victim he identifies himself with all the victims of human history. As we see in the judgment scene in Matthew's Gospel, "just as you did it to one of the least of these who are members of my family, you did it to me" (Matt 25:40). He invites us to recognize in ourselves our own most victimized part, so that, like the good Samaritan, who could recognize himself in the broken body of a Jew on the roadside, we too might be moved to compassion for the victims of violence and greed in the world. As priest he offers himself in the face of violence, to break down its endless spiral, by freely embracing his victimhood. If Jesus were simply a victim of such sacrifice he would be one more in a long line of such victims of violence. What transforms this act of sacrifice is the fact of Jesus' "priesthood," Jesus' act of self-sacrificing love, which transforms his death into the life-giving Spirit active through his resurrection

Now much has been written and will continue to be written about the real presence of Jesus in the eucharist and the suitability of denoting the eucharistic change as transubstantiation. No doubt this is an important discussion and a significant aspect of Catholic faith, as defined at the Council of Trent (DS 1636, 1642). Yet this discussion can only be preparatory to a further question as to the manner of Jesus' presence in the eucharist. Is Jesus present as the glorious risen Lord of history? Or as the promised Son of Man coming in judgment of sinful humanity? Or is there another manner of presence that Jesus manifests to us in the eucharist? Here the uniform presupposition of the bishops of Trent can be summarized in the words of Pius XII in his encyclical *Mediator Dei*: "at the words of consecration Christ is made present upon the altar *in the state of victim*" (DS 3850 [emphasis added]). It is as victim—risen, yes, but still bearing the wounds of the cross—that Jesus is made present in the eucharist.

As victim he confronts us with both our own acts of victimization and with the vulnerable, broken, and bruised part of ourselves, our own innermost victim. In the terms of the parable of the good Samaritan (Luke 10:25-37), he is not the priest or the Levite who walk on the other side; nor is he the helpful stranger, the good Samaritan; no, he is the one broken by the roadside, beaten by brigands. He is the woman caught in adultery, the scapegoat of a crowd's angry self-righteousness (John 8:1-11). He is the hungry and thirsty one, the stranger seeking comfort, the one without clothes and shelter, sick and imprisoned (Matt 25:31-46). In our own day she is the victim of sexual violence, in the family or the church; he is an impoverished African owing first world bankers more than he could ever earn in a dozen lifetimes. His face is ever changing, but his plight is always the same. And as Matthew's Gospel reminds us, it is on the basis of our attitudes and actions toward him as victim that we will ourselves be judged (Matt 25:31-46).

In terms of our own acts of victimization, the eucharistic presence of Jesus as victim calls us to repentance and conversion. It is a continual call to compassion for the victim and a challenge to put an end to all sacrifice, to truly make the sacrifice of Jesus once for all (Rom 6:10; Heb 7:27; 9:26). In terms of our own innermost victim, the eucharistic presence of Jesus is one of healing solidarity. As victim Jesus identifies with that broken part of ourselves and offers us his healing love. In hope he leads us forward to the time when our own innermost victim will be able to rise again to full life, as Jesus did in the resurrection. In this way through our participation with the sacrifice of the eucharist we can partake in the fruits of the life, death, and resurrection of Jesus. In this way the eucharist captures the essence of the religious and moral dimensions of the life of the church.

THE CULTURAL DIMENSION OF EUCHARIST

The liturgical celebration of the eucharist cannot be reduced to the consecration and reception of the sacrament. These elements are embedded in a ritual setting that creates a new world of meaning for those who participate. Through the prayers of the liturgy, the reading of Scripture, the singing of hymns and psalms, the celebration of the eucharist becomes a platform for informing a worldview, shaping the ways we think and feel about our faith, our interactions with others, the world in which we live. All these elements reflect meanings and value shaped and informed by our Christian faith, a living tradition of faith. There is one element of the liturgy, however, that has the specific task of moving from this Christian worldview to the life situation of its audience, the task of mediating between Christian meanings and values and the dominant cultural meanings and values of the particular situation in which the liturgy is celebrated. This element is the homily: "By means of the homily the mysteries of the faith and the guiding principles of the Christian life are expounded from the sacred text, during the course of the liturgical year; the homily, therefore, is to be highly esteemed as part of the liturgy itself ... it should not be omitted except for a serious reason" (*Sacrosanctum Concilium* 52).

Throughout the centuries the homily has been the means whereby the

Christian message has been "translated" into the language and context of the day. We can still refer to the great homilies of the early church fathers as they struggled with the various heresies of their day. More recently we have had the homilies of Pope John Paul II and Archbishop Oscar Romero as examples of mediating the Gospel message to the culture of the day. Let us consider the example of Romero and his outspoken homilies, which led eventually to his martyrdom at the altar of a hospital chapel, while saying Mass.

Romero carried out his ministry during a time of brutal oppression in El Salvador. Those who stood up for the rights of the poor, for justice for the workers, met with frequent violence and at times death. Though Romero was from a conservative background, his perspective underwent a radical change when his friend Jesuit priest Rutilio Grande was killed for his opposition to the repressive government and his fight for the rights of the poor. Romero himself then became an outspoken champion for the rights of the poor, which led eventually to his own death (March 24, 1980).[28]

Romero's homilies are a lesson in mediating the gospel message into a context of injustice and violence. On the one hand, he emphasizes the importance of working for peace and adopting the methods of nonviolence. On the other, he identifies the injustices that ravaged his country and demanded action to set them right. At a time when to speak of the rights of the poor was to be labeled a communist, he highlighted the greater danger of capitalism: "But there is an 'atheism' that is closer at hand [than Marxism] and more dangerous to our church. It is the atheism of capitalism, in which material possessions are set up as idols and take God's place."[29] He rejected a purely spiritualized form of the gospel that refused to be concerned with the plight of the poor and suffering:

> It is very easy to be servants of the word without disturbing the world: a very spiritualized word, a word without any commitment to history, a word that can sound in any part of the world because it belongs to no part of the world. A word like that creates no problems, starts no conflicts. What starts conflicts and persecutions, what marks the genuine church, is the word that, burning like the word of the prophets, proclaims and accuses: proclaims to the people God's wonders to be believed and venerated, and accuses of sin those who oppose God's reign, so that they may tear that sin out of their hearts, out of their societies, out of their laws—out of the struc-

---

28. For a full account of the life of Romero, see James R. Brockman, *Romero: A Life* (Maryknoll, N.Y.: Orbis Books, 2005).

29. Homily on November 15, 1978, available at http://www.justpeace.org/romero2.htm (accessed July 3, 2006).

tures that oppress, that imprison, that violate the rights of God and of humanity.[30]

Romero clearly identified the evil that was dominating his community. He brought the power of the gospel to bear on that evil through his eucharistic homilies, which mediated gospel meanings and values to the heart of the context of his community. He did so without fear or favor and eventually he paid the price with his life.

Of course this was an extreme context of violence and oppression. Still the homily remains for many people the only time in which they can hear the gospel translated into the context of their lives. This is not an accidental aspect of the eucharistic liturgy but intrinsic to its full articulation as our participation in the saving mystery of Jesus.

THE SOCIAL DIMENSION OF EUCHARIST

Just as the cultural dimension of the eucharist presumes a community of meaning shaped by the prayers, Scripture readings, and homily of the liturgy, so too the social dimension presumes an actual community that gathers, prays, listens, and seeks to build a common life of justice integrity and peace. It is easy to idealize the communal life of the Christian community such as we find in Acts 4:32-35, and we know that the actuality often falls far short of the ideal. A good illustration of this can be found in the first letter of Paul to the Corinthians. Paul is writing to a community that is experiencing deep divisions and conflicts over a number of issues—disputes over food offered for sacrifice (1 Cor 8:1-12), over liturgical practices involving women (11:2-16), over immoral conduct of its members (5:1-13), over the place of marriage (7:1-16), over apostolic authority (9:1-27), over divisions between rich and poor at the eucharistic table (11:17-34). These disputes were obviously quite heated, and Paul invokes all manner of techniques, from cajoling to assertions of apostolic authority, to get the community back on track. The popular notion of some type of idyllic, loving, peaceful community at the beginning of Christianity is, on this evidence, an idealistic fantasy.

As Paul's letter informs us, within this difficult community the celebration of the eucharist was a serious problem. Rather than being a source of unity, the celebration had become a scandal of division. What was the problem that Paul identifies? Basically that the rich were eating their fill, while the poor

---

30. Homily on December 10, 1977, available at http://www.justpeace.org/romero4.htm (accessed July 3, 2006).

were getting nothing: "For when the time comes to eat, each of you goes ahead with your own supper, and one goes hungry and another becomes drunk" (11:21). Faced with this scandal, Paul admonishes them, pointing out that by embarrassing the poor—"do you show contempt for the church of God and humiliate those who have nothing?" (11:22)—they are failing to "discern" the body of Christ—"all who eat and drink without discerning the body, eat and drink judgment against themselves" (11:29). In this way they can be numbered "among those who murdered Jesus":[31] "Whoever, therefore, eats the bread or drinks the cup of the Lord in an unworthy manner will be answerable for the body and blood of the Lord" (11:27). This is strong condemnation indeed.

Paul is arguing that in shaming the poor the Corinthians are invalidating their eucharistic practice: "When you come together, it is not really to eat the Lord's supper" (11:20). In shaming the poor they have the blood of Jesus on their hands. Does this mean that Jesus is sacrificed again by the failures of the community in Corinth? Yes and no. Certainly not in the sense that Jesus suffers on the cross again, but in the sense that the meaning Jesus gives to his death, as expressed in the Last Supper, is invalidated by their actions. Jesus' sacrifice is once for all. Inasmuch as we continue to sacrifice the poor, as did the community in Corinth, we ignore the moral imperative of the Last Supper: "Do this as a memorial of me"; that is, be agents of self-sacrificing love, not of other-sacrificing violence and greed. The "once for all" is a moral imperative to the whole Christian community. The sacrifice of Jesus is meant to put an end to all sacrifice, and Christian communities are meant to be antisacrificial, in the sense of putting an end to all acts of victimization.

In this snapshot from the early church we can grasp something of the significance of the social dimension of the eucharist. There is a certain realism that recognizes that the life of the Christian community will not completely transform society, at least not immediately. However, the normal distinctions and divisions that may exist in the wider social order should not be carried over into the community's celebration of the eucharist. On the other hand, there may be instances when the actions of some members of the community are so beyond the bonds of Christian community that such people should be excluded from the community's celebration of the eucharist. Paul himself had such a case when a man and his mother-in-law were living as husband and wife, a scandal "not found even among the pagans" (1 Cor 5:1). These people were to be excluded from the community. A more recent example is that encountered in some Latin American countries where people who were

---

31. Jerome Murphy-O'Connor, "The First Letter to the Corinthians," *The New Jerome Biblical Commentary*, ed. Raymond E. Brown et al. (Englewood Cliffs, N.J.: Prentice Hall, 1990), 810.

known to have been torturers working for repressive governments were also members of the church. To engage in torture is the very antithesis of the meaning of the eucharist.[32] Far from working toward the end of victimhood, the torturer is actively engaged in creating new victims with scant regard for justice and human dignity. The church has no option but to exclude such people from their eucharistic celebration until they truly repent of their previous actions. Indeed churches in various Latin American countries did formally excommunicate those involved in torture on behalf of repressive governments.[33]

CONCLUSION

In this chapter we have considered the various dimensions of the mission of the church and how these are manifested in its eucharistic celebration. We have paid particular attention to the challenges that the church's mission presents to us personally, culturally, and socially. Still we know that we and others often fail to meet that challenge, and then we are faced with the problems of forgiveness and reconciliation. This too is an important element of the mission of Jesus, which we shall take up in the next chapter.

QUESTIONS FOR REFLECTION

1. The text above states that "the study of the church (ecclesiology) is the prolongation of the theology of grace into human history." How does this help us better to understand the nature of the church?
2. People today often say "Jesus, yes; church, no." How much is the church essential to the fulfillment of the mission of Jesus? How essential are the institutional aspects of the church to that fulfillment?
3. Vatican II speaks of the eucharist as the "source and summit" of our Christian life. In what sense is it the "source," and in what sense the "summit"?
4. It is sometimes said that the eucharist is incomplete everywhere in the world as long as anyone is hungry anywhere in the world, and Ghandi once said: "There is so much hunger in the world that God could appear only in the form of bread." How does this help us better understand the implications of our eucharistic celebrations?

---

32. Similar comments could be made about those who perpetrate sexual abuse, particularly of minors. As with torture, it is the antithesis of the meaning of eucharist. That various church officials have failed to recognize this is a major scandal.

33. For an account of the situation in Chile during the reign of Augusto Pinochet, see William T. Cavanaugh, *Torture and Eucharist: Theology, Politics, and the Body of Christ* (Oxford: Blackwell, 1998).

SUGGESTIONS FOR FURTHER READING AND STUDY

Bosch, David. *Transforming Mission: Paradigm Shifts in Theology of Mission*. Maryknoll, N.Y.: Orbis Books, 1991.

Brockman, James R. *Romero: A Life*. Maryknoll, N.Y.: Orbis Books, 2005.

Fuellenbach, John. *The Kingdom of God: The Message of Jesus Today*. Maryknoll, N.Y.: Orbis Books, 1995.

Lamb, Matthew L. *Solidarity with Victims*. New York: Crossroad, 1982.

Lonergan, Bernard J. F. "The Origins of Christian Realism." In *Second Collection*, edited by William F. Ryan and Bernard Tyrrell, 239-62. Toronto: University of Toronto Press, 1996.

Meyer, Ben. *The Early Christians: Their World Mission and Self-Discovery*. Wilmington, Del.: Michael Glazier, 1986.

Ormerod, Neil. "A Dialectic Engagement with the Social Sciences in an Ecclesiological Context." *Theological Studies* 66 (2005): 815-40.

———. "Eucharist as Sacrifice." In *The Eucharist: Faith and Worship*, edited by Margaret Press, 42-55. Homebush: St Pauls, 2001.

Stark, Rodney. *The Victory of Reason: How Christianity Led to Freedom, Capitalism, and Western Success*. New York: Random House, 2005.

8

Forgiveness and Reconciliation

THE ABILITY TO FORGIVE is often thought of as the paradigmatic example of Christian virtue. The teaching of Jesus is full of exhortations to forgive. When asked by Peter whether he should forgive seven times, Jesus responds by saying that he should forgive seventy-seven times (Matt 18:21-22). The parable of the unforgiving debtor is a powerful statement that we must forgive our brothers or face the consequences (Matt 18:23-35). On the other hand, the parable of the prodigal son is an equally powerful expression of the forgiveness of God (Luke 15:11-35). Perhaps most tellingly Jesus pronounces forgiveness from the cross to those who have executed him, "Father, forgive them; for they do not know what they are doing" (Luke 23:34). Finally the risen Jesus breathes forth his Spirit on the disciples, empowering them to forgive, "If you forgive the sins of any, they are forgiven them" (John 20:22-23).

It all seems so simple that one might wonder what all the fuss is about. For many people, however, particularly those who have survived sexual or physical abuse as children, forgiveness is far from a simple matter. Not only have they suffered the immediate effects of the abuse, but for decades after the event they continue to suffer from a variety of effects, such as self-hatred, guilt, suicidal thoughts, and depression, all symptoms of posttraumatic stress. To suggest to people who have suffered in this way that they should just forgive the perpetrators of this abuse can seem like an insult designed to minimize their sufferings and to protect the perpetrator from the consequences of his actions.[1]

Beyond the acute sufferings of individuals, there are the historical sufferings of oppressed peoples, sufferings whose origins have been lost in history but whose memories have been kept alive by continued repetition of acts of violence and revenge. These cycles of violence weave a fatal mix of hatred and retribution, of guilt and responsibility that become impossible to unpick. What does forgiveness mean to "Catholic" republicans and "Protestant" unionists in Northern Ireland? Or to Israelis and Palestinians in the Middle

---

1. The use of the male pronoun is deliberate, as most perpetrators of sexual and physical abuse are male.

East? Who should take the first step and how should one respond to it? And even in cases where guilt and responsibility are relatively clear-cut—for example, the Holocaust during the Second World War—do current generations bear guilt for the acts of their ancestors, and what does forgiveness mean for a generation now dead?

In light of such situations the Christian preaching on forgiveness suddenly becomes much more complex. In this chapter we shall explore some of that complexity as it relates in the first place to the situation of the individual victim of the sin of another, and then move on to consider the more complex matters of historical and social victimization. Finally, we shall consider a theological understanding of reconciliation in light of the saving work of Jesus.

FORGIVENESS AND THE INDIVIDUAL

All of us are called to forgive others for the countless minor inconveniences and irritations of everyday life. This person speaks too loudly; another does not attend to personal hygiene, while a third never listens to what I am saying. All this is part of the stuff of life, coping with the limitations and shortcomings of others. Imagine what life would be like if we could not forgive these, if each such encounter led to growing hostility and eventual violence. The very fabric of society would be torn apart if we were not able to transcend such minor irritations.

There are other situations, however, that are much more difficult to deal with. Take a case—sadly not so uncommon—of a person sexually abused as a child. The abuser may be a father, an older brother, an uncle, a grandfather, or a trusted person such as a priest or a scout leader. They are persons of relative power (parental relationship, age difference, position of respect), who know that their power will protect them from being revealed. Their victim will not be believed and can easily be manipulated through threats and fear not to say anything. Silence is the perpetrator's greatest ally. The memory of that abuse may even be suppressed or denied,[2] but it emerges in midlife, bringing with it all the symptoms of posttraumatic stress—depression, suicidal thoughts, nightmares, flashbacks, panic attacks, and so on. Self-esteem plummets and the victim's world begins to fall apart. A victim begins to realize the horror of the abuse that has been perpetrated. A victim's whole life has been shaped by the abuse: educational opportunities, patterns of substance abuse, choice of

---

2. This is not the place to enter into debate about the issue of false memories of abuse. I assume that there can be false memories of abuse, but there can also be false denials by abusers. Not all memories are false, just as not all denials are true.

partners (often abusive men or women who replicate patterns of the early abuse), employment history—all have been affected by early childhood abuse. Victims start to name their abuse, and their abuser, as the source of the tragedy of their lives. Enormous anger can well up in victims, a reactive anger at all that has been taken from them by their abuse.[3]

One of the most frequent responses to this new-found voice of the victim, particularly in Christian circles, is the call to forgive the perpetrator. Forgive and forget; put the past behind you; look at how upset you have made your (alleged!) perpetrator; why are you making up these stories about him? You'll ruin his life, his career, and what about all the good things he has done for you and others? And all this anger is so destructive. It is not Christian to be so angry! In such circumstances, we have to ask, Is it the Christian thing to forgive? And what might forgiveness mean?

Of course, it is easy to cite any number of scriptural texts that speak of the importance of forgiveness. In fact it is a constant theme in the Gospels. The case may look open and clear-cut that the victim should forgive the perpetrator. Nonetheless, many of these texts on forgiveness deserve a closer look. Jesus begins his mission with a message of repentance and conversion, not forgiveness (Mark 1:15). Many of the parables that Jesus relates about forgiveness contain elements of relative power difference. In these parables the direction of forgiveness is from the more powerful to the less powerful. The father forgives the prodigal son, while the older brother withholds his forgiveness through resentment (Luke 15:11-32). When Jesus himself forgives, it is viewed as signifying his own power and authority (Mark 2:5-12). Further, when the early Christian community is dealing with the sins of one of its members, it may confront the sinner with his actions and offer forgiveness, but forgiveness itself is dependent on the repentance of the sinner (Luke 17:4). And Jesus keeps his most strident criticisms for religious leaders who fail to show mercy to the people they lead (Matt 23:23).

This puts a different slant on the position of the victim of sin that we speak of in our examples above. The perpetrator was a powerful figure in the life of his victim. In the complex process of recovery from abuse, the original dynamics of the relationship can easily recur—the victim feels powerless in relation to the perpetrator; the victim feels once more like the child who suffered abuse, afraid and defenseless. It is often not difficult to manipulate such a person into forgiving the perpetrator. The slightest sign of remorse (as dis-

---

3. See Janet Pais, *Suffer the Children: A Theology of Liberation by a Victim of Child Abuse* (New York: Paulist Press, 1991), for a fulsome and theologically insightful account of the effects of child abuse and the processes of recovery.

tinct from genuine repentance),[4] and the victim may be more than willing to forgive simply to put the whole matter behind him or her. The victim still feels under the power of the perpetrator, whose needs and feelings are paramount, while the victim's feelings count for nothing. Under such circumstances the suggestion and at times even the demand to forgive the perpetrator amount to little more than a repetition of the original abuse. It is a way of silencing the victim and preserving the power and privilege of the perpetrator.

Further, the perpetrator may have no intention of repenting in such a circumstance. For whatever reason—his own history of abuse and suffering may be a mitigating factor—the perpetrator is held in the power of his own sinfulness.[5] Quick forgiveness provides an easy escape for the perpetrator from taking responsibility for his actions or from the demands of conversion. In fact, he may not even be interested in accepting forgiveness, because to accept forgiveness would be to acknowledge his own sinfulness and abuse of his victim. This is the last thing he is interested in acknowledging. His whole life has been built on the lie of his own invulnerability, his own ability to control his victims' reactions. His acceptance of his victims' accusations would demolish his world, and his achievements would be exposed as built of the sufferings of his victims.

There is a further complication when the perpetrator of the abuse is dead. The perpetrator thus escapes from responsibility and the demands of repentance. Under such circumstances, what does it mean to forgive someone who has never asked for forgiveness and can no longer effectively repent of his sins? Under these circumstances the Christian message of forgiveness needs careful nuancing. For the victim it can easily lead to a revictimization, a repetition of the original experience of the abuse. Are these really the outcomes Jesus expects with his emphasis on forgiveness? Or have we misread this teaching or misplaced its emphasis?

I would argue that there are sufficient grounds in the scriptural material to distinguish between an act of forgiveness as gracious condescension from above—that is, from the more powerful to the less powerful, as when God forgives us—and the very different experience and context of the situation of the less powerful who is sinned against by a more powerful figure. The more powerful figure may not ask for forgiveness, may not even acknowledge that he has done anything wrong. He may even reject such a suggestion out of

---

4. As a colleague once stated to me, remorse is what you feel in the back of the police car. It is not the same as genuine repentance, which seeks to make reparation. Remorse is more a matter of suffering and pain at being exposed for one's action.

5. Such mitigation is real but does not absolve the perpetrator, just as we all remain responsible for our sins, despite the mitigation due to the "sin of Adam."

hand. In such a context the Christian message of forgiveness might mean something completely different.

In the first place, it will not mean any action that diminishes or minimizes the actions of the more powerful perpetrator. A movement toward forgiveness can occur only where the truth of the plight of the victim, the one who is less powerful, is clearly acknowledged and accepted. Anything less than this will effectively revictimize the victim and is fundamentally unacceptable. God does not ask the victim to prolong his or her suffering. God asks the perpetrator to acknowledge his sins. When slapped in the face by the high priest's guard, Jesus does not rush to forgive. He confronts the one who assaults him with the truth of his action: "If there is something wrong in what I say, point it out. Otherwise, why do you strike me?" (John 18:23).

In the second place, the victim of sin is not responsible for the plight of the perpetrator once he has been exposed. The fact that the perpetrator's world is falling apart, that he is suffering from shame and remorse, is not the fault or responsibility of the victim who names the abuse and speaks the truth. The sufferings of the perpetrator are the simple consequence of his own sinfulness. God is handing him over to the divine wrath (Rom 1:18-32), from which he can escape only through an act of genuine repentance. The victim cannot be called upon to alleviate the suffering of the perpetrator if this means silencing the victim or denying the truth of the abuse.

In the third place, it may occur that in some cases the pattern of perpetrator and victim is reversed when the victim makes the abuse public, names it, and identifies the abuser. There may be a significant shift in the power relationship between the two. The heart of the victim may become full of hate and driven by revenge. The victim may seek to extract suffering on the basis of "eye for eye, tooth for tooth" (Exod 21:24). Certainly the Christian message of forgiveness is not compatible with such an outcome. Far more common, however, is the situation where the supporters of the perpetrator rally around him, protect and support him. All the attention and care are directed toward the perpetrator of abuse, because this is the nature of social power. To believe that a powerful person is capable of doing great harm means that our world is unsafe. There is a socially driven imperative to believe that powerful persons are worthy of our esteem. Powerful people continue to be trusted even after their abusive actions have been made public. The victim, on the other hand, does not experience the support and protection of the community. In such a situation, the simple request of the victim for acknowledgment on the part of the perpetrator will be viewed as an act of revenge. Such a construal should not be accepted.

Finally, there does come a time when the victim of sin needs to move on. There is a danger that victims adopt their status as victim as a permanent "get out of jail free" card. They act as if they deserve everyone's sympathy and solicitation forever; their needs are paramount and no one else's really matter. To go down this track is for them to become abusive in their relationships with others. Even where the perpetrator is not even asking for forgiveness, there needs to be a movement in the heart of the victim to let go of the past. Just as the suffering of an exposed perpetrator is not the responsibility of the victim, neither is the perpetrator's continued hardness of heart. The movement needed in the victim cannot be dependent on any repentance on the part of the perpetrator. Forgiveness in such a circumstance may amount to no more than a handing over to God, an act that has more to do with releasing the victim from the past than it has to do with the plight of the perpetrator. However, the timing of such a movement is a complex question of the interaction of human freedom and divine graciousness acting to heal the victim of sin. It has its own rhythms, which resist any external control.[6] It cannot be dictated to or imposed by those outside. It may take years to achieve.

At the least I hope this material suggests that the simple message of forgiveness is not as simple as it might seem. To suggest immediately that someone needs to forgive the one who has sinned against him or her may not be the most helpful suggestion, nor is it the most "Christian" thing to do. We need to look not only at the sin but at the relative power difference between sinner and sinned against. We must attend to the psychological dynamics involved, in both sinner and sinned against. Grace completes and perfects nature, but it is no magical solution to the patient unfolding of forgiveness and healing in the cases we have considered above.

SOCIAL AND POLITICAL DIMENSIONS OF RECONCILIATION

We shall now turn our attention to the more complex question of reconciliation, where we are dealing not just with individual abuse or injustice, but large-scale social and political violence perpetrated over some generations. What does the Christian message of forgiveness and reconciliation mean in these circumstances? Let us consider the example of South Africa.

For decades the people of South Africa lived in a regime that actively sanctioned racial discrimination against black African and "colored" people (i.e., generally those of of Indian or mixed descent). This system of "apartheid," or separate development, led to the segregation of the races, unequal access to

---

6. Robert M. Doran notes that "the healing that is mediated by such love [i.e., human love mediating the love of God] has a rhythm that is far beyond the control of the one who loves" (*Theology and the Dialectics of History* [Toronto: University of Toronto Press, 1990], 244).

education and heath services, and a lack of economic opportunities for the majority of people, creating situations of poverty and violence in the appalling conditions of the "black homelands." Over decades resistance to this regime grew both internally and internationally. Those who opposed the regime internally, people such as Nelson Mandela and other members of the African National Congress (ANC), were imprisoned or died in unusual circumstances (for example, the case of anti-apartheid activist Steve Biko, who died in prison in 1977[7]). Nonetheless, internal armed struggle and external sanctions combined to bring down the apartheid regime and replace it with a black majority government elected by the whole populace. The formerly oppressed majority were now to be given the reins of power. How would they respond to their former oppressors?

History is littered with examples of the oppressed becoming in their turn the oppressors of their former enemies. Too often violence begets violence, spiraling into generations of suffering, revenge, and hatred. The new black majority government, under the inspirational leadership of Nelson Mandela, was determined to avoid the cycle of recrimination and revenge that so often accompanied such a historical transformation. The government established a Truth and Reconciliation Commission. The aims of the commission, established by an act of the South African Parliament were as follows:

to promote national unity and reconciliation in a spirit of understanding which transcends the conflicts and divisions of the past by:

(a) establishing as complete a picture as possible of the causes, nature and extent of the gross violations of human rights which were committed during the period from 1 March 1960 to the cut-off date, including the antecedents, circumstances, factors and context of such violations, as well as the perspectives of the victims and the motives and perspectives of the persons responsible for the commission of the violations, by conducting investigations and holding hearings;

(b) facilitating the granting of amnesty to persons who make full disclosure of all the relevant facts relating to acts associated with a political objective and comply with the requirements of this Act;

(c) establishing and making known the fate or whereabouts of victims and by restoring the human and civil dignity of such victims by granting them an opportunity to relate their own accounts of the violations of which they are the victims, and by recommending reparation measures in respect of them;

---

7. See http://www.sahistory.org.za/pages/people/biko,s.htm (accessed July 3, 2006), for an account of his life and death.

(d) compiling a report providing as comprehensive an account as possible of the activities and findings of the Commission contemplated in paragraphs (a), (b) and (c), and which contains recommendations of measures to prevent the future violations of human rights.[8]

The commission operated through three committees:

1. The *Human Rights Violations Committee* whose task it was to "investigate human rights abuses that took place between 1960 and 1994 . . . [to] establish the identity of the victims, their fate or present whereabouts . . . the nature and extent of the harm they have suffered; and whether the violations were the result of deliberate planning by the state or any other organization, group or individual."

2. The *Reparation and Rehabilitation Committee* whose task was to "provide victim support to ensure that the Truth Commission process restores victims' dignity . . . to formulate policy proposals and recommendations on rehabilitation and healing of survivors, their families and communities at large . . . to ensure non-repetition, healing and healthy co-existence."

3. The *Amnesty Committee* whose task was to "consider that applications for amnesty were done in accordance with the provisions of the Act . . . being granted amnesty for an act means that the perpetrator is free from prosecution for that particular act."[9]

What we find in this process is a powerful recognition of the need for social reconciliation together with an effective mechanism for achieving this goal. It is important here to distinguish between the personal needs of individuals affected by the abuses of apartheid, such as the needs we have identified above in the previous section of this chapter, and the needs of the community as a whole. The processes of the Truth and Reconciliation Commission were not based on the repentance of the perpetrators of abuse. Many came forward to gain amnesty who displayed no real repentance, their arrogance unbroken. The aim of the process was not their repentance, but the telling of the truth of what happened. What had been done in the darkness was to be brought to light. The truth was to be brought out into the open. Often this involved relatives discovering for the first time the fate of their loved ones. Some of the stories were so horrific that those who sat on the commission wept. And sometimes the process did seem to bring about genuine conversion on the part

---

8. Promotion of National Unity and Reconciliation Act, 1995, from http://www.doj.gov.za/trc/legal/act9534.htm (accessed April 19, 2005).

9. From http://www.doj.gov.za/trc/trccom.htm (accessed April 19, 2005).

of the perpetrators of past violence. But the truth of the past violence could no longer be kept silent.[10]

Of course some perpetrators used the mechanism of amnesty to escape from the punishment of their crimes. And some victims would like to have exacted a greater price from the perpetrators than the commission would allow for. However, the goal of the commission was not to solve all the individual problems but to provide a way forward for the whole of society that would break the back of the cycle of violence and revenge. It could offer the victims a voice to break the silence. It could not offer complete justice. Some perpetrators may have escaped human justice, but the truth of their actions was there for all to see. The stigma and shame of exposure were the best the commission could offer.

South Africa was one of a number of countries to establish such a process after decades of severe political unrest with long term histories of political violence and the abuse of power. Others such as Argentina, Chile, East Timor, Ecuador, El Salvador, Ghana, and Nigeria have instituted similar processes in an attempt to overcome a history darkened by political violence and the abuse of power.[11] We can discover in this process a real manifestation of grace operating within the social dimension of human existence. Processes such as these seek to "make right" the large-scale disruption of the social order that occurs with prolonged social and political violence. It seeks to heal the social divisions and restore some sense of social unity and the ability to move forward.

HISTORICAL VIOLENCE AND
THE PURIFICATION OF MEMORY

In the instances of social and political violence we have considered, both victims and perpetrators live in a continuing social context that, unless it is dealt with constructively, will spill over into an ongoing cycles of violence and destruction. However, there are cases where the original violence or abuse of power is not part of the present historical context, but arises from past acts that are no longer the direct responsibility of the present generation. Sometimes such acts have consequences that may stretch for centuries. The original perpetrators have gone to meet God's justice, but their descendants live in a continuing uneasy relationship with the descendants of the original victims.

---

10. Copies of the victims' statements can be found at http://www.doj.gov.za/trc/hrvtrans/index .htm (accessed July 3, 2006).

11. A fuller list can be found at http://www.usip.org/library/truth.html (accessed July 3, 2006), with links to the appropriate Web pages of the various organizations.

Do they share in some "primal guilt" for the sins of their forebears? Can the descendants of the victims make claims against the descendants of the perpetrators in the name of justice?

It is not difficult to think of examples of this type of question. European settlement in North America displaced the Native American First Nation peoples, leading to their violent dispossession from the land and potential loss of cultural identity and social structure, creating conditions of poverty, drug abuse, and communal violence within Indian communities. A similar story can be told of the Aboriginal peoples of Australia, who were similarly dispossessed and to this day still suffer problems of poverty, poor health, a lack of education, drug abuse and communal violence. These problems persist despite the efforts of various governments to "repair" the situation through social welfare schemes directed toward these communities. One could also instance the situation of the descendants of slavery in the United States. The African American population still suffers a higher level of social problems such as unemployment, poverty, violence, and drug abuse than the white population.

It is easy for the present generation to disclaim any responsibility for the plight of the current descendants of the victims of past injustice. Most of the current generation rarely meets descendants of the original inhabitants of the land, and no one today owns slaves. It is easy to shift blame to the descendants of the original injustice. They are, it is claimed, lazy, less intelligent, and irresponsible, so their current plight is their own fault. Or one may dismiss responsibility as lying completely in the past. "Yes, our forebears were wrong in what they did, but what they did is not my fault. I have done nothing wrong, and no claim can be made against me for their wrongs."

However, matters are not so simple. We may not have participated in the crimes of the past, but we continue to enjoy the benefits of those past actions. Nations have been built on the blood of displaced peoples, whose descendants walk among us, often in our shadows, as a constant and uncomfortable reminder of the sins of our own ancestors. We enjoy the wealth of those nations while the descendants of the original inhabitants live in poverty and desperation. Can we so easily absolve ourselves of complete responsibility?

These types of questions were brought to a head when Pope John Paul II initiated a remarkable event in the life of the church. He asked forgiveness for the past sins of the church and its members. These were identified as sins committed in the service of truth (one might think of those burned at the stake for witchcraft, or the case of Galileo), sins committed in relation to the division within Christianity (for example, in relation to the schism with the Eastern Church and later with the Reformation), sins against the people of Israel (the sorrowful history of anti-Semitism in Christian Europe culminating in the Holocaust), sins resulting from a lack of respect for the culture and religions of other peoples (evident in various missionary endeavors that demonized local cultures), and sins against the dignity of women (for example, the marginalization of women from positions of responsibility in the Church). Many of these sins relate to matters that are centuries old and are not necessarily the result of the actions of individuals alive today, yet their memory continues to haunt the church, and their effects are still felt in the present situation with ongoing division, scandal, and resentment. Commenting on this initiative of John Paul II, the International Theological Commission noted:

> The Church is invited to "become more fully conscious of the sinfulness of her children." She "acknowledges as her own her sinful sons and daughters" and encourages them "to purify themselves, through repentance, of past errors and instances in infidelity, inconsistency and slowness to act." The responsibility of Christians for the evil of the time is likewise noted, *although the accent falls particularly on the solidarity of the Church of today with past faults.*[12]

In fact, there were some in the church who resisted this call from the pope. They felt it would give ammunition to the enemies of the church, or that the church of the present is not responsible for the actions of the past, or that we simply should not imply that the Church is sinful. However, these objections did not deter John Paul II from implementing this initiative.

The themes of solidarity and reparation are the keys to this sense of reconciliation. Yes, we may not have committed the originating sin, but we are in continuing solidarity with those who perpetrated this sin. This has strong parallels with an understanding of original sin, which has traditionally been understood as a solidarity that goes all the way back "to Adam." We are all implicated in it. Because our present situation has been built on these sinful foundations, we need to acknowledge this past history and seek to repair the damage done (that is, we need to make reparation). To achieve this, John Paul II introduced the notions of the purification and healing of memory. Purification and healing of memory implies a frank acknowledgment of the sins of the past. It honors the sufferings of the past by bringing them to the light of present consciousness. These sufferings often live on in the memories of present descendants as a continuing unacknowledged cancer that eats away at their lives. Purification and healing of memories allow both parties to be reconciled and their relationship repaired.

---

12. "Memory and Reconciliation: The Church and the Faults of the Past" (International Theological Commission, 2000), no. 1.3 (emphasis added). The inner quotations are from the apostolic letter *Tertio Millennio Adveniente*.

RECONCILIATION AND THE WORK OF JESUS[13]

So far we have focused our attention on the ways in which sin and evil fracture the human community and so give rise to the need for forgiveness and reconciliation. However, sin and evil also fracture our relationship with God, who is the source of all our life and freedom. Sin distorts our living and imprisons our freedom in ways that our own freedom is powerless to repair. How do we envisage the work of reconciliation and forgiveness between humankind and God? We shall now consider a more sustained theological reflection on the work of reconciliation and the work of Jesus, taking a text from the Letter to the Colossians as our starting point:

> Through him God was pleased to reconcile to himself all things, whether on earth or in heaven, by making peace through the blood of his cross. And you, who once were estranged and hostile in mind, doing evil deeds, he has now reconciled in his fleshly body through his death, so as to present you holy and blameless and irreproachable before him. (Col 1:20-22)

Reconciliation as Divine Initiative

The first and most important thing to note about reconciliation according to this text from Colossians is that it is a divine initiative. God is the agent of reconciliation, which is achieved through the saving actions of Jesus. God is both the active agent of reconciliation and the one with whom we are reconciled. God seeks our reconciliation, not because of anything we have achieved or deserve but as a purely gratuitous act on the part of the divinity. As Paul states, "But God proves his love for us in that while we still were sinners, Christ died for us" (Rom 5:8).

While this is a fundamental statement of a Christian understanding of reconciliation, it needs to be reinforced because so often people feel that God has distanced Godself from us, that somehow the divine anger needs to be appeased by us before we can approach God. In fact, as we noted earlier, it is impossible to square this image of an angry god needing to be appeased, with the true God who takes the initiative in the process of reconciliation. This is the image of God that Jesus portrays as the father in the parable of the prodigal son. The father takes the initiative, while the younger son is still a long way

---

13. This material has appeared in modified form in Neil Ormerod, "Reconciliation and the Paschal Mystery," in *Reconciliation: A Hunger in Society and the Church*, ed. Gerard Moore (Strathfield: St. Pauls, 2004), 41-53.

off. The only anger is that of the elder son, who expresses anger at the father's extravagance in celebrating the return of the younger son. It is the father, not the elder son, who is our model of God! (Luke 15:11-32).

It is possible to multiply biblical verses to reinforce this message. First Timothy 2:4 tells us that God wants all people to be saved. The Johannine witness reminds us that "God so loved the world that he gave his only Son" (John 3:16) and that "God is light and in him there is no darkness at all" (1 John 1:5); that is, in God we do not find the darkness of resentment, self-righteousness, and anger that would prevent God from actively seeking reconciliation with us. Put simply, it is never the sinner whom God rejects, only the sin, the evil "no-thing" to which God responds with creative love and an offer of forgiveness to the sinner.

Nonetheless, we are confronted with the fact that experientially we feel distance between God and ourselves. This distance can be felt as rejection, alienation, and estrangement. We may feel as if we live under the divine anger (Rom 1:18-32). This is evident when people may approach sacramental reconciliation with a sense of threat and reproach from God. Indeed God may be experienced as an accusing figure who sits in judgment on our human weaknesses. This takes us to our next theme emerging from our text.

Estranged from God—Original Sin

The text from Colossians speaks of our being estranged from God. This, of course, reminds us that our initial situation with regard to God is never neutral. We are born into a life of estrangement, of alienation from God. This is not a matter of personal sin, but is more analogous to the form of the social and historical contexts we examined above. Classically this is expressed by the doctrine of original sin, which reminds us that, however we understand it, our estrangement is the result of human actions, which we trace all the way back to "Adam," not God's actions. From the beginning we find ourselves not simply distant from the creator but turned away from God, facing in the wrong direction, as it were, because of forces mediated through our human history of sinfulness, our solidarity in Adam. This initial situation is not our own personal fault; it is not the result of any personal sin on our part. Rather, it finds its origins from the beginning of human history, "in Adam."

While there are many issues that need to be investigated with regard to the doctrine of original sin, particularly in light of the theory of evolution, one simple thing needs to be stated. As we argued earlier in chapter 4, the doctrine of original sin states that we are the victims of another's sin. Adam sins, and we all suffer; we are the victims of Adam's sin. The situation of alienation that we experience is the result of the evil deed of another, not our own act. This state of victimhood is prior to any act of will on our part and is the root source of our own personal "evil deeds." This simple observation can become an invitation to explore what modern psychology has uncovered about the experience of victimhood and the impact of innocent suffering imposed on victims by their perpetrators.[14]

Often the doctrine of original sin is interpreted as saying that something is wrong with you because of the sin of Adam. But in fact it is more a matter of "something is wrong, and you have been wronged, because of the sin of Adam." The analogy used by Aquinas is of the shame felt by a family because of a criminal forebear (*ST* I-II, q. 18, a. 1). As we explored in chapter 4, it may be more helpful to consider the plight of the victim of childhood abuse. Such a child experiences feelings of guilt and responsibility, but in fact has been deeply wronged. I suggest that it involves a considerable change in perspective to view the doctrine of original sin as a statement of the universal victimhood of humanity, rather than to view it as simply a statement of our original and universal corruption. It allows us to identify the impetus of God's reconciliation as grounded in divine compassion. The compassion of God reaches out to humankind, since each one of us individually has suffered loss as a result of Adam's sin.

This interconnection between the reconciliation achieved by Jesus and original sin is further confirmed in the theology of Thomas Aquinas. Aquinas asks whether the purpose of the incarnation is to deal with our actual sins or more to deal with original sin. As we noted in chapter 5, he argues that the more important purpose of the incarnation is to deal with the problem of original sin (*ST* III q. 1, a. 4).[15] Though the primary sacrament reconciling us from our basic estrangement with God is and remains baptism, it is clear that for many Christians there is an ongoing existential concern with a sense of alienation from God. In pastoral settings pastors may be aware that it is this more primitive sense of estrangement that brings people to the sacrament of reconciliation. It may show itself as ongoing anxiety or fear despite repeated confession of relatively minor matters; it may be a pervasive sense of dread in

---

14. There is a growing body of literature on which one could draw here. Apart from the profound and disturbing works of Alice Miller, such as *Banished Knowledge: Facing Childhood Injuries* (New York: Anchor Books, 1990), there are a large number of books that outline the impact of being a victim. Perhaps the most notable work is Judith Herman, *Trauma and Recovery* (New York: Basic Books, 1992).

15. "In this way original sin, through which the entire human race has been infected, is greater than any actual sin, proper to an individual person. From this standpoint the intent of Christ's coming was chiefly to take away original sin."

relation to God or an excessive sense of unworthiness unconnected to actual behavior. In such a situation the sacrament of reconciliation may more appropriately involve a reappropriation of the grace of baptism, through a reaffirmation of God's offer of friendship and the gift of that perfect love which "drives out fear."

Hostile in Mind—Reactive Anger

Again, our text identifies for us one of the major symptoms that indicate our sense of estrangement from God, that is, "hostility in mind." As events surrounding various sexual-abuse scandals have confirmed, there is no pain as deep, no anger as sharp as unacknowledged injustice and suffering.[16] Our text speaks of this anger as hostility in the mind, an enmity and distrust oriented toward God and toward the world. Previously we considered the perspective of original sin as a statement of our original victimhood, an alienation or estrangement produced within us by the sin of another (Adam). This state is an injustice and a suffering; we have been robbed of our state of "original justice" and we must now "suffer death," involving feelings of vulnerability and weakness. The result in us is a reactive anger, an anger that is saying, "I am worth more than this; why have I been sold short?" Yet to whom this anger is to be directed we do not know. Is it toward our parents? To the outsiders, the strangers? To God perhaps?

Unacknowledged or repressed, this anger can become contempt. As child psychologist Alice Miller notes, "Contempt for those who are smaller and weaker thus is the best defense against a breakthrough of one's own feelings of helplessness: it is an expression of this split-off weakness."[17] Often such anger or contempt is misdirected to the nearest available target, usually someone we love. A common misdirected target of our anger is in fact oneself. Not only is the target misdirected, but the source of the anger is misidentified, as somehow coming from God. God is then experienced as remote, angry, and unapproachable, a being who needs to be appeased so that he will turn away his wrath. Such an angry god cannot be the agent, the initiator of reconciliation; instead he is the angry father figure from whom we need protection.

Here we see that fundamental questions about the nature of God arise. Is

---

16. One need only note the recent outbreak of sexual-abuse scandals in the church, both in Australia and North America. In one notable Australian case the resulting pain and anger led to the resignation of the Australian Governor General, who in his previous role as an Anglican bishop had failed to deal adequately with a case of abuse.

17. Alice Miller, *The Drama of the Gifted Child* (New York: Basic Books, 1990), 67.

God the powerful abusive figure who stands behind all the perpetrators of abuse? Is God responsible for the whole human history of sin and suffering? Should we be angry with God? Will God respond to our anger like so many perpetrators of abuse, with threats of even greater anger and violence unleashed against us, as envisaged in so many apocalyptic scenarios? Or will God respond with compassion and forgiveness to our human brokenness?

It might now be a good idea to deal with those biblical texts which do refer to the anger of God, particularly in the first chapter of Paul's Letter to the Romans. I cannot go into the necessary exegetical and systematic detail here, but I will refer to the conclusions of some theologians. Raymund Schwager states in his account of the various texts of Romans that speak of the divine anger:

> The representation of direct punishment by an external authority is not once indicated by Paul. The anger consists entirely in the fact that God hands people over to the dynamic and inner logic of those passions and of that depraved thinking which they themselves have awakened by their turning away from God. Thus God's anger means that God fully respects the evil that people do with all its consequences.[18]

James Alison comes to a similar conclusion:

> [Paul] continues by pointing out that the effect of this revelation of the goodness of God is simultaneously to make apparent the injustice of humans, who by their injustice keep truth a prisoner to injustice, and this is described as the wrath of God. That is: the wrath of God is not understood as something which God does actively, but is rather the condition of human involvement in the murderous lie . . . God is described as handing us over to ourselves: this is the content of the wrath.[19]

Doing Evil Deeds

In this drama of salvation we are not simply victims of the evil deeds of others; we make our own contribution to the problem. We must make no bones about the fact that the destructive acts done by ourselves as a result of suffering from such a reactive anger are evil deeds, as spoken of in our text. The

---

18. Raymund Schwager, *Jesus in the Drama of Salvation: Toward a Biblical Doctrine of Redemption* (New York: Crossroad, 1999), 165.

19. James Alison, *Raising Abel: The Recovery of Eschatological Imagination* (New York: Crossroad, 1996), 46-47.

often-random lashing out at some innocent bystander is wrong, sinful, and just plain evil. We need only think of the September 11 attacks (2001) or the Bali bombing (2002), and perhaps even the second war against Iraq. To identify the psychological origins of the anger in injustice and suffering does not justify the evil deeds that flow from it. When we do so justify them we end up excusing evil and robbing people of their personal responsibility for their actions. Increased recognition of the effects of abuse, for example, has led some to excuse the violence of victims in later life, when they themselves become abusive.[20] Such excusing does not break the cycle of violence and abuse.

Two things, however, should be kept in mind. Our text speaks of "doing evil deeds"; it does not speak of "evil people." There is no justification here for labeling anyone as an "evil person."[21] To do so verges on ontological dualism, as we noted in chapter 2. The text quite correctly distinguishes between the person and the person's acts. Again, we may recall the saying "Love the sinner; hate the sin." Indeed, in a very real sense the evil deeds that we perpetrate have an impact not only on others but also on ourselves. Inasmuch as we do such deeds, we become the victims of our own evil deeds, as our world becomes increasingly violent, isolated, and filled with hate and alienation from God and others. This is the hell into which we fall through sin, a situation that God is doing everything possible to avoid. Yet in the end, as Schwager notes, "God fully respects the evil that people do with all its consequences."[22]

The second thing to note is that the reactive anger is not evil in itself, though the deeds that flow from it may be. Here I would like to draw a parallel between this reactive anger and the way in which the Catholic tradition handles the question of concupiscence. The Council of Trent deals with the question of concupiscence, the material element of original sin, in its decree on original sin (DS 1510-16). In responding to the position of the reformers that concupiscence is sin, the bishops at Trent stated that while it comes from sin (Adam's) and inclines to sin (ours), it is not sin "in the sense of real and actual sin in those reborn" (DS 1516). Here we can grasp an analogy with reactive anger. Reactive anger from unacknowledged injustice and suffering is

---

20. We witness numerous examples of this in public life, but perhaps the most recent and most powerful arose in the aftermath of September 11. Although it is valid to ask questions about how much U.S. foreign policy may had led to the "anger" of the terrorists, this should in no way excuse or minimize the responsibility of those who personally made the decision to hijack planes and fly them into buildings.

21. Again it is worth drawing attention to the political rhetoric, post–September 11, of terrorists being "evil." Such a stance is antithetical to the Christian understanding of human beings, who are not ontologically constituted as evil but remain always open to the possibility of conversion.

22. Schwager, *Jesus in the Drama of Salvation*, 165.

not sin. It clearly comes from sin, the sin of others; it clearly inclines to sin as long as it is not dealt with. But it needs the healing of compassion, not the fire of condemnation.

This is an important pastoral issue. It is all too easy to be put off by reactive anger and to make hasty judgments that "anger is bad." This leads to poor pastoral practice. Where people really need an attentive ear and a compassionate response they often attract condemnation and rejection. Nor is it helpful when pastors themselves deny and repress their own reactive anger, again because "anger is bad." Inevitably such repressed anger emerges in inappropriate and destructive ways, usually from behind a mask of self-righteousness.

Holy, Blameless, and Irreproachable—Restorative Justice

We began this reflection with a focus on the divine initiative toward reconciliation. Now we can consider the purpose of God's initiative, the goal God seeks to achieve. Reconciliation with God involves the total transformation of the sinner. Whereas before the sinner was estranged, hostile, and doing evil deeds, now the sinner is present before God as holy, blameless, and irreproachable. This involves a real transformation of the sinner, a new creation, which removes our heart of stone and puts within us a heart of flesh (Ezek 36:26). There are two things to draw out from this.

The first concerns the question of "blamelessness," or "being without blame." Wherein is the source of blame in the first place? Many would experience this as a blame that comes from God, a consequence of the divine anger. Yet, according to the Johannine author, this is not the case. He states:

> By this shall we know that we are from the truth, and will reassure our hearts before him whenever our hearts condemn us; for God is greater than our hearts, and he knows everything. Beloved, if our own hearts do not condemn us, we have boldness before God. (1 John 3:19-21)

This is the condemnation not of an external judge but of our own hearts, or what some psychologists might call the superego. God is greater than this blame and can quieten our accusing heart. In this context it is worthwhile recalling the notion of the Satan. As we have already noted, in Hebrew the term "Satan" means the adversary or the accuser. In legal language, the accuser is the one who puts before the court the accusation against the accused. In the perspective developed here, the accuser is the voice within continually blaming us, running us down with a multitude of accusations, loading us with guilt. Psychologically the role of the Satan is that of the superego running out of control. It is this voice that God can silence.

The second is to observe that this action of God is in part a restorative justice. We often hear talk about the tension between God's justice and mercy. It is stated that God's justice punishes the sinner, while God's mercy tempers God's justice. Yet justice demands not only a punishment of the sinner but a restoration to the victim. We are all both sinner, inasmuch as we lash out from our reactive anger, and victim, inasmuch as we have lost our innocence because of the sin of Adam. The healing of our reactive anger can come about only through a restorative justice, restoring in us all that has been lost in Adam.[23] Through God's act of reconciliation we become a new creation and we are restored to our initial state, holy, blameless, and irreproachable.

Through the Blood of the Cross: Identification with the Victim

Finally, we enter into the heart of the paschal mystery. How is all this achieved through the death of Jesus, the blood of the cross? The history of theology has promoted various responses to this question, and our search for a satisfactory response continues as we saw in chapter 5. We shall now bring that earlier material to bear on the question of reconciliation.

The first concerns Jesus' own identification with the victim in us all. In the parable of the last judgment in Matthew's Gospel, Jesus makes clear his identification with the broken, the poor, and the victims of human history: "whenever you do it to the least, you do it to me" (see Matt 25:31-46). Through Jesus, God is reaching out to that victim in us all, standing with us through a divine act of solidarity. The act of solidarity extends to Jesus experiencing the full brunt of our human victimhood and our reactive anger, that is, death, a violent death at the hands of sinners. Provocatively Paul states that "for our sake [God] made him to be sin who knew no sin" (2 Cor 5:21),[24] and the Apostles' Creed speaks of Jesus' "descent into hell" (also 1 Pet 3:18). These phrases express symbolically the extent of Jesus' identification with the victim in us all.

Second, this language of victimhood finds its correlate in—though in fact it is often masked by—the language of sacrifice. Scripture and liturgy refer to the death of Jesus as a sacrifice, and so it is. But if we are to retain this language, let us recognize that it is not the divine anger that is being appeased but our own reactive anger, from which we lash out and damage others and

---

23. We might recall the words of the hymn by Australian poet James McAuley, "By your kingly power of risen Lord, all that Adam lost is now restored"; see *Australian Hymn Book* #306.

24. According to the exegetical study of Leopold Sabourin, this verse refers to the "sacrifice for sin, that is, God makes Jesus a victim of a sacrificial act"; see S. Lyonnet and L. Sabourin, *Sin, Redemption and Sacrifice: A Biblical and Patristic Study* (Rome: Biblical Institute Press, 1970), 187-289.

ourselves. As a revelation of the extent of divine love, of Jesus' and God's solidarity with the victim, the crucifixion of Jesus has the power to heal our reactive anger and to restore that which Adam lost for us. It is an acknowledgment and sharing of our unjust suffering, freely undertaken. Such is the extent of God's love, even to the point of descending into the hell of that suffering. Still, this "power to dissolve" is not automatic, requiring from us open acknowledgment that we are both victim *and* sinner, both crucified *and* crucifier. None of us is purely victim, for we have all sinned (Rom 5:12-21), and without an acknowledgment of our own complicity in the history of human sin, the healing power of the paschal mystery is not available to us.

Third and finally, Jesus presents us with a model to be followed. While Jesus is in one sense the victim of human sinfulness, in another sense he is not. Although he is clearly "done away with" by the Jewish and Roman authorities,[25] he does not interiorize the reactive anger that is the source of human sinfulness. He does not experience estrangement from God or hostility in mind, despite all that is done to him. His response is to turn the other cheek, to pray for forgiveness for those who wrong him. Even in the resurrection he does not turn against those who abandoned him, but offers them renewed fellowship. I think that this postresurrection experience of Jesus is the ground for the Johannine witness statement that "in him there is no darkness, only light," no darkness of hostility and revenge, only the light of compassion and forgiveness. In all this Jesus is a model of redemptive suffering that disarms the power of evil through creative love. He invites us to conform ourselves to this model so that we may make up in our own bodies the sufferings lacking in those of Christ (Col 1:24).

CONCLUSION

The reconciliation achieved between humanity and God through the death and resurrection of Jesus releases a power for healing of all the personal, social, and historical alienations and broken relationships that continually mar our human existence. Still, this is no automatic solution, operating like a computer program correcting spelling mistakes. It is an unfolding reality in human history, with many threads often apparently left untied. Perpetrators and victims often die before any meaningful reconciliation is possible. Where is justice then? Surely the demands of both justice and mercy call out for something more than the partial and frail imitations of justice that are attainable in this

---

25. See in particular the interpretative framework provided by the parable of the wicked tenant (Matt 21:33-45).

life. We need an eschatological vision that can sustain our hope beyond the limits of this life. We shall consider this is the next two chapters.

QUESTIONS FOR FURTHER REFLECTION

1. In what ways can the supposed Christian "demand" to forgive be used to silence victims and undermine the call for justice?
2. The great German Lutheran theologian Dietrich Bonhoeffer speaks of "cheap" grace and "costly" grace. Can there be "cheap" forgiveness and "costly" forgiveness? Can you give examples of each?
3. How can we work for reconciliation and forgiveness for deeds that took place in previous generations, such as the displacement of indigenous peoples or slavery?
4. In chapter 5 we considered the notion of original sin in terms of our universal victimhood of the sin of Adam. How would the notion of restorative justice help us better understand God's saving actions in the death and resurrection of Jesus?

SUGGESTIONS FOR FURTHER READING AND STUDY

Alison, James. *Raising Abel: The Recovery of Eschatological Imagination*. New York: Crossroad, 1996.

Herman, Judith. *Trauma and Recovery*. New York: Basic Books, 1992.

International Theological Commission. "Memory and Reconciliation: The Church and the Faults of the Past" (2000).

Miller, Alice. *Banished Knowledge: Facing Childhood Injuries*. New York: Anchor Books, 1990.

Moore, Gerard, ed. *Reconciliation: A Hunger in Society and the Church*. Strathfield: St Pauls, 2004.

Pais, Janet. *Suffer the Children: A Theology of Liberation by a Victim of Child Abuse*. New York: Paulist Press, 1991.

Schwager, Raymund. *Jesus in the Drama of Salvation: Toward a Biblical Doctrine of Redemption*. New York: Crossroad, 1999.

9

Death and the Afterlife

DEATH IS PERHAPS THE MOST AMBIGUOUS of all human experiences. Each of us must realistically face the prospect of our own death, yet at the same time we will tend to eliminate from our language anything as stark as "he died," using euphemisms such as "he passed away" or "she is no longer with us." Death has a finality about it that we find difficult to comprehend. The ones we loved are no longer with us and we wonder about the possibility of their continued existence in some form. Is there life after death? Do the dead still relate in some fashion to the living? Are there rewards and punishments for a life lived in virtue or vice? Or is the universe indifferent to our moral struggles? These are profound questions that have implications for the totality of our living, and all religious traditions and various philosophical systems seek to address them in one way or another. Belief in life after death is common to many, but not all, religions, as is belief in rewards and punishments. The Christian tradition has responded to these questions, too, though not always with a uniform voice, as we shall see. There are underlying anthropological assumptions that tend to color our responses, even in our common adherence to Christian faith.

LIFE AFTER DEATH

When we consider portrayals of life after death in film (for example, *Ghost*, or the final scenes of *Titanic*, or even *Bill & Ted's Bogus Journey*), one might wonder what all the fuss is about. Life seems to go on much as usual, except for the fact that the dead are no longer visible to the living. They continue to see, hear, and feel, though for some reason they are not able to touch the living or be heard or seen by them. They even take on the shape they had in life. Death appears as a simple transition from one state to the next, which, although it may be painful beforehand, leaves the departed "soul" in a fairly robust state. The underlying assumption of such portrayals seems to be a form of dualistic anthropology, in which the soul is a separate substance from the body, death separates the soul from the body in an almost physical sense, and the soul itself is conceived as a form of refined matter, much as the Stoic philosophers did.

This conception is so common that many might be surprised how far it is from the biblical conception of life after death and from Catholic thought on these issues. Let us begin with the Old Testament, move on to the New Testament, and then consider the question from a more philosophical perspective.

Some would say that the Old Testament, or at least the Torah, has no conception of life after death. The conservative Jews of Jesus' time, the Sadducees, who followed the Torah strictly, did not believe in resurrection and hence had no clear concept of life after death. When you die, that is it. From this perspective, the best one can hope for is a long life and a good family to carry on one's name and tradition. Beyond the Torah—for example, in the Psalms—we do find references to Sheol or the Pit, the place of the dead. Here the dead endure a shadowy existence, cut off from the living and from God (Ps 6:5). There are no punishments, rewards, or fellowship with others. The rich and the poor, the good and the bad all meet the same fate. It is not as if the biblical authors did not believe in rewards and punishments, but they were to be found in this life, not the next.[1]

As we have already indicated, this approach started to fall apart during the Maccabean Revolt. For the first time in their history the Jews were suffering, not because of their lack of fidelity to the Law but precisely because of their fidelity. How could God allow such suffering to his faithful elect? The "solution" that emerged was belief in life after death, through which rewards to God's faithful could be imparted—at this stage the writers did not conceive of a resurrection for the wicked (2 Macc 7:14). It is the form of life after death, however, that should capture our attention. The Jewish authors did not think of death as the release of the soul from the body, which would free it from the limitations of physical existence. Such a dualistic conception was far from their understanding of human existence. Rather, life after death could only mean bodily life, a life where "body and soul" are formed into a single living human being. For this stage of Jewish belief, a "disembodied soul" was not a human existence, more a half life, like that of the shades in Sheol. Real postmortem life, human life, must be embodied life, what N. T. Wright refers to as "life after 'life after death.'"[2] We are not angels, and even in death a life without a body is hardly worthy of the name.

This is the horizon that was operative at the time of the New Testament.

---

1. This is perhaps most evident in the Book of Job. In the end, Job is rewarded for his constancy by the return of his earthly blessings. The notion of a postmortem reward is not fully in the horizon of this book.

2. N. T. Wright, *The Resurrection of the Son of God*, vol. 3 of *Christian Origins and the Question of God* (Minneapolis: Fortress, 2003), 31.

While some Jews (the conservative Sadducees) did not believe in a resurrection (Matt 22:23), and hence did not believe in any form of life after death, the Pharisees did believe in the resurrection of the body (Acts 23:6), as emerged during the Maccabean period. In his debate with the Sadducees, Jesus affirms the reality of resurrection (Matt 22:23-33), and for Christians Jesus' own resurrection from the dead settles the matter in the affirmative. Nonetheless, any reading of the New Testament resurrection narratives, or of Paul's account of bodily resurrection in 1 Corinthians 15, should be enough to remind us that we are dealing with mystery. These are not accounts of a resuscitated corpse, but of encounters with the risen Lord of history, whose bodiliness can no longer be tied down in easily quantifiable terms. For example, Karl Rahner speaks of the relationship of the soul to the material order as pan-cosmic, while Wright prefers to speak of the resurrected body as transphysical.[3] It would be easy, perhaps too easy, to read these New Testament texts like some modern movie script of ghostly appearances, disappearances, and interactions with the living. Rather, they speak of Jesus as fully alive, in a new and mysterious relationship with the material world, but one in which he is able to express his presence in tangible and active forms. Jesus continues as an active agent in human history, through his body which is the church, through his body which is the eucharist, and in ways that are simply beyond our comprehension.

We shall now turn our attention to some of the philosophical concerns underlying this problem. As we shall see they closely parallel the discussion above.

THE PLATONIC CONCEPTION OF SOUL

The Platonic (or at least Neoplatonic versions of it) conception of the soul is essentially dualistic.[4] The person is constituted by a union of two distinct substances: a spiritual substance (soul) and a material substance (body). The immateriality of the soul means that it enjoys a natural immortality, and the soul is the essential reality of the person. Personal immortality, life after death, is an immediate consequence of the spiritual nature of the soul. This position generally denigrates the body as imprisoning the soul, which is released from

---

3. Karl Rahner, *On the Theology of Death* (New York: Herder & Herder, 1961), 22-23; Wright, *Resurrection of the Son of God*, 477.

4. See Joseph Ratzinger, *Eschatology, Death and Eternal Life*, ed. Aidan Nichols, trans. Michael Waldstein (Washington, D.C.: Catholic University of America Press, 1988), 140-46, for a discussion of the distinction between the Platonic and Aristotelian conceptions of soul.

its bondage to matter in death. Death becomes liberation. On this conception of human existence resurrection of the body makes no sense. Nonetheless Neoplatonism has had an enormous impact on Christianity through the writings of Pseudo-Dionysius, Augustine, and others. The monastic theology of the Middle Ages was largely Neoplatonic in character and lived with the tension between the inherent dualism of the position and Christian beliefs in the goodness of creation and the resurrection of the dead. It is fair to say that many Christians still adopt this dualistic position in an unreflective and uncritical manner. Although they may accept resurrection of the body, they would find it difficult to fit into their worldview.

THE ARISTOTELIAN CONCEPTION OF SOUL

For Aristotle, on the other hand, the soul is the form or intelligibility of a living thing, so all living things have a soul; what distinguishes the human soul from others is that it is a rational soul. It can understand and reason and so is spiritual in nature. We have explored this spiritual aspect in chapter 2, where we spoke of it in terms of the human search for meaning, truth, and value. However, the soul always remains the form of a living thing and so requires a body for its proper operation. This is particularly evident in the dependence of the intellect, our ability to understand, on the imagination (phantasm), or the senses. There can be no understanding and possibly no memory without phantasm. Given the close union between body and soul, Aristotle was in fact pessimistic about the possibility of survival of the soul after death. For Aristotle, matter individuates us, so without matter we just have general "form." Some Arab commentators on Aristotle, the Averroists, concluded that there was a single human soul, with which we merged at death.

In a way the position of Aristotle is much closer to that of the Old Testament than writers who draw a sharp distinction between biblical and philosophical conceptions might assume. For Aristotle, the purpose of the soul is to inform a living body. If it is not doing so, it is not performing its natural function. Death threatens the existence of the soul because the soul no longer serves any purpose. The possibility of life after death, of personal immortality, simply cannot be taken for granted from Aristotle's account. Indeed, when Aquinas began to deploy Aristotelian philosophy in his writings he was accused of denying the immortality of the soul, which led to his condemnation by some church authorities.[5]

---

5. On this basis the "Christian Aristotelianism" of Aquinas was condemned three years after his death by the Archbishop of Canterbury, Robert Kilwardby; see Frederick Charles Copleston, *Aquinas* (Harmondsworth: Penguin, 1975), 243.

Aquinas responded to these criticisms by arguing that, though the soul of a human being is dependent on the operation of the senses, still it has its own operation, which cannot be reduced to those senses. The operation of understanding transcends material conditions, since potentially we can understand anything. This operation is "spiritual," that is, not material, and so the human soul is spiritual in nature. Moreover, when I understand something, it is clear that others do not necessarily understand it, so the understanding is mine. My soul is not the same as anyone else's. Aquinas deduces from this that my soul can in fact survive death and that this soul is an essential constituent of my personal existence. Still, for Aquinas I am not my soul;[6] my personal identity is that of the union of my body and soul.

Given the intimate unity of body and soul, that the soul is immortal *and* the form of a living human being, Aquinas's position almost demands a resurrection as the only proper form of life after death. A soul separated from the body is in an "unnatural" state, and no such unnatural state can be permanent. Perfect human happiness and justice demand the reuniting of body and soul in a resurrection. Despite the naturalness of the resurrection, however, it is something achieved not by nature but by the power of God.[7]

DEATH AND SIN

The conception of the intimate relation between body and soul corresponds to much of our natural reaction to death. Death is a wrenching experience, not a simple transition. The disembodied soul is in an unnatural state. Removed from its body, how can it know anything? How can it remember anything?[8] Without access to the senses, the soul is cut adrift from the world, from relationships, and possibly even from God. The biblical witness concerning death affirms this "unnatural" quality of death. Such a separation of body and soul cannot be part of God's original intention. It must be the result of sin: "Therefore, just as sin came into the world through one man, and death came through sin, and so death spread to all because all have sinned" (Rom 5:12). Here Paul is picking up on the mythological material of Genesis that has

---

6. *Super Epistolam Pauli Apostoli* (Turin: Marietti, 1953); *Thomas Aquinas: Selected Philosophical Writings*, trans. Timothy McDermott (Oxford: Oxford University Press, 1993), 192.

7. This position is argued more fully in Montague Brown, "Aquinas and the Resurrection of the Body," *Thomist* 56 (1992): 165-207.

8. The question of memory, which we take to be so central to personal identity, is a major issue. It is increasingly clear that the proper operation of memory is dependent on the proper functioning of our brain's biochemistry. Without that proper functioning, as in cases of dementia, memory is severely degraded.

death (or no further access to the "tree of life") seen as part of God's punishment of Adam and Eve for their sin. Death is now a punishment for sin. According to a premodern Christian understanding, Adam and Eve would not have died if they had not sinned.

From an evolutionary perspective, however, it is clear that death was an ever-present reality for all biological creatures prior to the advent of sin. Not only have individual living things died, but even whole species have gone extinct. And it is difficult to know what it might mean to think of human beings, as biologically constituted, being "immortal" if Adam and Eve had not sinned. Would our bodies not have burnt in a fire? Would poisons not have affected our biochemistry? Would falling rocks not have crushed our bodies? And would blood not have drained out of our open wounds? As finite biological beings, we could still be affected by physical, chemical, and biological actions that might lead to the destruction of our bodies. It would seem that the connection between sin and death is more mythological than literal, more exploratory than explanatory.

One direct exploration of the connection between sin and death is to raise the question of meaning. What does death mean to one who is sinless? Conversely, what does death mean to the one who has committed sin? On the side of sinlessness, the Johannine Jesus speaks of his death as "going to the Father" (John 16:17). Similarly in the case of Mary, preserved free from sin, the church speaks of her assumption body and soul into heaven (*Lumen Gentium* 59). We might argue from these instances of sinlessness that where sin is present it robs death of its integrity, of its original inner meaning, a meaning we find revealed in the cases of Jesus and Mary. As a result of sin, death becomes ambiguous in character. We cannot say that for us death is simply a return to the Father; it is not just being taken "body and soul into heaven," at least not in any unambiguous sense. Death for us is inextricably bound to judgment, accusation, separation, and pain; it is not an unambiguous possibility of return, but the ambiguous possibility of judgment and ensuing punishment. The inner meaning of death has changed because of sin, and so the reality of death has changed. The death that we experience is the result of sin. Apart from the cases of Jesus and Mary we have no direct access to what death would be like "without sin," though we may witness approximations to it in the dying of people of strong faith.

The relationship between death and sin is not, however, the final word that faith can speak on the subject. Paul continues drawing his parallels between the sin of Adam and the obedience of Jesus:

> If, because of the one man's trespass, death exercised dominion through that one, much more surely will those who receive the abundance of grace

and the free gift of righteousness exercise dominion in life through the one man, Jesus Christ. (Rom 5:17)

So if there is linkage between sin and death, we must also expect a linkage between grace and death. The theological writings of Karl Rahner and Ladislaus Boros point in the direction of such a linkage.[9]

The first thing that Rahner wants to dispel is the notion that death is simply a transition from one state to the next, like changing horses midstream. As we have already seen in relation to Aquinas, Rahner stresses the unity of spirit and matter, and death hits at the very heart of this unity.

> Death is an event which strikes man in his totality . . . Man is a union of nature and person. He is a being who possesses, on the one hand, antecedent to his own personal and free decision and independent of it, a specific kind of existence with definite laws proper to it and, consequently, a necessary mode of development; on the other hand, he disposes freely of himself and is, in the last analysis, what he himself, through the exercise of his liberty, wills himself to be. Death must consequently possess for him a personal and natural aspect. In the doctrine of the Church, the natural aspect is expressed by saying that death is the separation of soul from body; its personal aspect by saying that it means the definitive end of our state of pilgrimage.[10]

But what about the personal aspect? How is it expressed in the reality of death? Here Rahner speaks of death as involving a personal response:

> In death something happens to him as a whole, something which, consequently, is of essential importance to his soul as well: his free, personal self-affirmation and self-realisation is achieved in death definitively. This should not be conceived as something occurring "with" death or "after" it, but as an intrinsic factor of death itself.[11]

Ladislaus Boros has taken up Rahner's suggestion to speak of death as involving a "final option." For Boros, the moment of death involves a personal act of the will, whereby it freely accepts or rejects "everything for which it had been striving already, right from the beginning." He also characterizes death as a "moment of truth," of self-presence and self-knowledge, whereby it can "come to itself and so posit in content and composition both its own nature and the infinite capacity that is an essential element in this nature."[12] Both the cogni-

---

9. Rahner, *On the Theology of Death*; Ladislaus Boros, *The Moment of Truth: Mysterium Mortis* (Montreal: Palm Publishers, 1965).

10. Rahner, *On the Theology of Death*, 13.

11. Ibid., 17-18.

12. Boros, *Moment of Truth*, 30, 35.

tional and volitional elements that Boros is seeking to identify give expression to the definitive element in death. They are not something that happens "after" death, but are constitutive elements of death itself. They are part of what is meant by the separation of body and soul.

While there is no empirical way of discerning whether there is such an intellectual and volitional element in death, we can get a suggestion of it in terms of the ways in which people deal with death, when they are caught in a long process of dying, as in a terminal illness. As death approaches, people settle into patterns of dealing with their coming death; they adopt a certain stance in relation to it. They may want to deal with "unfinished business," heal significant relationships from the past, and find an inner peace. There may be a new sense of self-knowledge that emerges at this time. Elisabeth Kübler-Ross in her famous work *On Death and Dying*, speaks of a final stage of acceptance,[13] but in some cases it might also be a final stage of resistance or fear. There emerges in the dying person a certain determinate attitude that they adopt toward their coming death. In this attitude we may witness in a more drawn-out manner the sort of inner decision that Boros is suggesting.

Joseph Ratzinger suggests that there is something of a Platonizing element in Boros's presentation. He suggests that Boros "secretly [considers] the human condition less than acceptable."[14] However, there are also some theological considerations that come into play. God is not a neutral agent in our dying. God wants all people to be saved (1 Tim 2:4), and Jesus sits at the right hand of the Father pleading for the salvation of sinners (Rom 8:34). It is not inconsistent with this understanding of God to think of the "one last chance" that the theory of a final option presents us with. Even in death itself God works for our salvation, offering us the final chance of salvation. This grace-filled offer still requires from us some form of response, a final movement of the will itself toward God. On this view, death could be our final providential moment of grace, a moment each and all experience. Death is judgment, not just for extrinsic reasons but because of the intrinsic nature of death as a final determination of our lives for (or against) God. It should also be noted that without grace a determination for God would simply be impossible, in death as much as in life. The final option is not a return to Pelagianism whereby we "save ourselves." God saves us through grace, and without grace any final option for God becomes impossible. Again, God is not a neutral judge (and certainly not a punitive judge), but always and everywhere God is a God of salvation.

There is an interesting element in the tradition that might be an acknowl-

---

13. Elisabeth Kübler-Ross, *On Death and Dying* (New York: Macmillan, 1969).
14. Ratzinger, *Eschatology, Death and Eternal Life*, 208.

edgment of some type of final option. The tradition speaks of the "grace of perseverance," a grace of persevering to the end (DS 1541). If grace is required until the point of death, is it not required in death itself? Nonetheless, the notion of a final option remains hypothetical, but attractive.

DEATH AND JUDGMENT

One of the most difficult things to grasp about death is its definitive character. A traditional theology viewed death as initiating a divine judgment on our life, a definitive act that determined for the rest of eternity what our final state of blessing or suffering would be. However, we might ask why death creates such a definitive moment for us? Rahner poses the question thus:

> Does God turn death into judgment because man himself in and through his death determines his own final condition, or does judgment follow death, because God has so ordained that it is this judgment, different in itself from death, and final happiness or unhappiness bestowed by God in this judgment, which brings about the finality of the personal attitude which death by itself could not produce?[15]

Clearly the notion of a final option adopts the first of these alternatives, but Rahner acknowledges that faith itself does not provide an answer to the question posed. What faith does tell us is that death does bring about something definitive in terms of any ongoing relationship to God and to the world.

This definitive character of death cuts across any simpleminded view of death as just a transition from one state to the next, where things carry on much as before. According to the position developed above, death is not transition; it is rupture, rupture from the world, from personal relationships and perhaps even from God. Any reestablishment of relationship must come not from us but from God, as a gift of divine grace, doing what human nature as disembodied cannot do for itself. Our response to such an offer is definitive because of the impact that such an unmediated experience of the divine has on our human freedom, an issue we can now consider in terms of heaven and the nature of the beatific vision.

HEAVEN AND THE BEATIFIC VISION

Ask any Christians what they think life will be like in heaven and they probably will not be able to say very much. While our Christian imagination brims

---

15. Rahner, *On the Theology of Death*, 29.

full of images of hell, heaven is much more difficult to envision. Even in the *Divine Comedy* of the great poet Dante, we find that his *Inferno* is much more interesting and popular than his *Paradiso*. Various saints warn us with images of hell, but not many attract us with images of heaven. The same could be said of the Scriptures, which are far more fulsome on hell than on heaven. Heaven is being "with Christ"; it is a banquet, a final consolation, a new heavenly city where God himself is the Temple. In more popular imagery, heaven is depicted as clouds and harps with little positively to appeal or attract us.

The theological problem of heaven is made more acute by Christian belief in the beatific vision.[16] Heaven is not just some earthly paradise where every material human want is fulfilled; heaven is the abode of God, the place where we see God face to face. Two scriptural verses stand out in this regard:

> Beloved, we are God's children now; what we will be has not yet been revealed. What we do know is this: when he is revealed, we will be like him, for we will see him as he is. (1 John 3:2)

> For now we see in a mirror, dimly, but then we will see face to face. Now I know only in part; then I will know fully, even as I have been fully known. (1 Cor 13:12)

These verses speak of an intimacy of divine presence that goes beyond any human experience of earthly fulfillment. However, they also create a problem for theological understanding, since any account of such an immediate vision of God is full of problems that remain to be overcome. The main problem here lies in our basic anthropology. We have already contrasted Platonic and Aristotelian anthropologies on the question of the relationship between body and soul. Now we can see a further consequence of the differences between these two positions.

For the Platonic conception of the soul/intellect in relation to its object, the basic position is one of confrontation of the knower with the known. The image behind this conception is ocular—the eye presents us with an "object" that is "out there" to be seen. The object confronts our senses as something other than ourselves. Such a position takes the "subject/object" distinction as primary and given in consciousness. The object stands over and against the subject. This position is "common sense" for most people, but it is not the position found in Aristotle and Aquinas.

For both Aristotle and Aquinas the relationship between subject and object is one not of confrontation but of assimilation. What proves the spiri-

---

16. For a fuller treatment than is possible here, see Anthony Kelly, *Eschatology and Hope*, Theology in Global Perspective (Maryknoll, N.Y.: Orbis Books, 2006), 159-80.

tuality of the soul/intellect is the fact that it is independent of materiality; what shows this is its ability to "become" what it knows, at least in an intentional sense. When we understand something, we do so because our intellect becomes the thing as understood. The understanding is "in us," not just in the object. So we know anything by assimilating into ourselves the form or intelligibility of the thing understood. In this account the subject/object distinction is not something given and immediate but something constructed through our growing knowledge of the world. Now while the Platonic conception of knowledge can envisage the beatific vision in terms of eternal contemplation of the divine essence on some type of analogy of sight, the Thomistic conception is much more difficult to comprehend, because knowledge by assimilation with the form is not really possible when the form is the divine essence. How can the intellect assimilate the divine form without becoming God?

The speculative difficulties involved in seeking to make some sense of the beatific vision are enormous. On my estimation, Aquinas's handling of this question in the *Summa Theologiae* is possibly the longest article in the whole *Summa*. Not only does he consider sixteen distinct objections, but he also provides six distinct sources of authority for the affirmative proposition that we do see God in his essence. In his positive account he suggests that the relationship between the divine essence and the individual soul is like the relationship between form and matter. This is the precursor to the speculations of Karl Rahner on "quasi-formal causality."[17]

We might also consider the actual "content" of the beatific vision. Does it entail, for example, an experience of the omniscience of God? Do the blessed in heaven "know" everything? Here Aquinas would deny that the beatific vision involves "seeing all that God sees" or more properly "understanding all that God understands." Even in the beatific vision we do not comprehend God, that is, completely understand God—only God fully understands God. Indeed, his conception of the beatific vision is "dynamic" rather than static: "Thus the knowledge . . . of the souls of the saints can go on increasing until the day of judgment, even as other things pertaining to the accidental reward" (*ST* Suppl. III q. 92, a. 3). One might say that the state of the blessed is dynamic and expansive, an ever-increasing consciousness of all that is. For Aquinas, however, this is a dynamism that definitely stops with the final judgment and resurrection of the dead, when we reach "the final state of things."

---

17. See David Coffey, *Grace: The Gift of the Holy Spirit* (Sydney: Catholic Institute of Sydney, 1979), 56-58, for a discussion of the relationship between quasi-formal causality, the beatific vision, and grace in the thought of Rahner.

Further, this relationship to God, which is the beatific vision, grounds the possibility of a communion not only with God but also with all creatures through God. We are able to relate to all others through God's relationship to them. Thus we speak of the "communion of saints" as a vital and loving reality contributing to the ongoing mission of the church on earth.

However, this vision of heaven is not egalitarian: some have a greater share in the light of glory than others. For Aquinas, heaven is a well-ordered society, ordered according to the merits of the saints. All enjoy heaven fully, but some have a greater capacity, a capacity developed in this life through the merits of a grace-filled virtuous life. Perhaps in our more democratic and egalitarian culture such an account is less appealing, but it does stress the permanent significance of this life and its consequences, something that is lost in a more egalitarian conception of heaven.

Finally we must ask, What is the impact on our freedom of such a beatific vision? If freedom is not about choice but about orientation to the good, what are the implications for freedom when the highest good, God in God's own being, is present immediately within our human consciousness? Surely nothing can compare with such an experience, and the thought of choosing against such a divine infinite goodness is in fact unthinkable. If we think of freedom as freedom of choice, then such a statement can only be read as the elimination or destruction of our freedom. If, however, we think of freedom in terms of orientation to the good, then it is the definitive establishment of our freedom. The only example we have of such an existence is that of Jesus himself, where the church believes not only that he did not sin, but in fact he could not sin (impeccability) as a consequence of the hypostatic union.[18]

HELL AND PUNISHMENT

The notion of hell involving the possibility of eternal damnation remains one of the great sticking points, or point of tension for many modern believers.[19] The question simply put is, How can a God of love condemn someone to eternal punishment? In responding it is not adequate to contrast the God of hellfire and brimstone of the Old Testament with the God of love revealed by Jesus in the New Testament. Many of our images of hell are in fact drawn

---

18. The logic of impeccability is clear. If Jesus can sin, then his supernatural relationship to God can be broken. This would imply that his union with the Logos is a moral union, not one of personhood, in contradiction to the teaching of Chalcedon. The psychology of impeccability is a different issue!

19. For a fuller treatment see Kelly, *Eschatology and Hope*, 138-58.

from the mouth of Jesus, for example, in Mark 9:47-48 Jesus warns, "And if your eye causes you to stumble, tear it out; it is better for you to enter the kingdom of God with one eye than to have two eyes and to be thrown into hell, where the worm never dies, and the fire is never quenched." The notion of hell is present in both Old and New Testaments. Moreover, the notion of hell is well attested in a large variety of religious traditions—Hinduism, Buddhism, Confucianism, and Islam to name a few.[20] This widespread belief points not necessarily to some universal revelation but to some underlying universal concern or experience to which a religiously attuned consciousness will inevitably respond: What are the consequences of my sins and failings? For if there are no consequences whatever, the moral life would seem to be pointless.[21]

We have already learned that the Old Testament had no clear conception of the afterlife. The principal notion is of Sheol, the underworld inhabited by the shades of the dead. This is a "washed-out" existence; the shades are not really alive, cut off from the living and from God. It is not necessarily a place of punishment or suffering in an active sense, more a place of absence or futility. The dead cannot praise God, so what is the point of existence! Some translations of the Old Testament will render Sheol as "hell" or "Hades." We have also seen how, under the pressure of persecution, Israel developed a notion of resurrection of the righteous whom God would raise from the dead so that they may be rewarded for their fidelity in the face of suffering. The same apocalyptic pressure gave rise to a sense that the wicked deserved punishment for their crimes.

Images of hell are not uncommon in the New Testament. Perhaps the most memorable account is found in the last judgment scene in Matthew 25, where we find the Son of Man separating sheep from goats, with the words:

> Then he will say to those at his left hand, "You that are accursed, depart from me into the eternal fire prepared for the devil and his angels; for I was hungry and you gave me no food, I was thirsty and you gave me nothing to drink, I was a stranger and you did not welcome me, naked and you did not give me clothing, sick and in prison and you did not visit me." (Matt 25:41-43)

Hell is the counterpoint of the kingdom of heaven, the consequence of evil deeds (see, e.g., the parable of Dives and Lazarus in Luke 16:19-31), of a lack

---

20. Though in Hinduism and Buddhism, both heaven and hell are temporary abodes, neither is the final state of the human condition. Confucianism is less definite but not unaware of the possibility.

21. This type of pointlessness is reflected in the Book of Ecclesiastes (e.g., 3:18-22).

of forgiveness (see the parable of the unforgiving debtor in Matt 8:23-35), of sins and crimes that exclude us from the Kingdom of God (1 Cor 6:9-10). Perhaps the most graphic images of hell can be found in the book of Revelation:

> Then another angel, a third, followed them, crying with a loud voice, "Those who worship the beast and its image, and receive a mark on their foreheads or on their hands, they will also drink the wine of God's wrath, poured unmixed into the cup of his anger, and they will be tormented with fire and sulfur in the presence of the holy angels and in the presence of the Lamb. And the smoke of their torment goes up forever and ever. There is no rest day or night for those who worship the beast and its image and for anyone who receives the mark of its name." Here is a call for the endurance of the saints, those who keep the commandments of God and hold fast to the faith of Jesus. (Rev 14:9-12)

These early Christian witnesses felt no contradiction between their proclamation of the good news of salvation and the consequences of human sin and failure to respond to the gospel or to live a moral life.

While the writings of the New Testament formed the horizon of belief among the early Christian communities, there were not a few who sought to push the boundaries of the question. Based on 1 Corinthians 15:28 and his own curious blend of Christian faith and Neoplatonic thought, Origen developed the notion that in the end God would be all in all, that hell would be emptied and even Satan himself would be reconciled to God. This teaching became known as *apocatastasis*, or the doctrine of universal salvation. Although Origen's position was later to be condemned, he was not alone in putting forward such speculation. Others with a similar position include Gregory of Nyssa, Clement of Alexandria, and Jerome, all of whom are saints of the church. More recently, universalist tendencies can be found in the writings of Karl Barth, Karl Rahner, and Hans Urs von Balthasar.

The issue of hell continues to "inflame" passions in various quarters.[22] There are justified concerns in balancing divine justice and mercy, righteousness and compassion. Within the broad debate it would seem that there are two basic assertions in relation to hell on which all are agreed:

- The Church teaches the existence of hell as a "state" of eternal punishment (*CCC*, no. 1035)
- The Church has never taught that any particular person is actually in hell.

---

22. A recent debate in *First Things* (culminating in May 2003) arose over the orthodoxy of the position of von Balthasar.

Some might argue that the existence of Satan and the punishment of the demons (fallen angels) does in fact place some beings in hell. However, from these two basic positions theologians have developed three different accounts.

1. Hell is a real (and realized) possibility for human beings. This is perhaps the "common teaching" of the Christian tradition. It would place in hell all those who die in a state of serious, unrepented (mortal) sin. The estimates of those damned to hell vary from the majority of the human race (Augustine's *massa damnata*) to a few recalcitrant sinners. Estimates probably reflect different degrees of optimism or pessimism in relation to the current historical context.

The difficulties people have with this position vary. First, there is the notion of God inflicting an eternal punishment for sins. Is this fair and just? How does it fit with Jesus' revelation of God's forgiveness and mercy? Second, we have problems already identified with the definitive fixity brought about by death. Why is repentance not possible after death? And what is the value of the punishment of hell if it cannot produce repentance? Finally, how is a final eschatological state possible with some part of creation in permanent and unresolved rebellion against God? How can God then be "all in all"? These problems are resolved in one of two distinct directions outlined below.

2. Hell is not a state of punishment but a metaphor for annihilation. Some argue that, rather than a state of punishment, hell is to be thought of as simply the annihilation of the sinner. At death, then, the sinner simply ceases to be. This position is adopted by a number of Protestant theologians, but also by Edward Schillebeeckx.[23]

This solution has a certain elegance. On the one hand, no punishment is as great as simple annihilation; removal of the gift of being is an obvious and complete repudiation of the sinner. And it is an eternal punishment, completely removing the sinner from the flow of time and even being. On the other hand, it removes the problem of an eternal process of conscious suffering on the part of the sinner, a suffering that has no redemptive goal or purpose in the sinners themselves. One might even refer to scriptural references to the "death of the soul," as distinct from the death of the body.[24]

Critics of this position can raise a number of objections. Some would find it hard to reconcile with the notion of hell as commonly taught. Some see it as excessively rationalistic, almost too neat, in the face of the mystery of God.

---

23. Edward Schillebeeckx, *Church: The Human Story of God*, trans. John Bowden (New York: Crossroad, 1990), 134-39.

24. These are loosely based on Rom 8:6; Eph 2:1-3; Col 2:13; Matt 10:28; and Rev 21:8 (which speaks of a "second death").

Finally, it is difficult to reconcile with the notion of the natural immortality of the soul, which has played an important role in Catholic thought. Here we might find why it is attractive to Protestant theologians who do not necessarily accept the natural immortality of the soul.

3. Modified universalism—hell as a real but unrealized possibility. Finally there is a position akin to apocatastasis that would see hell as a real but unrealized possibility. Taking a lead from the absence of any condemnation of a person to hell, this position views hell as a real possibility (realized perhaps in the demons) but never actual in the case of human beings. For example, Edith Stein, recently canonized St. Teresa Benedicta of the Cross by John Paul II, thought the likelihood of going to hell as "infinitely improbable" in light of God's prevenient grace,[25] while St. Thérèse of Lisieux proclaimed belief in hell but entertained the possibility that hell is empty.[26] This position would then consider the Gospel material on hell as a "threat discourse," something that highlights the dangers of human freedom separated from God.

A further modification in von Balthasar's writings is that we must hope that all are in fact saved. We must pray and act for the salvation of all, as an element of Christian hope (*CCC*, no. 1058). The "rightness" of this position is evident in the horrific notion of hoping or praying that someone be condemned to hell. Avery Dulles quotes material from John Paul II that points in this direction:[27]

> Christian faith teaches that in taking the risk of saying "yes" or "no," which marks the (human) creature's freedom, some have already said no. They are the spiritual creatures that rebelled against God's love and are called demons (cf. Fourth Lateran Council). What happened to them is a warning to us: it is a continuous call to avoid the tragedy which leads to sin and to conform our life to that of Jesus who lived his life with a "yes" to God.
>
> Eternal damnation remains a possibility, but we are not granted, without special divine revelation, the knowledge of *whether or which* human beings are effectively involved in it. The thought of hell—and even less the improper use of biblical images—must not create anxiety or despair, but is

---

25. Cited by Hans Urs von Balthasar, *Dare We Hope: "That All Men Be Saved"?*, trans. David Kipp and Lothar Krauth (San Francisco: Ignatius Press, 1988), 219-21. "All merciful love can thus descend to everyone. We believe that it does so. And now, can we assume that there are souls that remain perpetually closed to such love? As a possibility in principle, this cannot be rejected. *In reality,* it can become infinitely improbable—precisely through what preparatory grace is capable of effecting in the soul."

26. See Schillebeeckx, *Church*, 136.

27. Avery Dulles, "The Population of Hell," *First Things* 133 (May 2003): 36-41.

a necessary and healthy reminder of freedom within the proclamation that the risen Jesus has conquered Satan, giving us the Spirit of God who makes us cry "Abba, Father!" (Rom 8:15; Gal 4:6) (*General Audience* talk of July 28, 1999)

There is no resolution of this difficult problem. We are dealing with fundamental issues of freedom, both divine and human, of grace and sin, forgiveness, compassion, and our human hardness of heart. This is the stuff of our human drama. With von Balthasar, perhaps the best we can do is hope that in fact, all are saved.

PURGATORY—A CATHOLIC THING

While belief in heaven and hell is part of the common Christian tradition, Catholics have long held a belief in a third postmortem state, that of purgatory.[28] Persons in purgatory are still "in process"; that is, they are moving "toward" the beatific vision, but because of the reality of sin in their lives, there is some impediment to their final enjoyment of that vision. Their state is "definitive" in that their salvation is assured. But there is still a need for transformation and growth, even after death. As with the case of infant baptism and original sin, belief in purgatory is built on the church's practice of praying for the dead, which led to the teaching, rather than vice versa. How does such prayer benefit the dead and what difference does it make? The doctrinal "answer" to these questions is belief in purgatory.

The first evidence we have of prayers for the dead is in the Second Book of Maccabees (12:43-46). After a battle between Jewish and pagan armies, Jewish fighters who had died in battle were found to have pagan amulets on their bodies—basically good luck charms. This was clearly an affront to God, but on the other hand they had died fighting for the survival of God's people. In addition, at this time speculation in relation to the afterlife was developing among the Jews. The response of the leader of the Jewish forces, Judas Maccabees, was: "It is therefore a holy and wholesome thought to pray for the dead, that they may be loosed from sins." This practice of praying for the dead continued in the early church; for example, the *Apostolic Constitution* (ca. fourth century C.E.) states:

Let us pray for our brethren who sleep in Christ, that God who in his love for men has received the soul of the departed one, may forgive him every

---

28. For a fuller treatment, see Kelly, *Eschatology and Hope*, 114-37.

fault, and in mercy and clemency receive him into the bosom of Abraham, with those who in this life have pleased God.[29]

There are also some scriptural texts, such as 1 Cor 3:11-15, that give some indication of a postmortem purification, but these are relatively minor and inconclusive, at least in the minds of Protestant and Orthodox Christians.

In the Catholic tradition the most definitive teaching on the existence of purgatory is from the Council of Trent (DS 1820; also *CCC*, no. 1030-32). At the time of the Reformation the issue of purgatory was inseparable from the complaints raised by the reformers about the selling of indulgences. Indulgences promised to "free souls from the punishments of purgatory"; the reformers equated this with works of righteousness and buying salvation. In light of this the council fathers affirmed the existence of purgatory and the practice and efficacy of prayer for the dead, while at the same time curtailing certain scandalous practices in relation to indulgences and unhelpful speculations that "do not make for edification" (DS 1820).

This, then, is the basic teaching in relation to the nature of purgatory. Our problem is to try to make some sense of it, as theologians seeking understanding of what is believed. Apart from the existence of purgatory, the elements that seem most significant are the following:

- Prayers for the dead, including indulgences, are efficacious.
- The postmortem state is one of suffering or purification for the effects of the sins in one's life.
- This suffering is "for a time"; that is, it is not eternal.

The first thing that we should note is that these elements seem to presume that the postmortem state is not atemporal or nontemporal. The prayers of the living are a temporal reality, and if they are indeed efficacious for the dead, then it means that there is some relationship between the dead and our temporal world. Similarly the very fact that the sufferings of purgatory are not "eternal" but have a beginning and an end would indicate that there is some temporal order in the postmortem state. If nothing else, the doctrine of purgatory should disabuse us of any assumption that the postmortem state is one of timeless eternity.[30] This is not to take up without some hesitation the notion of spending a number of "days in purgatory" or of indulgences being a release from so many "days in purgatory," as was once promoted in popular

---

29. Quoted in the *Catholic Encyclopedia*, at http://www.newadvent.org/cathen/12575a.htm (accessed April 14, 2006).

30. The International Theological Commission rejected an atemporal understanding of the postmortem state; see "Some Current Questions in Eschatology," *Irish Theological Quarterly* 58 (1992): 215-16.

Catholic piety. But it is to recognize, as we have argued before, that there is an ongoing relationship between the living and the dead one that in some sense "defines" their present state. This notion of a relationship between the living and the dead may also help us understand the other two aspects of purgatory noted above. How do we understand the notion of suffering and the efficacious nature of prayer for the dead?

Let us begin with the notion of the suffering of the dead. Common teaching often refers to the "temporal effects of sin" in relation to purgatory. What might this mean? We know that the evil people do has its consequences in history, in the lives of people and communities. Sin impacts persons, making their own sinfulness more likely; it distorts societies through sinful structures; it distorts cultures through their justification of sinful structures (ideologies). The effects of sin radiate out through human history and do not end simply because a person has died. In a very real sense we are still feeling the "effects" of the sin of "Adam and Eve," and certainly the effects of Adolf Hitler, Josef Stalin, and Pol Pot.

What is the relationship of the sinner who has died to the history of the consequences of their own sinfulness? How do they experience it? Are the dead active agents or passive in relation to the world? Passivity is itself a form of suffering. The dead may indeed "suffer" the consequences of their evil in the world, to which they are related, through their inability to do anything about it, through the awareness of their own personal responsibility for this evil. They suffer their own powerlessness; they suffer out of the love they have for those who are affected by their actions. This passivity is evident in the position of Aquinas that those in purgatory cannot even pray for the living (*ST* II-II q. 83, a. 11). Rather, they are in need of our prayers.

The second aspect of this is more internal and has to do with questions of psychological continuity. In a traditional theology of grace, while God's grace is operative in the sinner, still there are "actual graces" prior to conversion proper, which create shifts or movements in the willingness of the sinner, so as to ensure that the psychological effects of conversion are not so dramatic as to cause serious breakdown. There is no reason to think that the same pattern does not pertain to our postmortem state. Most of this process can be thought of as letting go of undue attachments, a reordering of our desires toward the highest good which is God, a purification of our motivations, and so on. Such processes are not automatic in this life, nor are they likely to be in the next. Again there is a certain passivity to such a process, it is something one "undergoes" or suffers.

This brings us to the final element, the one that underpins the whole doctrine of purgatory, that of prayers for the dead. What does it mean to pray for the dead? Here again we might quote the opinion of Aquinas especially in relation to indulgences, that the primary effect of an indulgence is on the person who performs it (IV *Sententiarum*, dist. xlv, q. ii, a. 3, q. 2). It is not difficult to relate this to what we have discussed above. If the dead suffer the effects of their sins in the world, the changes in us brought about by our prayers can be part of the healing of that evil through:

- Promoting forgiveness in us for the person who has died—our lack of forgiveness may "bind" a person to their sins.
- Taking on some responsibility for the evil they have done to others—repairing the damage done (reparation).

Through actions such as these we may indeed lessen the suffering of those who have died.

There are other eschatological issues that need to be explored, particularly in relation to notions of final judgment, general resurrection, and the relationship of the world to come to the present world. We shall take up these issues in the final chapter of this book.

AFTERLIFE IN OTHER TRADITIONS

We have already noted differences between Christian and early Jewish conceptions of the afterlife, as well as differences between Catholics and other Christians. For example, Judaism has a variety of positions on the afterlife from resurrection to basic agnosticism, while Catholics alone believe in purgatory, though Orthodox Christianity has a parallel notion of tollgates wherein the soul is "educated" or purified for heaven. Islam, too, believes in a system of rewards and punishments, of heaven and hell, based on a moral calculus of the good and evil deeds one does in one's life. However, the reward of heaven is not viewed as a product of divine grace, but more as a just reward for one's moral achievements. Here it differs from Christian belief.

One of the things that clearly differentiates Western and Eastern religious beliefs with regard to the afterlife is Eastern belief in reincarnation. Both Hinduism and Buddhism have some sense of life continuing beyond death, not just through rewards and punishments, but through the reinsertion of the soul into the movement of life, through its reincarnation as another living thing. However, these two major religions have very different understandings of the significance of reincarnation.

For the Hindu believer, reincarnation is part of the great cycle of life, in which the soul is reborn again and again, as it moves along the path of perfection, until it reaches union with God and achieves a cosmic consciousness. Hinduism has been quick to adopt modern evolutionary language because it reflects the Hindu understanding of spiritual development. One's progress on the path to perfection is measured through one's accumulated karma, which is, like some Islam ideas, a matter of a moral calculus, based on one's good and evil deeds. Of course one might regress because of one's evil deeds, but ultimately progress toward perfection is assured.[31]

Undoubtedly many in the West are finding belief in reincarnation an attractive alternative to traditional Christian beliefs concerning the definitive nature of death and judgment. It seems to offer a form of hope that Christian belief cannot match. It is interesting to note, then, that for Buddhist adherents, the cycle of birth and rebirth is something one wishes to be freed from. While Buddhism holds to some form of reincarnation—though not perhaps in the more popular and vulgarized sense commonly portrayed—it views the cycle as part of the illusion in which we are trapped and from which we must be freed. Buddhist practice is aimed at breaking the cycle of birth and rebirth by release from karma through enlightenment, leading to nirvana, the extinction of all desire. This is very different from the Hindu conception of the ultimate goal of union with the Creator.

From the perspective we have developed above, it would be easy to read belief in reincarnation as based on a dualistic anthropology. Whether this is a fair construal demands a more sympathetic entry into the thought of these great religions. However, it does raise important questions about the ground of human identity and the relationship between spirit and matter, soul and body. One may also question whether the notion of reincarnation lessens the moral seriousness of the present life. Herein lies the strength on the Western account that death brings judgment with eternal consequences.

CONCLUSION

In this chapter we have considered issues of individual eschatology, of death, judgment, heaven, purgatory, and hell. However, the Christian tradition places our eschatological fate in a much larger framework, that of the resurrection of the dead and the emergence of a new heaven and a new earth. In our first chapter we explored a contemporary vision of the nature of the universe, which requires a reimagining of our traditional understandings of the doctrine of creation. So too, in our final chapter, a contemporary vision of the nature of the universe requires us to reimagine our eschatological doctrines in relation to resurrection and the final consummation of the universe.

---

31. An account of Hindu belief can be found at http://hinduwebsite.com/reincarnation.htm.

QUESTIONS FOR REFLECTION

1. How credible is belief in life after death? What arguments might we mount for believing that something of our personal identity survives death? Or is it just a matter of "faith" in God's action without any rational basis?
2. How essential is belief in the existence of hell for the Christian life? Can the cosmos still be a place of justice if there is no hell? Or is the notion of hell an empty threat?
3. Anthony Kelly speaks of purgatory in terms of the "realism of hope."[32] How does belief in purgatory express a more realistic account of human beings and their struggle with evil than would a tendency to eliminate the notion of purgatory altogether?
4. Belief in reincarnation has become increasingly popular in the West. What are the gains and losses associated with belief in reincarnation? Why would Buddhism seek escape from the endless cycle of death and rebirth?

SUGGESTIONS FOR FURTHER READING AND STUDY

Balthasar, Hans Urs von. *Dare We Hope: "That All Men Be Saved"?* Translated by David Kipp and Lothar Krauth. San Francisco: Ignatius Press, 1988.

Boros, Ladislaus. *The Moment of Truth: Mysterium Mortis.* Montreal: Palm Publishers, 1965.

Brown, Montague. "Aquinas and the Resurrection of the Body." *Thomist* 56 (1992): 165-207.

Dulles, Avery. "The Population of Hell." *First Things* 133 (May 2003): 36-41.

International Theological Commission. "Some Current Questions in Eschatology." *Irish Theological Quarterly* 58 (1992): 209-43.

Kelly, Anthony. *Eschatology and Hope,* Theology in Global Perspective. Maryknoll, N.Y.: Orbis Books, 2006.

Rahner, Karl. *On the Theology of Death.* New York: Herder & Herder, 1961.

Ratzinger, Joseph. *Eschatology, Death and Eternal Life.* Translated by Michael Waldstein. Edited by Aidan Nichols. Washington, D.C.: Catholic University of America Press, 1988.

Wright, N. T. *The Resurrection of the Son of God.* Vol. 3 of *Christian Origins and the Question of God.* Minneapolis: Fortress, 2003.

---

32. Kelly, *Eschatology and Hope,* 114.

10

The End of All Things

WE BEGAN THIS WORK WITH A REFLECTION on the nature of the cosmos as revealed by modern science. The findings of science, particularly in the fields of cosmology and evolutionary biology, have forced theology to demythologize biblical accounts of creation and seek to integrate those findings into our Christian worldview. Despite the resistance of so-called creation science and proponents of "intelligent design," most theologians have accepted the necessity of this integration. In this chapter we must turn our attention to another area where there exists a major disparity between a Christian worldview and the findings of modern science. This concerns questions of the end of all things. How does the world end? Indeed, what do we even mean by the "end of the world" in light of the findings of modern science? Or is there simply no connection between scientific accounts of the future of the cosmos and our traditional eschatological imagination?

TRADITIONAL ESCHATOLOGY

"We believe in the resurrection of the dead and the life of the world to come." We affirm these words each time we profess our common faith in the Nicene Creed. Yet few would seek to examine the meaning of this profession beyond a very general sense of "life after death." As we saw in an earlier chapter, questions of life after death are very complex, particularly if one is seeking to eliminate any residual dualism from one's intellectual perspective. However, the closer one holds to the unity of human existence as body and soul, and the more one upholds the fundamental orientation of the human spirit to materiality, the more complex become the questions one needs to address about the cosmos as a whole. This is the case particularly in light of modern conceptions of the age and size of the universe together with recent analyses of the final state of the universe.

These are not problems Christian faith has ever had to face in the past. Within a biblical imagination the whole of creation consisted of a vast tent (firmament) stretched over the land to separate the waters above from the waters below and so create dry land (Gen 1:1-4). The biblical conception of the world was relatively limited in scope, so that the idea of the "end of the world" was simple to accept. God could literally "pull the plug" on creation, as occurred in the "great flood" at the time of Noah (Gen 5-8). The later apocalyptic writings of the Old and New Testaments replaced a watery end with more vivid imaginings, with the end of the world bringing fiery judgment to sinners and blessed peace to the righteous.[1] These writings present images of a new heaven and a new earth which arise out of the ashes of the present world. There the dead shall see God face to face, and in their resurrected bodies live in the heavenly city, in communion with God and with one another.

This same basic imagination can be found throughout the history of Christian thought. For example, Thomas Aquinas taught that the resurrection of the dead would not come about until all the heavenly spheres had ceased their motion:

> Hence it would be contrary to the order established in things by Divine providence if the matter of lower bodies were brought to the state of incorruption, so long as there remains movement in the higher bodies. And since, according to the teaching of faith, the resurrection will bring men to immortal life conformably to Christ Who "rising again from the dead dieth now no more" (Rm. 6:9), the resurrection of human bodies will be delayed until the end of the world when the heavenly movement will cease. (*ST* III Suppl. q. 77, a. 1)

The problem is that this imagination is so tied to an outmoded cosmology as to be scarcely credible to a modern scientific worldview. The fact that we repeat such imaginings, particularly those drawn from the Bible, in our Christian worldview is indicative of the huge split we maintain between our faith and the resources of contemporary culture. There is an assumption within our classical Christian imaginations that can no longer be allowed to pass uncrit-

---

1. Contemporary fascination with the "rapture" found in some Evangelical and Pentecostal groups is still firmly wedded to this limited biblical imagination. It has not begun to take into account the findings of modern science. "The belief in rapture—the certainty that the end-time is near—has become widespread in the United States. Consider the current rage on the Christian right, the 'Left Behind' series. The upcoming book in the series is titled *Armageddon*. The publisher's blurb reads, 'No one will escape Armageddon and few will live through the battle to see the Glorious Appearing.' These publications are targeting children. The Left Behind industry has a 'Kids Series.' A blurb from the publisher: 'With over ten million copies sold, Left Behind: The Kids Series is a favorite for all ages. Following a group of teens that were "left behind," and are determined to stand up for God no matter what the costs, they are tested at every turn.' At the Left Behind web site (http://www .leftbehind.com/), they have a video promotion for *Armageddon* replete with footage of American troops in Kuwait." From http://www.publiceye.org/apocalyptic/bush-2003/austin-providence.html (accessed July 13, 2006).

ically. It is the assumption that the end of human history marks the end of cosmos, an assumption buried in the neat phrase "the end of the world." But which "world" are we talking about?

END OF HISTORY, END OF COSMOS?

It is often noted that biblical thinking is more historically oriented than cosmologically oriented. It rejects the cyclical view of the world (often a feature of more cosmologically oriented cultures, as referred to in chapter 3), which it tends to identify with paganism, to embrace a more linear view, one with a beginning, a middle, and an end. The beginning is evident in the material of Genesis 1-11, which moves from paradisal origins to a period of increasing violence and despair over human activities. The middle is the history of God's chosen people beginning with the story of Abraham (Gen 12), chosen as God's instrument to turn around human history, moving through the gift of the Torah, the prophetic critique of Israel's failures, and a messianic longing for God to fulfill the divine promises and bring the redemptive process initiated in Abraham to its completion. From a Christian perspective this history is proleptically completed in the ministry, death, and resurrection of Jesus and continued in the history of the church (particularly in Acts). Increasingly this history is viewed biblically in conflictual apocalyptic terms, a conflict between powerful forces of evil (in Christian literature captured in the symbol of the Antichrist [1 John 2:18, 22; 4:3]) and God's faithful remnant, who suffer persecution at the hands of these evil forces. In the apocalyptic imagination this conflict takes on a cosmic dimension, a conflict between the angels and demons battling over the fate of the entire creation (Daniel; Book of Revelation). History is not just "secular history" but ultimately has theological significance.[2] In the end victory is gained not through human achievement, which proves inadequate to the task, but through divine intervention, which snatches victory or at least vindication from the jaws of defeat. God's enemies are punished in the fires of hell, while the righteous enjoy the rewards of new life. History as we know it is brought to an end, with the coming of the Son of Man as judge of all humanity. God's kingdom will come; peace and justice will reign; every tear will be wiped away; and every sadness will be removed. Not only has human history come to an end, but the whole cosmos is implicated, leading to a "new heaven and a new earth," a new Jerusalem, where God *is* the temple in which we worship (Rev 21:22).

---

2. "Apocalyptic language was ... an elaborate metaphor system for investing historical events with theological significance." N. T. Wright, *The Resurrection of the Son of God*, vol. 3 of *Christian Origins and the Question of God* (Minneapolis: Fortress, 2003), 96.

It was relatively easy to maintain this linkage between the end of human history and the end of cosmos while our cosmos remained relatively small. Indeed, this was the case even up until the end of the nineteenth century.[3] The biblical world consisted of the earth, the waters above and below, and lights in the sky to mark the seasons and time of day. The Ptolemaic universe was a bit bigger, placing the earth at the center with the sun, the moon, and a few planets circling around within the heavenly spheres. Copernicus may have placed the sun at the center, but still the cosmos remained a small affair. Newton's universe was marginally bigger, as people discovered more planets within our solar system and realized that the stars were much farther away than previously recognized. Growing observation displaced the sun from the center to take its place in the outer reaches of the galaxy we call the Milky Way. All this time, it remained at least partially plausible that the end of human history might be linked in some way to the end of the cosmos. However, it was only at the turn of the twentieth century, thanks to the work of Edwin Hubble, that science began to reveal just how big, and how old, the universe really is.[4] Our galaxy, with its 100 billion stars, is just one of another 100 billion galaxies that we can presently observe. The size of the universe is staggering, in comparison with the very limited imaginations of the early biblical writers. It becomes increasingly unlikely that the end of human history would be of any consequence to the rest of the cosmos, which would continue on its merry path with barely a hiccup to note our passing.

The problem is made more difficult if we attempt to absorb the insights of Einstein's theory of relativity. Einstein's theory of special relativity argues that certain features of space and time are relative to observers. Distance and time shift as observers move relative to one another. The truth of Einstein's theory has been verified to remarkable accuracy in experiments with subatomic particles, whose rate of decay varies precisely as predicted with their motion relative to laboratory observer. One of the many consequences of Einstein's theory is that the simultaneity of spatially removed events is also relative to observers. Two observers moving relative to each other will not be able to agree that spatially removed events are simultaneous with one another. There is no universal measure of time on which all observers will agree.[5]

---

3. It was only toward the middle of the nineteenth century that scientists were able to measure the distance to the nearest stars (apart from the sun).

4. Hubble was the first to prove the existence of galaxies other than our own. He also discovered the expansion of the universe, a fundamental observation for all subsequent cosmology.

5. Matthew L. Lamb, "Nature, History, and Redemption," in *Jesus Crucified and Risen: Essays in Spirituality and Theology in Honor of Dom Sebastian Moore*, ed. William Loewe and Vernon Gregson (Collegeville, Minn: Liturgical Press, Michael Glazier, 1998), is one of the few theologians to recognize this.

This observation is important when we ask questions about the relationship between the end of the cosmos and the end of history. The end of human history, when it does come either through our own stupidity (ecological disaster) or violence (nuclear weapons), or through cosmic events (asteroids impacting, or the sun going supernova), will be a relatively distinct temporal event. The end of the cosmos, on the other hand, cannot be a distinct temporal event in the same way. The universe cannot "blink out of existence" because this would imply a common, nonrelative measure of simultaneity, in violation of special relativity. The effect of any temporal event can spread out only at the speed of light. It would seem, then, that the notion that the end of human history would be identical to the end of the cosmos may be simply incoherent.

It is fair to say that our Christian imaginations have simply not caught up with these scientific perspectives. Most of us, theologians included, still live imaginatively in a three-dimensional Newtonian universe rather than the four-dimensional space-time universe uncovered by Einstein.[6] In general the differences this might make to our theology are minimal; however, there is one question that does need exploration where the distinction between the end of human history and the end of cosmos makes a big difference. The question is, When do we think of the resurrection of the dead as occurring? When we speak of resurrection at the end of the world, what exactly is our reference point? Finally we have to realize how completely new this question is. It can only seriously arise in the modern era when we realize the real distinction between the end of human history and the end of the cosmos.

THE RESURRECTION OF THE DEAD

Of course, the more Platonic our thinking, the less interested we are in such a question. If resurrection is viewed as just a religious metaphor for "life after death," conceived in terms of the continued existence of our spiritual soul (and nothing more), then the fate of both human history and the cosmos is of little interest to us. The material universe is like an eggshell, something we discard as we emerge into a new spiritual form of existence. Matter no longer matters and only spirit survives.

It seems to me, however, that this sells short Christian belief in the resurrection of the dead. Throughout this work we have emphasized the funda-

---

6. More recent theories of the physical universe speak of ten or eleven dimensional space-time configurations, for example, the attempts at theories to unify electromagnetic, weak and strong nuclear forces and gravity as found in string theory; see B. Greene, *The Elegant Universe: Superstrings, Hidden Dimensions, and the Quest for the Ultimate Theory* (London: Jonathan Cape, 1999).

mental unity of body and soul. This is clearly part of the biblical understanding of human existence, and it is further supported by the philosophical account of human existence given by Thomas Aquinas. Further, modern biology is making ever clearer the close connections between mind and brain. The human spirit is not a separate substance from our bodies; it is a higher-order integration of all our physical, chemical, biological, and psychic systems, on which it depends for its proper operation, particularly operations of memory, understanding, and reasoning. A disembodied soul may possess a natural immortality, but *of its own natural resources* its capacities to remember, to understand, and to reason are severely compromised. Its natural orientation is to the material world, and the grace of beatitude does not destroy this orientation but completes and perfects it. Hence the need for resurrection, not just as a purely spiritual event, but as something that reestablishes the relationship between the soul and the material order.[7]

RESURRECTION VERSUS IMMORTALITY OF THE SOUL

It has become common to claim an opposition between notions of resurrection and natural immortality of the soul. Often this opposition is expressed in terms of some supposed opposition between biblical revelation and Greek philosophy.[8] We have already indicated the inadequacy of this opposition in other areas and here again it is misplaced. Some argue that resurrection is simply a miracle of God and so does not require any notion of natural immortality. God can raise me up by simply recreating me, with all my memories and other relevant attributes. However, such a notion of resurrection is indistinguishable from replication. If God can recreate me, God can also create multiple copies of me with all my memories and other attributes. Unless there is a spiritual component which is an essential constituent of my existence that survives death, a spiritual component that is then reunited to materiality, then it is not me that is being resurrected but rather a replica of me that God creates. Resurrection in fact requires the natural immortality of the soul to be meaningful.[9]

---

7. This position is argued in more detail in Montague Brown, "Aquinas and the Resurrection of the Body," *Thomist* 56 (1992): 165-207.

8. The position was famously articulated by Oscar Cullmann, *Immortality of the Soul: Or, Resurrection of the Dead? The Witness of the New Testament* (London: Epworth Press, 1960).

9. Wright makes the same point when he notes, "The concepts 'resurrection' and 'immortality' are not in themselves antithetical . . . Granted how the word 'immortality' has been used, it may be misleading to use for [an] intermediate state; but in so far as that state involves some kind of personal

The problem we face is one of timing. When do we place the general resurrection of the dead? The traditional answer—at "the end of the world"—raises more problems than it solves. Do we mean the end of the cosmos, however we might measure this, or do we mean the end of human history, an event we can plausibly locate sometime in the near future (cosmically speaking)?

Some seek to solve this question by abolishing it. Resurrection is then said to occur "immediately"; that is, the dead are raised immediately by God.[10] Either this is conceived as a "spiritual" event, or, while it may be "future for us" in our temporal existence, it is immediate in terms of our experience, for we experience no temporal gap between our death and our resurrection. This is a "neat" solution in that it makes any gap between the end of cosmos and end of history irrelevant, since our lack of any conscious experience of such a gap means that it makes no real difference to us how long the gap might be. However, it also renders meaningless any notion of the natural immortality of the soul, since on this account the immortality would be "unconscious," which really defeats the significance of any such immortality.[11]

If, however, we seek to maintain the notion of natural immortality of the soul and the necessity of resurrection as the reestablishment of intimate connection with the materiality, then the question remains, When do we locate the general resurrection of the dead?

Let us explore the possibility that the resurrection is at the end of the cosmos when, as Aquinas states, "the heavenly movement will cease" (*ST* III Suppl. q. 77, a. 1). Now just as theology has been forced to abandon literal readings of Genesis in relation to the creation of the world and work with modern scientific accounts of creation, so too in the area of eschatology we should begin to reevaluate our Christian imaginings about the end of the world and begin to consider what science is telling us about cosmic unraveling. Given the fact that God established the world according to scientific processes, there is no reason to expect that the final stages of the universe will be anything other than according to those same processes. Just as creation is not a series of divine interventions, as proposed by so-called "scientific cre-

identity which has not been removed by bodily death the term is not inappropriate" (*Resurrection of the Son of God*, 164). Similarly, Gregory of Nyssa views immortality of the soul and resurrection of the body as intimately linked (John L. Drury, "Gregory of Nyssa's Dialogue with Macrina: The Compatibility of Resurrection of the Body and Immortality of the Soul," *Theology Today* 62 [2005]: 210-22).

10. See, for example, Hans Küng, *Eternal Life? Life after Death as a Medical, Philosophical, and Theological Problem* (Garden City, N.Y.: Doubleday, 1984).

11. The statement of the International Theological Commission strongly defends the position that there is an interim period prior to resurrection that involves continued consciousness on the part of the soul. See International Theological Commission, "Some Current Questions in Eschatology," *Irish Theological Quarterly* 58 (1992): 221.

ationism" or "intelligent design," so too the end of all things is likely to occur according to the inner dynamics already discernible through the insights of modern science. If that is in fact the case, then the "end of the cosmos" is an event billions of years in the future (a Big Crunch), if indeed it can be thought of as an event at all, since in some cosmologies the "heavenly movement" simply never ceases. We shall consider two major scenarios in the next section below, but in none of the commonly accepted possibilities are we looking at a short time frame.

The advantage of placing resurrection at the end of the cosmos is that, given the power of God and that we are starting literally with a clean slate, we can say anything we like about resurrection. God can recreate a new heaven and a new earth *ex nihilo*, discarding the old as simply no longer relevant. The difficulty is attempting to find some meaning in the interim state, the gap of billions of years between our own personal death and the final resurrection of the dead. What does one do with all that time? What is the meaning of such a large gap? In the absence of a human presence, does the universe continue to have theological significance? It makes the above suggestion of there being no conscious experience of the gap, or no interim period, look very attractive.

The alternative is to view the general resurrection as being at the end of human history, as marking the completion of all human existence in its current form. While human history in its current form has drawn to a close, human beings as resurrected have an ongoing, meaningful, and effective participation with the rest of cosmic history. The new heaven and the new earth, then, are not a creation *ex nihilo*, but rather the transformation of our existing cosmos into a new and higher form of existence, suggested by Wright's use of the term "transphysical."[12] Is this plausible or have we entered into the realm of science fiction?

The advantage of this position is that it affirms the ongoing value of the present material cosmos. It is not simply a shell to be discarded, but is taken up into a new mode of existence, resurrected existence, so that the history of human relationship to the cosmos does not come to an end with the death of the last remaining human being. Matter matters, especially for the ongoing resurrected state of human beings who by the power of God are brought back into an active relationship with the material order. The difficulty with this position remains one of confronting what it is that science tells us about the end of the cosmos. If resurrection involves an ongoing relationship with the material universe as we currently know it, then the fate of that universe is a matter of theological interest. What, then, does science say about the fate of the universe?

---

12. Wright, *Resurrection of the Son of God*, 477.

COSMIC ESCHATOLOGY

Just as cosmology has forced us to shift our imaginations about how the world began, so too cosmology is forcing us to shift our eschatological imagination as well. What, then, does cosmology tell us about the ultimate fate of the physical universe, and should this be a matter of concern for theology?

While in the early twentieth century cosmologists drew on the Second Law of Thermodynamics to argue that the universe would end in a state of "heat death" with the eventually dissipation of all energy to its lowest, uniform level across the universe, more modern accounts are more complex and difficult to conceptualize. We know that the universe is in a state of expansion at present. It has been so since the "Big Bang" some fifteen billion years ago. However, the end result of this process of expansion is not clear. Will the universe continue to expand forever—whatever "forever" might mean for a physical universe? Or will its expansion cease, to be followed by a "Big Crunch," whereby the universe will, at some time in the future, collapse back down to a superheated mass, similar to that from which the original Big Bang emerged? The answers to such questions depend on the total mass of the universe, which is not so easy to ascertain. If the overall mass of the universe is large enough, eventually the force of gravity might well be enough to induce a Big Crunch. If the mass is less than a critical level it will expand forever. The matter of the universe will dissipate into fundamental nuclear particles, and even this may disintegrate into energy spread over more and more vast regions of space.[13]

At face value neither of these would seem to be an attractive scenario. The long-term prospects for some type of continuing involvement in cosmic history through the resurrection of humanity do not seem very likely. Indeed, it would be more than tempting to revert to a more "spiritual" understanding of resurrection simply as a way of avoiding the problem. Is there any way, let alone any point, in conceiving of continued human engagement with a cosmos whose fate is either to collapse into a fiery ball or to dissipate into ultimate oblivion?

Things are not that simple, however. Physicist Frank Tipler has been investigating the possibilities present within the universe for continued order and meaning in the various cosmic scenarios that face us. Tipler's approach reads like science fiction, with the deployment of self-replicating von Neumann machines which "embody" human meanings and values and spread throughout the galaxy and eventually the universe.[14] At each stage of future cosmic

---

13. See John D. Barrow and Frank J. Tipler, *The Anthropic Cosmological Principle* (Oxford: Oxford University Press, 1988), for an analysis of various scenarios.

14. John von Neumann was one of the great mathematicians of the twentieth century. He conceived of the idea of self-replicating machines or "universal constructors," which were computers designed to construct new versions of themselves.

evolution these machines could, with appropriate technological advances, find the necessary surplus energy to continue to manipulate matter, even to the point of "resurrecting" human beings through computer simulations. Eventually the whole cosmos would be brought under "intelligent" control, reaching what Tipler refers to as the "Omega point" of cosmic evolution.[15]

It is of course not my intention to endorse Tipler's suggestions, which many might consider verge on a caricature of genuine Christian belief. On Tipler's account, resurrection is a technological achievement, not a gift from God. However, his work does represent a steadfast refusal to adopt a "spiritualized" account of resurrection that would make the ongoing existence of the universe after the death of the last human being a matter of no theological interest. This is the question that remains for us to consider. To find some answer we might turn to the only clear account of resurrection that we know of, that of Jesus, and see what it might teach us.

THE RESURRECTION OF JESUS—WHAT DOES IT TEACH US?

We have considered two distinct scenarios in relation to resurrection. One stresses the discontinuity between our current state and our resurrected state. God raises us up from the ashes of the old world, starting as it were with a clean slate. The other stresses the continuity between our current state and our resurrected state. The new heaven and the new earth emerge in the midst of the present cosmos, transforming it from within. Does the resurrection of Jesus help shed any light on these options?

Certainly in the resurrection of Jesus we find elements of continuity and of discontinuity. There is a strong element of continuity in terms of personal identity. It is Jesus who is raised from the dead; it is Jesus who initiates a new relationship with his disciples (Matt 28:9, 18; Luke 24:15); it is Jesus who breaks the bread and opens up the Scriptures on the road to Emmaus (Luke 24:25-30). But there is a discontinuity in the form of existence. The risen Jesus is not a revivified corpse; his appearances and disappearances do not conform to those of a normal bodily existence (Luke 24:31; John 20:19); even his closest friends find it difficult to recognize him (John 20:11-16). In 1 Corinthians 15 Paul attempts to give expression to these elements of continuity and discontinuity, but one would be hard pressed at the end of the day to say that he sheds much light on the precise nature of the resurrection:

---

15. Frank J. Tipler, *The Physics of Immortality: Modern Cosmology, God, and the Resurrection of the Dead* (New York: Anchor Books, 1994). Tipler's work has generated considerable debate, both from scientists and from theologians. Wolfhart Pannenberg has expressed qualified support of Tipler's theories, though a number of authors on both sides of the science/theology divide have been highly critical.

But someone will ask, "How are the dead raised? With what kind of body do they come?" Fool! What you sow does not come to life unless it dies. And as for what you sow, you do not sow the body that is to be, but a bare seed, perhaps of wheat or of some other grain. But God gives it a body as he has chosen, and to each kind of seed its own body. Not all flesh is alike, but there is one flesh for human beings, another for animals, another for birds, and another for fish. There are both heavenly bodies and earthly bodies, but the glory of the heavenly is one thing, and that of the earthly is another. There is one glory of the sun, and another glory of the moon, and another glory of the stars; indeed, star differs from star in glory. So it is with the resurrection of the dead. What is sown is perishable, what is raised is imperishable. It is sown in dishonor, it is raised in glory. It is sown in weakness, it is raised in power. It is sown a physical body, it is raised a spiritual body. If there is a physical body, there is also a spiritual body. Thus it is written, "The first man, Adam, became a living being"; the last Adam became a life-giving spirit. But it is not the spiritual that is first, but the physical, and then the spiritual. The first man was from the earth, a man of dust; the second man is from heaven. As was the man of dust, so are those who are of the dust; and as is the man of heaven, so are those who are of heaven. Just as we have borne the image of the man of dust, we will also bear the image of the man of heaven. (1 Cor 15:35-49)[16]

There is another element of continuity and discontinuity in terms of the ongoing presence of Jesus with his church. If we follow the Lukan account, then the risen Jesus ascends into heaven with the promise that he will return at the end of time (Acts 1:9-11). For John, too, Jesus must return to the Father (John 20:17). For Matthew, however, the risen Jesus promises his eternal presence to the disciples, without any suggestion of withdrawal or ascension (Matt 28:20). Paul talks of the church as the body of Christ (1 Cor 12:12-27), and Jesus speaks of the blessed and broken bread as his body (Matt 26:26-28).

One thing, however, that is constant in this whole account is that the risen Jesus is not detached from his church or from the world. Luke may have Jesus ascend, but he also has the risen Jesus confront Paul with his actions in persecuting the church (Acts 9:3-5). Jesus may be "in heaven," but he pleads for sinners at the right hand of the Father (Rom 8:34). At the final judgment Jesus reveals his continual personal identification with the poor, the imprisoned, the hungry, and the naked and judges us in terms of our response to their needs (Matt 25:31-46). Is this identification "general" or "specific"? Does he identify with the poor in some general way, and only with each individual

---

16. See Wright, *Resurrection of the Son of God*, 312-60, for an analysis of the complexity of this passage. In particular Wright rejects any suggestion that takes this passage as denying the physicality of the resurrection.

because of this generic identification, or does he know and love each one of them personally, so that he identifies specifically with one and all? Is Paul correct when he claimed that "the Son of God ... loved *me* and gave Himself for *me*" (Gal 2:20)? It would seem that for the authors of the New Testament, Jesus had an ongoing, active, and intentional relationship with human history.

However, the story does not end there. The risen Jesus not only has a role in the ongoing history of the church, and humanity more generally; his resurrection is of cosmic significance: "as a plan for the fullness of time, to gather up all things in him, things in heaven and things on earth" (Eph 1:10). "Therefore God also highly exalted him and gave him the name that is above every name, so that at the name of Jesus every knee should bend, in heaven and on earth and under the earth" (Phil 2:9-10). "Through him God was pleased to reconcile to himself all things, whether on earth or in heaven, by making peace through the blood of his cross" (Col 1:20). The whole of creation is brought under the reign of Christ, not just our human history. The incarnation and resurrection are events predestined before time to bring the whole of creation together under God.

Before we proceed with this, there are two issues that require clarification. The first is the misunderstanding, not uncommon, that the humanity of Jesus somehow becomes inactive or irrelevant with the resurrection. It is as if the resurrection of Jesus eliminates the humanity of Jesus and replaces it with his divinity. An apologetic theology would often argue that the resurrection "proves" the divinity of Jesus. As is clear from the anthropology developed in this work, however, the resurrection in fact proves Jesus' full humanity. Human beings require resurrection, and the resurrection of Jesus is required for him to be a continuing agent in human history. The human consciousness of Jesus continues as a human consciousness and is not absorbed into or eliminated by his divine consciousness.[17]

The second issue regards the commonly stated notion that the risen Jesus "transcends space and time." Rahner, for example, speaks of the resurrected state as pan-cosmic, as no longer bound by the limitations of space and time.[18] Again, this notion needs to be critically reevaluated in light of contemporary understandings of the nature of the universe. Clearly Rahner's notion of a pan-cosmic relationship is an advance on an a-cosmic existence, with all its Platonic overtones.[19] We need to ask, however, whether the risen Jesus is no

---

17. The human consciousness and divine consciousness of Jesus remain distinct, as a consequence of Chalcedon's distinction between the two natures of Christ. See, for example, Bernard J. F. Lonergan, *The Ontological and Psychological Constitution of Christ*, ed. Frederick E. Crowe and Robert M. Doran, trans. Michael G. Shields, Collected Works of Bernard Lonergan 7 (Toronto: University of Toronto Press, 2002). This distinction is not abolished by the death and resurrection of Jesus. Otherwise Jesus' resurrection cannot be a model for our resurrection.

18. Karl Rahner, *On the Theology of Death* (New York: Herder & Herder, 1961).

19. Peter C. Phan notes that "in his later systematic writings on death, [Rahner] quietly dropped

longer bound by the spatio-temporal structure of the universe? Strictly speaking, an agent who transcends space and time can also act backwards in time, another consequence of Einstein's theory of relativity.[20] Are we to think of the risen Jesus as active prior to his own death, or his own birth? Does he exercise a reverse temporal causality? Here again, the distinction between the human and the divine in Jesus is very important. While the divine consciousness of Jesus, the consciousness of the Logos as the second person of the Trinity, does transcend space and time, it is not at all clear that this is the case for the human consciousness of Jesus, even the risen Jesus.

If this is the case, then the "Christification" of the universe is still in process, not just because human history is still caught in the dialectic of grace and sin, but also because the human consciousness of the risen Jesus does not yet encompass the universe as a whole. In this regard, Peter Chirico contrasts the type of conception of the resurrection commensurate with a static worldview, with the type commensurate with a dynamic worldview. A static worldview gives rise to the concept of a static unrestricted subject who:

> would be one whose self-differentiation would be conceived as totally developed in regard to the world in which he lived. Every capacity of this subject within that world would be developed to its fullest extent possible ... The static fully developed subject would live in a static world and would fully grasp himself and the world.[21]

On the other hand, a dynamic worldview gives rise to the concept of a dynamic unrestricted human subject who "would constantly be expanding within a constantly expanding world, a world whose intelligibility would be ceaselessly increasing." Chirico argues that the risen Jesus exists as such a dynamic unrestricted human subject.

We might also ask questions about the traditional notion of the communion of saints. It is clearly part of Catholic tradition to pray to those who it holds have been taken into divine intimacy with God in heaven (especially in the case of Mary the Mother of Jesus [*CCC*, no. 2675]). There is a strong sense that the saints "intervene" on our behalf, that our prayers to them are not in vain, and that through their mediation divine favor may be granted us. In

---

this theory [of the pancosmic soul] or at least no longer espoused it with his initial enthusiasm" (*Eternity in Time: A Study of Karl Rahner's Eschatology* [Selinsgrove: Susquehanna University Press, 1988], 114).

20. Of course, time travel is a common theme in many science fiction stories, but the paradoxes involved of reverse causality—for example, killing one's own father before one is conceived—make it a most unlikely possibility.

21. Peter Chirico, *Infallibility: The Crossroads of Doctrine* (Kansas City: Sheed Andrews & McMeel, 1977), 155-56.

extraordinary cases this may mean miracles, events that seem to go beyond our normal expectation of what is possible. Are such actions personal or impersonal, intentional or unintentional? Do they arise from a real sense of personal relationship with the one who prays? Do they represent a real, active, and personal relationship between those in the "church triumphant" and those in the "church militant"?

This is most notable in the church's teaching on Mary, "assumed body and soul into heaven." Consider the formal decree of this teaching:

> Consequently, just as the glorious resurrection of Christ was an essential part and the final sign of this victory, so that struggle which was common to the Blessed Virgin and her divine Son should be brought to a close by the glorification of her virginal body, for the same Apostle says: "When this mortal thing hath put on immortality, then shall come to pass the saying that is written: Death is swallowed up in victory." Hence the revered Mother of God, from all eternity joined in a hidden way with Jesus Christ in one and the same decree of predestination, immaculate in her conception, a most perfect virgin in her divine motherhood, the noble associate of the divine Redeemer who has won a complete triumph over sin and its consequences, finally obtained, as the supreme culmination of her privileges, that she should be preserved free from the corruption of the tomb and that, like her own Son, having overcome death, she might be taken up body and soul to the glory of heaven where, as Queen, she sits in splendour at the right hand of her Son, the immortal King of the Ages. (Pius XII, *Munificentissimus Deus*, [1950], DS 3902)

One might notice immediately the strong parallels between the language of assumption and the language of resurrection. One gets the strong impression that while Jesus may be the "firstborn" of the new creation (Col 1:18) and exemplar of all our resurrections (Rom 8:29), nonetheless, resurrection is not restricted to Jesus alone (see also Matt 27: 50-53 for a more scriptural example).

What conclusions may we draw from this discussion? I would suggest that resurrection of the dead is not into an a-cosmic state, nor a pan-cosmic state, but into a state of ongoing, active, and effective relationship with human history, and beyond that with the ongoing processes of the whole cosmos. This is not something brought about by one's own "natural" powers, but through the power of God operating through and in those who have died. The new creation of the resurrection does not involve the discarding of the old order, but rather its being taken up in a new and more creative way. Through resurrection the history of the cosmos can be open to become part of an ongoing human history in ways we may find difficult to imagine.

FINAL JUDGMENT

The New Testament refers frequently to a not-too-distant judgment, a judgment that will involve the return of the Son of Man, who will come in glory to "separate the sheep from the goats." As the Nicene Creed affirms: "He will come again in glory to judge the living and the dead, and his kingdom will have no end." Often this is viewed as initiating a general resurrection of the dead: "We look for the resurrection of the dead, and the life of the world to come."

The problem that confronts us is what exactly the purpose of this general final judgment might be. If there is judgment at death for each individual, what purpose does such a final judgment hold? Does it simply duplicate each individual judgment or is there something else that is the object of judgment in this final setting?

The first thing that needs to be demythologized is the type of Hollywood apocalyptic scenario, where Jesus in his second coming appears in the clouds dispensing bolts of lightning on God's enemies. Much of this arises from an imagination that is almost premodern in nature. For example, where exactly will Jesus appear? Over Washington? Moscow? London? Jerusalem? Wherever he appears, half the world will be in daylight, the other half in nighttime.[22] Most will certainly not be able to see him, if this is how we imagine his second coming.

Moreover, we need to ask, as Rahner does in relation to the connection between death and personal judgment,[23] Does the second coming of Jesus initiate final judgment and the "end of the world," or does the "end of the world," understood as the end of human history in its current form, initiate final judgment? Perhaps we are looking at some type of final assessment of human history as a whole coming at the end of human history, something that is not just the sum of its individual parts (personal judgments)? Just as sin has a transpersonal and historical element, so too final judgment may well embrace these transpersonal and historical elements as a final estimation of the human race as a whole.

Just as Rahner argues for an intrinsic connection between death and personal judgment, I would argue for an intrinsic connection between the final judgment and the end of human history. The end of human history could come about from a variety of reasons. It is not unlikely that we will be the

---

22. This obvious point seems to have eluded Aquinas's premodern cosmology as he argues that the resurrection will be at night (*ST* III Suppl q. 77, a. 3).

23. Rahner, *On the Theology of Death*, 29.

arbiters of our own fate, as the means of mass destruction become easier to create and the sources of conflict take on an increasingly global reach. Alternatively, our present inability to tackle our growing ecological problems could be the deciding issue.[24] Such an end to human history would itself be a form of judgment, a judgment on the deep-seated nature of the problem of evil, both in the individual and in human history as a whole. It would also be a time of testing, of trial, with a corresponding temptation to despair and hopelessness. Indeed, we might well pray, "do not bring us to the time of trial" (Luke 11:4).

Second, we must consider the divine response to such a human calamity. Would this apparent triumph of evil in human history be the last word, a final whimper with no one left to hear it? Or would it be the occasion for the coming of God's definitive Word to pronounce a judgment that redeems all that was good and true in our difficult, troublesome history, even while casting aside the destructive elements that brought human history to its end? If God is indeed the creator God and Lord of history, then it is fitting that the end of history be intrinsically linked to judgment and the second coming of Christ.

Third, if all that is true and good in human history is to be redeemed at the end of history, can this mean anything less than the resurrection of the dead? The pattern of suffering, death, and final vindication through resurrection is, after all, the pattern of Jesus himself. Should we expect anything less for the totality of human history itself? None of this implies that the end of human history would be a good thing, or an end to be sought after. Indeed it would be nothing less than an appalling evil and an indictment on human history. The resurrection is not about justifying the evil but about redeeming and vindicating the good that evil seeks to destroy. It is the divine response of drawing good out of evil, a *creatio ex nihilo*. And it clearly indicates that the hope of human history does not lie in human hands, as in the liberal myth of progress or a communist dream of a workers' paradise or in Frank Tipler's notion of resurrection through cybernetic reconstruction.[25] Our hope lies in God alone.

While the precise content of this final judgment remains open, the criteria are clearly spelled out in Matthew's Gospel:

---

24. Wolfhart Pannenberg describes "apocalyptic ideas of a destruction of our earthly environment by the misuse of technology" as "more compelling" possibilities for the end of history than biblical scenarios taken literally (*Systematic Theology*, trans. Geoffrey W. Bromiley, 3 vols. [Grand Rapids: Eerdmans, 1991], 3:590).

25. Tipler, *Physics of Immortality*. A preliminary form of the argument is worked out in conjunction with Barrow in Barrow and Tipler, *Anthropic Cosmological Principle*.

> Then the king will say to those at his right hand, "Come, you that are blessed by my Father, inherit the kingdom prepared for you from the foundation of the world; for I was hungry and you gave me food, I was thirsty and you gave me something to drink, I was a stranger and you welcomed me, I was naked and you gave me clothing, I was sick and you took care of me, I was in prison and you visited me." (Matt 25:34-36)

What this passage reveals is Jesus' complete sense of solidarity with the poor, the dispossessed, the weak, and the vulnerable in human history. Human history, from the perspective of the powerful, the rich, and the strong, will be turned on its head. They will no longer be able to "call the shots" or "take control of the situation." Rather, they will be brought low:

> And Mary said,
> "My soul magnifies the Lord, and my spirit rejoices in God my Savior,
> for he has looked with favor on the lowliness of his servant.
> Surely, from now on all generations will call me blessed;
> for the Mighty One has done great things for me, and holy is his name.
> His mercy is for those who fear him from generation to generation.
> He has shown strength with his arm; he has scattered the proud in the thoughts of their hearts.
> He has brought down the powerful from their thrones, and lifted up the lowly;
> he has filled the hungry with good things, and sent the rich away empty.
> He has helped his servant Israel, in remembrance of his mercy, according to the promise he made to our ancestors, to Abraham and to his descendants forever." (Luke 1:46-55)

How will human history be judged on such criteria? How does human history look to indigenous peoples who have been dispossessed of their land and their culture, through colonization and economic exploitation? How does it look to the millions of poor in Africa, stricken by AIDS, who do not have access to expensive drugs and other treatments? How does it look to slum dwellers in the sprawling cities of third world countries who must eke a living out of the garbage of the rich elites of those countries? Will they be as generous to us in their assessment of human history as we have been to them in the living of that history? The parable of Dives and Lazarus hangs over the whole of human history (Luke 16:19-31).

In his perceptive work *Raising Abel*, James Alison tells a moving parable of the eschatological reconciliation of Abel with his brother Cain.[26] Cain is

---

26. James Alison, *Raising Abel: The Recovery of Eschatological Imagination* (New York: Crossroad, 1996), 132-34.

drawing to the close of his life, after a lifetime of struggle with the violence his murder of Abel unleashed. He lives in fear and under a cloud of guilt for the primordial murder of his brother, a murder born not of hatred but of envy, a "devastating excess of love that grasps at being."[27] As he struggles yet again to go to sleep, he notices an intruder entering into his bare hut. He fears that this intruder will unleash the final act of violence against him; the intruder is young and strong in comparison with his frailty and age. But the intruder reveals himself to be his brother Abel, returned from the dead. This encounter between Cain and Abel, between brother murderer and murdered brother, is not a pleasant one for Cain, as it revives all his memories of the distant event and the way in which it shaped the rest of his life's journey.

> Nevertheless, the young brother doesn't let him off this strange trial, for in this court, the younger brother is victim, attorney, and judge, and the trial is the process of unblaming the one who did not dare to hear an accusation that never comes. Strangely, as his memory takes body, the old man begins to feel less and less the weight of the threatened end, which he had almost heard roaring about his ears. And he is right to lose that feeling, for the end has already come, but not as threat: it has come as his brother who forgives . . . [I]n this . . . does the Christian faith consist: in the return of Abel as forgiveness for Cain, and the return of Abel not only as a decree of forgiveness for Cain, but as an insistent presence which gives Cain time to recover his story.[28]

Indeed, we can witness this same drama unfolding in the accounts of the resurrection of Jesus. We have become so familiar with the story of the resurrection of Jesus as "good news" that we forget the implications this resurrection might have held for his disciples. These are the ones who deserted Jesus at the time of his greatest need. Peter had denied him three times. All this occurred after their protestations that they would stick with him to the end (Matt 26:30-35). If you were one of his disciples, how would you react to suggestions that Jesus had risen from the dead? We are all familiar with the story of the disciples on the road to Emmaus, but we do not always attend to the fact that they have already heard news that Jesus is risen (Luke 24:22-24). They do not hang around to celebrate, but head off in the opposite direction, along the road to Emmaus. The risen Jesus may well provoke fear for the disciples. How will he react to their desertion and betrayal? Will be bring vengeance and punishment? Rather, what we hear is a constant refrain, "Do not be afraid; peace be with you" (Matt 28:10; Luke 24:37; John 20:20, 21, 26). Jesus brings

---

27. Ibid., 133.
28. Ibid., 134.

not punishment but the offer of forgiveness. Thomas, the one who doubts the truth of the resurrection, must confront the reality of the suffering that Jesus endured—"place your hands in my wounds" (see John 20:27)—in order for this forgiveness to penetrate his heart. Like the parable of Cain and Abel above, he encounters that reality not as blame and guilt but as an outpouring of love and forgiveness through the "insistent presence" of the risen Lord.

Can we find in this a model for the final judgment of human history, a judgment where the victims are judge? The complexity of the model is evident when we realize that we are all in our own way both victim and perpetrator, both sinner and sinned against. Only in Jesus do we find the pure and spotless victim (Heb 9:14; 1 Pet 1:18-19), the one who through a voluntary act of solidarity has identified himself with that which is victim in us all. Through this act of identification he becomes Abel to our Cain, not in accusation (the role of Satan) but in mediating forgiveness and reconciliation to the whole of human history. This is the final judgment of human history, where the voices of the victims are finally heard, where restorative justice is finally effected, and where a new and glorious human community can live to the glory of God, in the radiance of their risen Lord:

> Then I saw a new heaven and a new earth; for the first heaven and the first earth had passed away, and the sea was no more. And I saw the holy city, the new Jerusalem, coming down out of heaven from God, prepared as a bride adorned for her husband. And I heard a loud voice from the throne saying, "See, the home of God is among mortals. He will dwell with them; they will be his peoples, and God himself will be with them; he will wipe every tear from their eyes. Death will be no more; mourning and crying and pain will be no more for the first things have passed away." . . . I saw no temple in the city, for its temple is the Lord God the Almighty and the Lamb. And the city has no need of sun or moon to shine on it, for the glory of God is its light, and its lamp is the Lamb. The nations will walk by its light, and the kings of the earth will bring their glory into it. Its gates will never be shut by day—and there will be no night there. People will bring into it the glory and the honor of the nations. (Rev 21:1-4; 22-26)

> The Spirit and the bride say, "Come." And let everyone who hears say, "Come." And let everyone who is thirsty come. Let anyone who wishes take the water of life as a gift. (Rev 22:17)

QUESTIONS FOR REFLECTION

1. For many Christians the notion of resurrection seems to have been displaced by a general notion of immortality. What does resurrection add to the general

sense of personal survival after death? How important are our bodies to our personal identity?

2. Is the notion of resurrection as a permanent and ongoing relationship with the material world credible in light of what we currently think about the fate of the material cosmos? How might Christian belief in resurrection challenge our current conceptions of the fate of the material cosmos?

3. Many Christians today speaks about a "rapture" that will take Christians up into heaven, based on a literal reading of 1 Thessalonians 4:16-17. How credible is the cosmology behind such a claim? For a critique of the concept of rapture, see http://www.ntwrightpage.com/Wright_BR_Farewell_Rapture.htm.

4. Hans Urs von Balthasar claims that we must dare to hope that all people are saved. Can we conceive of a situation in which the Nazis and those executed in the gas chambers, Jews and others, are reconciled? Slave owners and their slaves? Rapists and their victims? What might final reconciliation mean to each side of this divide?

SUGGESTIONS FOR FURTHER READING AND STUDY

Alison, James. *Raising Abel: The Recovery of Eschatological Imagination*. New York: Crossroad, 1996.

Cullmann, Oscar. *Immortality of the Soul: Or, Resurrection of the Dead? The Witness of the New Testament*. London: Epworth Press, 1960.

Drury, John L. "Gregory of Nyssa's Dialogue with Macrina: The Compatibility of Resurrection of the Body and Immortality of the Soul." *Theology Today* 62 (2005): 210-22.

International Theological Commission. "Some Current Questions in Eschatology." *Irish Theological Quarterly* 58 (1992): 209-43.

Phan, Peter C. *Eternity in Time: A Study of Karl Rahner's Eschatology*. Selinsgrove: Susquehanna University Press, 1988.

Rahner, Karl. *On the Theology of Death*. New York: Herder & Herder, 1961.

Ratzinger, Joseph. *Eschatology, Death and Eternal Life*. Translated by Michael Waldstein. Edited by Aidan Nichols. Washington, D.C.: Catholic University of America Press, 1988.

Tipler, Frank J. *The Physics of Immortality: Modern Cosmology, God, and the Resurrection of the Dead*. New York: Anchor Books, 1994.

Bibliography

Alison, James. *The Joy of Being Wrong: Original Sin through Easter Eyes*. New York: Crossroad, 1998.

———. *Raising Abel: The Recovery of Eschatological Imagination*. New York: Crossroad, 1996.

Aristotle. *Nicomachean Ethics*. Translated by W. D. Ross. Oxford: Oxford University Press, 1980.

Augustine. *The Confessions*. Translated by Maria Boulding. Vintage Spiritual Classics. New York: Vintage Books, 1998.

Balthasar, Hans Urs von. *Dare We Hope: "That All Men Be Saved"?* Translated by David Kipp and Lothar Krauth. San Francisco: Ignatius Press, 1988.

———. *Theo-Drama: Theological Dramatic Theory*. 5 vols. San Francisco: Ignatius Press, 1988-98.

———. "Women Priests? A Marian Church in a Fatherless and Motherless Culture." *Communio* 22 (1995): 164-70.

Barrow, John D., and Frank J. Tipler. *The Anthropic Cosmological Principle*. Oxford: Oxford University Press, 1988.

Barth, Karl. *The Epistle to the Romans*. Translated by Edwyn Clement Hoskyns. London: Oxford University Press, 1933.

Bartlett, Anthony W. *Cross Purposes: The Violent Grammar of Christian Atonement*. Harrisburg, Pa.: Trinity Press International, 2001.

Bellah, Robert Neelly, Richard Madsen, William M. Sullivan, Ann Swidler, and Steven M. Tipton. *Habits of the Heart: Individualism and Commitment in American Life*. Berkeley: University of California Press, 1985.

Bhaskar, Roy. *A Realist Theory of Science*. Atlantic Highlands, N.J.: Humanities Press, 1978.

Boff, Leonardo. *The Maternal Face of God: The Feminine and Its Religious Expressions*. San Francisco: Harper & Row, 1987.

Boros, Ladislaus. *The Moment of Truth: Mysterium Mortis*. Montreal: Palm Publishers, 1965.

Bosch, David. *Transforming Mission: Paradigm Shifts in Theology of Mission*. Maryknoll, N.Y.: Orbis Books, 1991.

Brockman, James R. *Romero: A Life*. Maryknoll, N.Y.: Orbis Books, 2005.

Brown, Montague. "Aquinas and the Resurrection of the Body." *Thomist* 56 (1992): 165-207.

Brown, Peter. *The Body and Society: Men, Women, and Sexual Renunciation in Early Christianity*. New York: Columbia University Press, 1988.

Burns, J. Patout. *The Development of Augustine's Doctrine of Operative Grace*. Paris: Etudes Augustiniennes, 1980.

Burrell, David. "Does Process Theology Rest on a Mistake?" *Theological Studies* 43 (1982): 125-35.

Byrne, Brendan. *Romans*. Sacra Pagina 6. Collegeville, Minn.: Liturgical Press, 1996.

Calvin, John. *The Institutes of Christian Religion*. Translated by Henry Beveridge. Edinburgh: Calvin Translation Society, 1845.

Catechism of the Catholic Church. 2nd ed. Strathfield, N.S.W.: St Pauls, 1997.

Cavanaugh, William T. *Torture and Eucharist: Theology, Politics, and the Body of Christ*. Oxford: Blackwell, 1998.

Chirico, Peter. *Infallibility: The Crossroads of Doctrine*. Kansas City: Sheed Andrews & McMeel, 1977.

Clifford, Richard J. "The Hebrew Scriptures and the Theology of Creation." *Theological Studies* 46 (1985): 507-23.

Clooney, Francis Xavier. *Theology after Vedanta: An Experiment in Comparative Theology*. Albany: State University of New York Press, 1993.

Cobb, John. *A Christian Natural Theology*. Philadelphia: Westminster Press, 1965.

Coffey, David. *Grace: The Gift of the Holy Spirit*. Sydney: Catholic Institute of Sydney, 1979.

Colombo, J. "Rahner and His Critics: Lindbeck and Metz." *Thomist* 56 (1992): 71-96.

Copleston, Frederick Charles. *Aquinas*. Harmondsworth: Penguin, 1975.

Cullmann, Oscar. *Immortality of the Soul: Or, Resurrection of the Dead? The Witness of the New Testament*. London: Epworth Press, 1960.

Curran, Charles. *Themes in Fundamental Moral Theology*. Notre Dame, Ind.: University of Notre Dame Press, 1977.

Dawkins, Richard. *The Blind Watchmaker: Why the Evidence of Evolution Reveals a Universe without Design*. New York: Norton, 1996.

Denzinger, Henricus, and Adolfus Schönmetzer, eds. *Enchiridion Symbolorum Definitionum et Declarationum de Rebus Fidei et Morum*. 36th ed. Freiburg im Breisgau: Herder, 1965.

Doran, Robert M. "The Analogy of Dialectic and the Systematics of History." In *Religion in Context*, edited by T. Fallon and P. Riley, 35-57. Lanham, Md.: University Press of America, 1988.

———. *Theology and the Dialectics of History*. Toronto: University of Toronto Press, 1990.

Doyle, Dennis M. *Communion Ecclesiology: Vision and Versions*. Maryknoll, N.Y.: Orbis Books, 2000.

Drury, John L. "Gregory of Nyssa's Dialogue with Macrina: The Compatibility of Resurrection of the Body and Immortality of the Soul." *Theology Today* 62 (2005): 210-22.

Duffy, Stephen. *The Dynamics of Grace: Perspectives in Theological Anthropology*. Collegeville, Minn.: Liturgical Press, 1993.

———. *The Graced Horizon: Nature and Grace in Modern Catholic Thought*. Collegeville, Minn.: Liturgical Press, 1992.

———. "Original Sin: Our Hearts of Darkness Revisited." *Theological Studies* 49 (1988): 597-622.

Dulles, Avery. "The Population of Hell." *First Things* 133 (May 2003): 36-41.

———. "Two Languages of Salvation: The Lutheran-Catholic Joint Declaration."
    First Things 98 (December 1999): 25-30.

Edwards, Denis. *Jesus and the Cosmos.* Homebush: St Paul's Publications, 1991.

Fagan, Sean. *Does Morality Change?* Collegeville, Minn.: Liturgical Press, 1997.

Faludi, Susan. *Backlash: The Undeclared War against American Women.* New York:
    Crown, 1991.

Fox, Matthew. *Original Blessing.* Santa Fe, N.M.: Bear, 1983.

Fredericks, James L. *Faith among Faiths: Christian Theology and Non-Christian Reli-
    gions.* New York: Paulist Press, 1999.

Freud, Sigmund. "Totem and Taboo." In *The Origins of Religion.* London: Penguin,
    1985.

Fuellenbach, John. *The Kingdom of God: The Message of Jesus Today.* Maryknoll, N.Y.:
    Orbis Books, 1995.

Geertz, Clifford. *The Interpretation of Cultures: Selected Essays.* New York: Basic Books,
    1973.

Girard, René. *I See Satan Fall like Lightning.* Maryknoll, N.Y.: Orbis Books, 2001.

———. *The Scapegoat.* Baltimore: Johns Hopkins University Press, 1986.

———. *Violence and the Sacred.* Baltimore: Johns Hopkins University Press, 1977.

Girard, René, Jean-Michel Oughourlian, and Guy Lefort. *Things Hidden since the
    Foundation of the World.* Stanford, Calif.: Stanford University Press, 1987.

Girard, René, and James G. Williams. *The Girard Reader.* New York: Crossroad, 1996.

Greene, B. *The Elegant Universe: Superstrings, Hidden Dimensions, and the Quest for the
    Ultimate Theory.* London: Jonathan Cape, 1999.

Gutiérrez, Gustavo. *A Theology of Liberation: History, Politics, and Salvation.* Translated
    by Sister Caridad Inda and John Eagleson. Maryknoll, N.Y.: Orbis Books, 1973.

Habermas, Jürgen. *Knowledge and Human Interests.* Translated by Jeremy J. Shapiro.
    2nd ed. London: Heinemann Educational, 1978.

Hartshorne, Charles. *Aquinas to Whitehead: Seven Centuries of Metaphysics of Religion.*
    Milwaukee: Marquette University Publications, 1976.

Herman, Judith. *Trauma and Recovery.* New York: Basic Books, 1992.

Horney, Karen. *Neurosis and Human Growth: The Struggle toward Self-Realization.*
    New York: Norton, 1991.

International Theological Commission. "Memory and Reconciliation: The Church
    and the Faults of the Past." 2000.

———. "Some Current Questions in Eschatology." *Irish Theological Quarterly* 58
    (1992): 209-43.

Jaki, Stanley L. *Science and Creation: From Eternal Cycles to an Oscillating Universe.*
    Edinburgh: Scottish Academic Press, 1974.

Kaufman, Whitley. "Karma, Rebirth and the Problem of Evil." *Philosophy East & West*
    55 (2005): 15-32.

Kelly, Anthony. *Eschatology and Hope.* Theology in Global Perspective. Maryknoll,
    N.Y.: Orbis Books, 2006.

Kübler-Ross, Elisabeth. *On Death and Dying.* New York: Macmillan, 1969.

Küng, Hans. *Eternal Life? Life after Death as a Medical, Philosophical, and Theological
    Problem.* Garden City, N.Y.: Doubleday, 1984.

Lamb, Matthew L. "Nature, History, and Redemption." In *Jesus Crucified and Risen: Essays in Spirituality and Theology in Honor of Dom Sebastian Moore*, edited by William Loewe and Vernon Gregson, 117-32. Collegeville, Minn: Liturgical Press, Michael Glazier, 1998.

———. *Solidarity with Victims*. New York: Crossroad, 1982.

Lawler, Michael G., and Thomas J. Shanahan. *Church: A Spirited Communion*. Collegeville, Minn.: Liturgical Press, 1995.

Loewe, William P. *The College Student's Introduction to Christology*. Collegeville, Minn.: Liturgical Press, 1996.

Lonergan, Bernard J. F. *Grace and Freedom: Operative Grace in the Thought of St. Thomas Aquinas*. Edited by Frederick E. Crowe and Robert M. Doran. Collected Works of Bernard Lonergan 1. Toronto: University of Toronto Press, 2000.

———. *Insight: A Study of Human Understanding*. Edited by Frederick E. Crowe and Robert M. Doran. Collected Works of Bernard Lonergan 3. Toronto: University of Toronto Press, 1992.

———. *Method in Theology*. London: Darton, Longman & Todd, 1972.

———. "The Natural Desire to See God." In *Collection*, edited by Frederick E. Crowe and Robert M. Doran, 81-91. Toronto: University of Toronto Press, 1988.

———. *The Ontological and Psychological Constitution of Christ*. Translated by Michael G. Shields. Edited by Frederick E. Crowe and Robert M. Doran. Collected Works of Bernard Lonergan 7. Toronto: University of Toronto Press, 2002.

———. "The Origins of Christian Realism." In *A Second Collection*, edited by William F. Ryan and Bernard Tyrrell, 239-62. Philadelphia: Westminster Press, 1975.

Lubac, Henri de. *The Mystery of the Supernatural*. London: Geoffrey Chapman, 1967.

Luther, Martin. *Lecture on Romans*. Edited by H. Oswald. Vol. 25 of *Luther's Works*. St. Louis: Concordia, 1972.

Lyonnet, S., and L. Sabourin. *Sin, Redemption and Sacrifice: A Biblical and Patristic Study*. Rome: Biblical Institute Press, 1970.

MacIntyre, Alasdair. *After Virtue: A Study in Moral Theory*. 2nd ed. Notre Dame, Ind.: University of Notre Dame Press, 1984.

Malkovsky, Bradley. "Advaita Vedanta and Christian Faith." *Journal of Ecumenical Studies* 36 (1999): 397-422.

Maloney, George. *A Theology of "Uncreated Energies."* Milwaukee: Marquette University Press, 1978.

May, Gerald. *Addiction and Grace*. San Francisco: Harper & Row, 1988.

McGrath, Alister E. *Iustitia Dei: A History of the Christian Doctrine of Justification*. 2 vols. Cambridge: Cambridge University Press, 1986.

McKenzie, John L. *Dictionary of the Bible*. London: Geoffrey Chapman, 1968.

Metz, Johannes Baptist. *Faith in History and Society: Toward a Practical Fundamental Theology*. Translated by David Smith. New York: Seabury Press, 1980.

Meyer, Ben. *The Early Christians: Their World Mission and Self-Discovery*. Wilmington, Del.: Michael Glazier, 1986.

Miller, Alice. *Banished Knowledge: Facing Childhood Injuries*. New York: Anchor Books, 1990.

———. *The Drama of the Gifted Child*. New York: Basic Books, 1990.

—————. *For Your Own Good: Hidden Cruelty in Child-Rearing and the Roots of Violence.* 4th ed. New York: Farrar, Straus & Giroux, 2002.

Moore, Sebastian. *Let This Mind Be in You.* London: Darton, Longman & Todd, 1985.

Neuner, Josef, and Heinrich Roos. *The Teaching of the Catholic Church.* Translated by Geoffrey Stevens. Edited by Karl Rahner. Cork: Mercier Press, 1967.

Origen. *Commentary on the Gospel According to John Books 1-10.* Translated by Roland Heine. Edited by Thomas Halton. Fathers of the Church 80. Washington, D.C.: Catholic University of America Press, 1989.

Ormerod, Neil. "Chance and Necessity, Providence and God." *Irish Theological Quarterly* 70 (2005): 263-78.

—————. "A Dialectic Engagement with the Social Sciences in an Ecclesiological Context." *Theological Studies* 66 (2005): 815-40.

—————. "Eucharist as Sacrifice." In *The Eucharist: Faith and Worship,* edited by Margaret Press, 42-55. Homebush: St Pauls, 2001.

—————. "Reconciliation and the Paschal Mystery." In *Reconciliation: A Hunger in Society and the Church,* edited by Gerard Moore, 41-53. Strathfield: St Pauls, 2004.

Pais, Janet. *Suffer the Children: A Theology of Liberation by a Victim of Child Abuse.* New York: Paulist Press, 1991.

Pannenberg, Wolfhart. *Systematic Theology.* Translated by Geoffrey W. Bromiley. 3 vols. Grand Rapids: Eerdmans, 1991.

Peck, M. Scott. *People of the Lie: The Hope for Healing Human Evil.* New York: Simon & Schuster, 1983.

Phan, Peter C. *Eternity in Time: A Study of Karl Rahner's Eschatology.* Selinsgrove: Susquehanna University Press, 1988.

—————. *Grace and the Human Condition.* Message of the Fathers of the Church 15. Wilmington, Del.: Michael Glazier, 1988.

Rahner, Karl. "Concerning the Relationship between Nature and Grace." In *Theological Investigations,* 1:297-317. London: Darton, Longman & Todd, 1961.

—————. *Foundations of Christian Faith: An Introduction to the Idea of Christianity.* New York: Crossroad, 1982.

—————. *On the Theology of Death.* New York: Herder & Herder, 1961.

—————. "The Sin of Adam." In *Confrontations,* 11:247-62. New York: Seabury Press, 1974.

Ratzinger, Joseph. *Eschatology, Death and Eternal Life.* Translated by Michael Waldstein. Edited by Aidan Nichols. Washington, D.C.: Catholic University of America Press, 1988.

Rees, Martin J. *Just Six Numbers: The Deep Forces That Shape the Universe.* New York: Basic Books, 2000.

Reynolds, Thomas. "Toward the Other: Christianity and Buddhism on Desire." *Journal of Ecumenical Studies* 39 (2002): 325-40.

Roberts, Louis. *The Achievement of Karl Rahner.* New York: Herder & Herder, 1967.

Ruether, Rosemary Radford. *Gaia & God: An Ecofeminist Theology of Earth Healing.* San Francisco: HarperSanFrancisco, 1992.

—————. *Sexism and God-Talk: Toward a Feminist Theology.* 10th anniversary ed. Boston: Beacon Press, 1993.

Schillebeeckx, Edward. *Christ, the Christian Experience in the Modern World.* London: S.C.M. Press, 1980.

———. *Church: The Human Story of God.* Translated by John Bowden. New York: Crossroad, 1990.

Schnackenburg, Rudolf. *The Moral Teaching of the New Testament.* Translated by J. Holland-Smith and W. J. O'Hara. London: Burns & Oates, 1965.

Schumacher, E. F. *Small Is Beautiful: Economics as If People Mattered.* New York: Harper & Row, 1973.

Schüssler Fiorenza, Elisabeth. *Bread Not Stone: The Challenge of Feminist Biblical Interpretation.* 10th anniversary ed. Boston: Beacon Press, 1995.

Schwager, Raymund. *Jesus in the Drama of Salvation: Toward a Biblical Doctrine of Redemption.* New York: Crossroad Pub., 1999.

Stark, Rodney. *The Victory of Reason: How Christianity Led to Freedom, Capitalism, and Western Success.* New York: Random House, 2005.

Stebbins, J. Michael. *The Divine Initiative: Grace, World-Order, and Human Freedom in the Early Writings of Bernard Lonergan*, Lonergan Studies. Toronto: University of Toronto Press, 1995.

Teilhard de Chardin, Pierre. *The Phenomenon of Man.* Rev. ed. London: Collins, 1977.

Tertullian. *Disciplinary, Moral and Ascetical Works.* Translated by Rudolph Arbesmann, Emily Daly, and Edwin Quain. Edited by Hermigild Dressler. Fathers of the Church 40. Washington, D.C.: Catholic University of America Press, 1977.

Tipler, Frank J. *The Physics of Immortality: Modern Cosmology, God, and the Resurrection of the Dead.* New York: Anchor Books, 1994.

Trible, Phyllis. *Texts of Terror: Literary-Feminist Readings of Biblical Narratives.* Philadelphia: Fortress Press, 1984.

Tschiggerl, Hans. "Two Languages of Salvation: Christian-Buddhist Dialogue with Aloysius Pieris, S.J." *East Asian Pastoral Review* 34 (1997): 225-54.

Vanneste, Alfred. *The Dogma of Original Sin.* Translated by E. Callens. Louvain: Nauwelaerts, 1975.

Vorgrimler, Herbert. *Understanding Karl Rahner: An Introduction to His Life and Thought.* New York: Crossroad, 1986.

Westermann, Claus. *Genesis 1-11: A Commentary.* London: SPCK, 1984.

Whitehead, Alfred North. *Process and Reality: An Essay in Cosmology.* Edited by David Griffin and Donald W. Sherburne. Corrected ed. New York: Free Press, 1978.

Wiedenhofer, Siegfried. "The Main Forms of Contemporary Theology of Original Sin." *Communio* 18 (1991): 514-29.

Winter, Michael M. *The Atonement.* Collegeville, Minn.: Liturgical Press, 1995.

Wiseman, James A. *Spirituality and Mysticism: A Global View*, Theology in Global Perspective. Maryknoll, N.Y.: Orbis Books, 2006.

Wright, N. T. *The Resurrection of the Son of God.* Vol. 3 of *Christian Origins and the Question of God.* Minneapolis: Fortress, 2003.

Young, Frances M. *The Use of Sacrificial Ideas in Greek Christian Writers from the New Testament to John Chrysostom.* Cambridge, Mass.: Philadelphia Patristic Foundation, 1979.

Index

Made in the USA
Middletown, DE
13 January 2022

58636975R00135